In Memoriam
Susan Strange

Contents

List of contributors

BAS J.M. ARTS
Lecturer
Department of Environmental Policy Sciences
Faculty of Policy Sciences
University of Nijmegen
The Netherlands

ERKKI BERNDTSON
Senior Lecturer
Department of Political Science
University of Helsinki
Finland

PHILIP G. CERNY
Professor of Government
University of Manchester
United Kingdom

STEWART R. CLEGG
Professor of Management
School of Management, Faculty of Business
University of Technology
Sydney
Australia

GERHARD GOEHLER
Professor of Political Theory
Department of Political Science
Free University of Berlin
Germany

HENRI GOVERDE
Associate Professor in Public Administration
School of Public Affairs
University of Nijmegen, and
Professor in Political Science

Wageningen University and Research Center
The Netherlands

MARK HAUGAARD
Lecturer
Department of Political Science and Sociology
National University of Ireland
Galway

HOWARD H. LENTNER
Professor of Political Science
Baruch College and the Graduate School,
City University of New York
United States

ELINA PENTTINEN
Ph.D. Student
Department of Political Science and International Relations
University of Tampere
Finland

HILMAR ROMMETVEDT
Head of Research
RF-Rogaland Research, Stavanger, and
Researcher
Norwegian Research Centre in Organization and Management,
Bergen
Norway

JAN VAN TATENHOVE
Lecturer in Political Science of the Environment
Department of Environmental Policy Sciences
University of Nijmegen
The Netherlands
and
Associate Professor
Department of Political Science
University of Amsterdam
The Netherlands

List of Tables and Figures

TABLES

FIGURES

Preface

This book was conceived and produced in order to provide an overview of current thinking and research on political power as we begin the new millennium, and is to be launched at the World Congress of the International Political Science Association in Quebec City in August 2000. The chapters included here represent the latest work of members of the IPSA Research Committee on Political Power (Research Committee no. 36), formerly the IPSA Study Group on Political Power. The Study Group was set up at the 1979 IPSA World Congress in Moscow and officially became a Research Committee in 1991. The contributions of participants in various group and committee meetings over the years have always demonstrated a healthy disrespect for disciplinary boundaries, on the one hand, and familiarity with and respect for the work of others in political science and the other social sciences, as well as history and other related disciplines, on the other.

In 1993, the group put together a special issue of the *International Review of Sociology* entitled *On Power*, edited by David A. Baldwin of Columbia University. Indeed, Professor Baldwin was the driving force of the group and later the committee for many years before stepping down as chair in 1994. Since that time, the committee has been chaired by Henri Goverde of the University of Nijmegen. The committee has organized panels of various kinds at all the triennial IPSA World Congresses, as well as holding meetings in between these congresses in order to examine and debate more focused issues at greater depth. In particular, especially with regard to the development of this book, we were invited to organize roundtable meetings at the University of Helsinki in December 1995 as part of the Fiftieth Anniversary of the Finnish Association of Political Science, and we held a lively colloquium at the University of Nijmegen in the Netherlands as part of the activities marking the Second Lustrum (Quinquennium) of Nijmegen's Faculty of Policy Sciences in May 1998. These panels and meetings have brought more continuity, cohesion and collaboration to the study of power as a complex and widespread phenomenon.

This book – *Power in Contemporary Politics: Theories, Practices, Globalizations* – developed out of the Nijmegen conference organized by Henri Goverde and has involved extensive collaboration and cross-fertilization among the authors as well as the editors. The contributors are grateful to the Faculty of Policy Sciences in Nijmegen, particularly the Nijmegen Centre for Business, Environment and Government, for its administrative support, accommodation and hospitality. Special thanks go to Lily van Wersch, Maurice Bogie and Annie van Bergen. The editors of the book are also grateful to the National University of Ireland in Galway, particularly the Department of Sociology and Politics and the Faculty of Arts, for hosting the final editorial meeting, organized by Mark Haugaard, in August 1999. Finally, our acquisitions editor at Sage Publishers, Lucy Robinson, offered early and continuing encouragement and support to this book, and her efforts have facilitated its timely appearance.

We dedicate the book to the late Susan Strange, a long-time participant in the Research Committee, who saw and understood the wider horizons of power, including those that were unspoken and obscure and those, both public and private, that cut across the boundaries of disciplines and the borders of nations. She did not suffer the intellectually timid gladly, and her driving force in the study of power in the contemporary world will be sorely missed.

General Introduction: Power in Contemporary Politics

Power has always been the most fundamental concept in the study of politics. Many other concepts are also vitally important to understanding the nature of politics, including justice, culture, equality, class, rational choice and many more. But in the history of political theory and political science since their origins in ancient Greece, power has constantly stood out as the single most important defining conceptual issue. With the development of the modern social sciences since the late nineteenth century, the problem of power has generally been seen as the very core of the emerging and developing discipline of political science as well as of cognate disciplines and subdisciplines such as political sociology, political economy, political anthropology, international relations and the like.

At the same time, the concept of power has not been static, philosophically or analytically. Indeed, the twentieth century was a cauldron not only of intellectual debates about power but also of an unprecedented range of empirical phenomena relevant to an understanding of political power – whether the total conflicts of the First and Second World Wars, the emergence and collapse of totalitarian states and revolutionary philosophies, the spread of capitalism to every nook and cranny of the globe, and the apparent triumph of liberal democracy, at least in principle if not always in practice. In this book, a range of authors assess the current state of debates on political power as we begin the twenty-first century. The book is divided into three parts, each of which tackles controversial contemporary issues about power.

The first part looks at the state of theorizing about the nature of power. Political power as a concept was itself in a state of flux at the turn of the millennium, as evidenced by the existence of a range of linked and cross-cutting conceptual debates such as these:

- between the power of particular agents 'over' other agents and power as a generalized capacity of political communities, systems and other structures and institutions;
- between power as force, violence or coercion and power as 'hierarchical structures of imperative coordination' (Clegg, Chapter 3 of this book);
- in the latter case, too, between power as direct hierarchical control and power as rules, knowledge and discourse;
- between power as something consciously 'exercised' and power as embedded in structures and generally veiled;
- between power and powerlessness;

- between 'power over' and 'power to';
- between having power and being able to *resist* power;
- and between power as a coherent, top-down phenomenon and a postmodern congeries of complex circuits of power swirling through social life.

The second part looks at some of the ways empirical political scientists have been attempting to reformulate the problem of power at an analytical level:

- the notion of power as constituted through *networks* rather than hierarchies (especially with regard to attempts to apply network analysis to public policy);
- the way interest groups use power as a strategic resource in national politics;
- and the growing influence of a relatively new type of cross-national interest organization, the nongovernmental organization or NGO.

The third and final part asks whether the changing international and transnational context within which political power increasingly exists, especially what has come to be known as globalization, not only alters the way power operates in the real world but also leads to a further reconceptualization of power in the light of some of the theoretical questions previously explored. In an epilogue, the editors look at the way this book was conceived and produced through the forum of the Research Committee on Political Power of the International Political Science Association. Of course, the chapters reflect the range of research interests of the members of that committee, and some important areas of study have inevitably been neglected here. Nevertheless, we believe the topics we have covered to be among the most salient and significant perennial issues and current debates about political power, and we hope that this book will provoke further discussion and debate not only on these topics but also on a range of others vital to the conceptualization and analysis of power.

POWER AS THE CORE OF POLITICS

The significance of power for the study of politics lies deep in its implicit and explicit ramifications for the study of social life in general. In particular, the very use of the notion of power as an analytical tool, a window on society or a frame of reference has implications for what we think of as the nature of social life itself. The study of social life in each of the social sciences is ultimately concerned with the relationship between the individual human being and society – or, to be more precise, between the individual and a range of different *social* categories, groups, structures, organizations and institutions of which the individual is ostensibly a member or at least some sort of participant, as well as the relationship amongst those categories, structures, etc., themselves. At the core is the issue of whether the relationship between the individual and society (and therefore amongst those groups and structures too) is one that is essentially *harmonious* or essentially *conflict-ridden* – an issue which is at one and the same time *normative* (i.e., concerned with what is good or bad, true or false, desirable or undesirable) and *empirical* (i.e., about examining in as objectively possible a fashion what really 'is' rather than what 'ought to be').

At one extreme is the view that society is a seamless web, that individuals are part of a divine or natural plan, or just that somehow, if left to nature, we would somehow fit into our 'proper' places, whether as cogs in a machine or parts of a quasi-biological organism or metaphysical 'absolute'. At the other extreme is the view that individuals are separate 'billiard balls', existing in inherent opposition to society and social organization. Of course, few social theories espouse either extreme (except perhaps some particularly totalizing religions on the one hand and Ayn Rand's so-called 'objectivism' on the other). Indeed, the very *raison d'être* of social theory is to identify how the individual and society actually interact in real life, looking at when, how and why people act more as individuals in some contexts and circumstances and more as 'social animals' (Aristotle) in others. In doing this, the social sciences focus primarily on the various structures and systems which not only (empirically) enable such interaction to take place over time and space and impose patterns on that interaction but also (normatively) promote some sort of 'better life' in which human potential at *both* levels might be maximized through politics.

The latter task at an intellectual level is of course that of political philosophy, but it is more generally reflected in and enacted through the myriad ways people attempt to pursue their values (or even just live their own lives) on an everyday basis. Some political theories see people as being naturally divided into macrosocieties (historically manifested in the modern world in *nation-states* for the most part), therefore enabling them to better realize and achieve common social values and the general welfare through coherently organized hierarchical or centripetal structures of power. Others like Marxism, for example, see people as being divided by capitalism into antagonistic economic classes in which the power of one class is entrenched through its economic as well as its political power, a situation that *prevents* the development of both individual freedom and social welfare – although that division will eventually come to an end with the achievement of true communism.

Yet other points of view such as liberalism see the very plurality of human life as providing a tableau of possibilities that can be realized through a division and diffusion of political power at different structural levels, as well as through the separation of politics from economics, the promotion of an independent civil society, and the like. Democracy – the core of which is that ultimate political power should be held and exercised of, by and for the people (Abraham Lincoln, *The Gettysburg Address*) – clearly means something different within each of these perspectives. Of course, all these perspectives (and many more) come in negative, pessimistic versions as well as more idealistic, optimistic ones. Such theories and practices are all bound together in *discourses* – the way ideas and understandings are represented and reproduced through language (or how people explicitly and implicitly make sense of their own worlds and the 'real world' in general). Discourses connote to those participating in them what is ostensibly real or unreal, what is therefore true or false, and therefore also what is good or bad. Thus at the heart of both empirical and normative analyses of politics and society is the question of what sort of basic, essential harmony or disharmony may or may not characterize the most fundamental relationship between individuals and society.

In this context, the very concept of power itself – in ways that are analogous to other concepts in the social sciences – in fact involves an *a priori* presumption that this relationship between individuals and society is of a particular type or has particular characteristics instead of others. Let us start with a fairly simple comparison with the discourse of neoclassical economics. Contemporary mainstream economics starts with a vision of society based on the notion of the market. In this context, individuals are essentially consumers making choices among alternative goods or assets available to them. Whether rich or poor, they look at what is available and decide what they want (preferences) and what they can afford (resources) – their utilities. Buyers and sellers then compare one another's market signals based on their different utilities. As a result of this comparison, a *price* is set (as at an auction) representing the mid-point at which the market 'clears' (or ought to clear) – i.e., at which whatever is available is sold out. Thus the market provides sellers with the highest prices they can realistically hope for and buyers with the lowest prices they can realistically hope for.

In this vision, a well-regulated and competitive market ought to provide for the *most economically efficient allocation of resources* in a society, i.e., the best products at the lowest prices. The market works, in Adam Smith's term, as an optimizing 'invisible hand', reconciling the different needs and wants of individuals with the overall efficiency of society as a whole. A genuinely competitive market punishes overpricing (monopoly rents) and the sort of out-of-control capital accumulation that Marx believed to be the driving force of capitalism, contrasting Marx's vicious circle of contradiction and revolution with a virtuous circle of increasing production and consumption for all. Interestingly, although such a Pollyanna-ish or Candide-like view of capitalism would have been considered laughable in the 1930s and 1940s – when a combination of the Great Depression, the memory of the First World War and the reality of the Second, Soviet communism and fascism all seemed to require *alternatives* to a collapsing capitalism – it is back today at the core of the so-called Washington Consensus on how to deal with the challenges of the post-Cold-War era, globalization and the millennium. Nevertheless, since the triumph in the 1980s of Thatcherism and Reaganism, such neoliberal economic discourse has become the dominant way of seeing politics and political power in the contemporary world. What it sees, in effect, is a world where a new harmony between individuals and society is indeed immanent (and, for some, imminent as well) through the global spread of neoliberal practices.

In contrast, the significance of power as an organizing concept for the study of politics – as a *discourse* of politics itself – lies in its implication that there is a much greater level of underlying *disharmony* between individuals and society. In fact, it implies that the very constitution of society itself – its infrastructure, its stability, its mechanisms of continuity and adaptation, its culture – depends first and foremost on the supposed fact (or truth, to adopt the language of the social theorist Michel Foucault, as analyzed in this book by Haugaard, Clegg and Penttinen) that some people are *dominated* systematically by others. In this context, progress in society derives not from some felicitous virtuous circle or invisible hand but from the continuing struggle of individuals and groups to improve their lot in a context of both continual manifest and deep latent conflict between them and others who have less or more power than they do.

In this sense, politics is not merely about power but also about *powerlessness* (Gaventa, 1980). In such a power-ridden world, stability and relative justice or fairness come not from some spontaneous auction-like process which reconciles alternative utilities in an ideal-rational sense, but from the painful and often problematic construction of mechanisms to keep conflict (and the relatively powerless) in check – through both formal political institutions and informal political processes. However, such structural mechanisms are always contingent upon the underlying relationships of power in society more widely. For example, they usually represent some sort of time-specific settlement or institutionalized truce in which some relatively powerless people come to accept that others have more power than they do, but also come to believe for one reason or another that such surplus power will be used to at least some extent for the common good or in the public interest and not merely for the personal aggrandizement of the power-holders (while accepting that some sort of extra economic or prestige benefits will accrue to the latter in return for their restraint in the use of that power). Such acquiescence is called legitimacy. A linked aspect of both power and powerlessness is that neither is necessarily nor primarily the result of some coherent system of power coordinated from the top. Rather, both are also embedded in multiple micro-level and meso-level[1] *circuits of power* interacting with and cutting across each other in everyday life.

From the perspective of a 'political analysis' therefore – if we accept that power is at the core of such an analysis – the rational choice economics of the market is sufficient to explain neither the empirical *nor* the normative aspects of the relationship between individuals and society. Nor is the role of culture, as in anthropology, nor the way the individual's mind works, as in psychology, nor the abstract study of intellectualized discourses, as in philosophy, nor the eclecticism of sociology (although the very flexibility of the last has allowed the generation of many insightful hypotheses). To understand society we must first of all understand it *politically*, that is to say we must focus first and foremost on power relations, according them epistemological priority over other conceptual issues – both in terms of the broader manifestations of power, such as the constitution of society itself from above, and more diffusely in terms of the micro-relations between individuals and groups from below.

NORMATIVE AND EMPIRICAL DIMENSIONS OF THE POWER DEBATE

These relationships take many forms, and all of them reflect the core paradox of social science – the ultimate impossibility of separating the twin dynamics of empirical analysis and normative judgment. In the first place, it is impossible to choose what to analyze, and how to analyze it, unless we make a normative judgment as to what is most *important* to study. As indicated in the example of neoclassical economics above, economists must come to a judgment of what is the truth about how the world is organized in economic, social and political terms before they can refine and apply their analyses in real cases. If they accept the neoclassical paradigm, then politics as power is relegated to the *pathology* of their study – i.e., how politics (as power) distorts market mechanisms and prevents them from working efficiently or properly (unless it is used merely to ratify or enforce the objective rules or principles of economics).

However, for political scientists and political sociologists (and many organizational analysts in business schools), such so-called distortions are part of the *normal* path of events and need to be studied and analyzed in their own right as having theoretical primacy over markets. In the latter case, markets may be seen by political liberals as *desirable* economic mechanisms, but they also need to be understood to be themselves rooted in and enabled by structures and institutions of power that determine the mix of social benefits and costs of the operation and shape the outcomes of those market mechanisms according to values chosen through *political* (power-driven) processes. If it is believed that the costs of markets are too high in terms of, for example, inequalities amongst human beings, and that the potential consequences are also too high in terms of such things as poverty, instability, conflict, welfare deficiencies and/or general unfairness or injustice, then analysts will pay not only more attention but also a *different kind* of attention to the political institutions, structures and processes that underpin, shape and facilitate economic processes.

At this point, the narrower role of normative judgment at an analytical level shades into its role in wider normative terms – in other words, not only what we think of as facts or truth for the purpose of *explaining* a phenomenon, but also what we consider to be a more or less *desirable* state of affairs, i.e., what constitutes the good, or justice, or the common (or public) interest. It becomes crucial to understand the range of discursively available alternative theoretical constructs or *paradigms* that exist – those more refined but complex lenses or windows through which people look at and try to understand the world. These constructs are available in a number of different forms. In the study of political philosophy, for example, they are thought to be found in the close, analytical, abstract study of how great thinkers have tried to refine and expand their systems of thought both historically and contemporaneously. Political philosophy is the most developed form of what Anthony Giddens has called 'discursive consciousness' (see chapters by Haugaard and Clegg). At the same time, however, people act in their everyday lives within the context of such ideas expressed less formally and abstractly, sometimes almost (but not quite) unconsciously – Giddens's alternative notion of 'practical consciousness'. People are only able to act in their everyday lives, to make decisions, to connect with other people and the world around them, in the context of normative concepts and judgments which to a great extent they *take for granted*.

In other words, in terms of the capacity of people to cope and to act as the core of human existence, there is just no getting away from normative ideas, whether at the discursive or at the practical level. Although very few people deal in such normative ideas at the purely discursive level, and very many operate overwhelmingly (but never entirely!) at the practical level, most people are betwixt and between. This is true of academics as well as, say, the ordinary voter. At various points (indeed, some theorists would say, at many important points) in our daily lives we need, merely in order to act in a coherent way, to be 'reflexive' – i.e., to *reflect* upon what we are doing and to somehow weigh, in whatever ways we can, the causes, underlying values and potential consequences of our own actions *or of the actions of others as they affect us* directly or indirectly. Human beings are by their very nature reflexive beings, although the extent of that reflexivity varies enormously in particular circumstances. Indeed much political and social theory is concerned primarily with debating the extent to which genuine reflexivity is in any real sense possible and/or desirable. Even in the major religions, the very fact that people can choose to *reject* God's will (in theory, the strongest form of external constraint) is usually seen to define their humanity – although that rejection may be seen as normatively bad in and of itself within those religions.

In the study of power, therefore, it is obvious from the start that the very employment of the concept itself is *value-loaded*. So, too, are all the other concepts used in social science that enable us to analyze and make sense of our world and our actions. We cannot even approach the idea of objectivity which has informed the philosophy of the natural sciences, especially in the nineteenth and twentieth centuries. And yet most social scientists accept the ethical need to *try* to be as objective as possible while at the same time (a) recognizing their limitations and (b) understanding the need to be as systematic as possible in analyzing the normative dimension too. Reflexivity is at the heart of social science itself, but it does not mean that we are merely prisoners of our basic emotions and raw opinions. It means *comparing different paradigms* and trying to see what way or ways of understanding an issue seems to make most sense in blending the normative and the empirical into some sort of coherent whole.[2] In this sense, ultimately, power and its central role in social structures and processes is not merely a prejudice, but a *hypothesis* (or, in terms of practical consciousness, a virtual hypothesis) – a hypothesis which people are continually testing in a reflexive way as they are forced to make decisions and to act in the real world (and in their different worlds, as the postmodernists say).

There are two main practical ramifications for the social scientist of this role of power as chief hypothesis in a reflexive process. The first and most obvious is that when social scientists, like all other people, make pronouncements about what they think is actually going on in the real world, they are choosing to accept certain facts and issues as significant and others as less so (or not at all). Political scientists tend, because of their general understanding of human nature, their training and the character of their discipline, to look at power first and to take it most seriously as the major issue. Economists look at the market first. Thus to economists, political scientists seem naive, because we are seen not to understand the way rational choice and the ideally spontaneous operation of the marketplace create opportunities for more efficient – i.e., normatively *better* – economic and therefore social outcomes. Economists are not exactly shy about expressing their opinions on public policy to governments, the media, etc.; indeed, they have dominated such public debates in recent decades. Ironically, political scientists – those who specialize in the study of politics as such – are often far less willing to express such broad normative political judgments (although there are significant exceptions, of course). To them, power is a highly complex matter, one which is a minefield for those who would pontificate on the substance of policy. Indeed, this book can in some ways be seen as a warning to those who would inveigh and proselytize in an oversimplified fashion about what governments should or should not do.

The second major ramification is more internal to the study of politics and the social sciences in general. That is to say that power is inextricably intertwined with a wide range of other conceptual and empirical issues, issues which arise in various chapters of this book, and issues which need to be seen in the wider context of power relationships. Each of these issues reflects the inseparability of, but difference between, the normative and empirical strands of social science analysis, and each requires a careful sensitivity to the reflexive dialectic, so to speak, between them. We will briefly mention some of these issues here. For the sake of simplicity – for undoubtedly the very choice of key terms and categories forms an essential part of the paradigmatic debate[3] – we will identify four types of issues and mention some of the more complex issues that make them up. The categories we will use are: power and people; power and institutions; power and knowledge; and power and force. Of course, all of these categories link and cut across each other in any real-time analysis.

Power and people

There are many strands which might comprise this rather broad category. Probably the most fundamental is the question of what role power plays in motivating actors, whether individuals or groups, to pursue particular goals and act in particular ways. The most important issue is whether people – whether biologically rooted in human nature or in some other way – are primarily *power-seekers*. Do people treat power as merely a means to an end (which would be important enough), or is it somehow an end in itself? Or if they are not primarily power-seekers, what role does power-seeking play in the wider, more complex amalgam of their basic needs and motivations?

Much of political science and political theory has focused on this question. It appears in the arguments of Thrasymachus in Plato's *Republic*, reappears in Machiavelli's *The Prince*, and reaches its zenith in the seventeenth century *Leviathan* of Thomas Hobbes. Hobbes argues, in line with the Renaissance biological rethinking of his day, that people have no deeper fundamental instinct driving them than pure physical survival. In this context, survival in a 'state of nature' broadly speaking goes to those individuals with more relative power over others in a 'war of all against all' wherein life is 'solitary, poor, nasty, brutish and short'. Nevertheless, people acting in concert *could* have the potential to achieve higher things, such as a more advanced level of civilization, if they can somehow *pool* their individual struggles for power in a way which provides for civil peace instead of endemic warfare. Such a 'social contract' would involve a delegation of individuals' power to a 'sovereign' (not limited to a personal king but more properly embedded in an institutionalized political structure of some sort) who (or which) would thereby enable everybody to be better off.

Therefore, for Hobbes and for much of modern political philosophy and political science, the empirical question of how to understand and analyze society and the normative question of how to make society better are inseparable but different, as diffracted and then refracted through the reflexive dialectic mentioned above. But does Hobbes's perspective, however compelling and insightful it may be in many ways, really capture the nature of power? John Locke at the end of the same century saw the same question as having to be resolved quite differently, with people retaining power (their 'natural rights') through certain civil rights and inalienable liberties, only delegating some peace-keeping powers to a government which could be recalled or even rebelled against if it misused its power. Adam Smith a century later saw the key to the question as one of limiting a government's power in the *economic* sphere in particular, as he believed that free markets rather than political rights as such were the key to realizing human potential and developing a better life (although he also believed that effective government regulation would be needed to prevent the misuse of markets by monopolists). In the nineteenth century, Karl Marx, as we have said, also saw the core of the power issue to be rooted in economics – or, more specifically, in the economic system called capitalism – in this case by giving the owners of the means of production lopsided economic *and* political power of a kind that would more or less be automatically or spontaneously misused to oppress the rest (whatever individual capitalists' personal intentions might be). Clearly each author makes a link between his view of *human nature* and the way power is distributed and used in society – judgments of truth or falsity being closely bound up in judgments of good and bad.

A number of normative as well as empirical implications flow from these sorts of considerations. The first is whether some particular kind of distribution of power is natural in society. Are some people or groups better fit for the exercise of power or somehow more deserving? Or on the contrary, to what extent do people have the capacity and or the right (or even duty) to *resist* the exercise of power by others? The question of resistance – its rightness, what sorts of constraints exist, the nature of oppression, and the possibilities of some sort of eventual emancipation – is at the core of many modern political philosophies, and is the central focus of postmodern analyses of power, too, as highlighted later in this book. But another crucial question is whether people are actually capable of acting in a genuinely non-power-seeking way. Are people altruistic or are they essentially selfish, always tempted to free-ride on the achievements of others? To what extent can people in general be emancipated (or emancipate themselves)? Can they be free spontaneously, or must they, in Jean-Jacques Rousseau's famous phrase, be 'forced to be free'? If they are emancipated from some forms of power, will other forms of power then emerge merely to create new constraints and forms of oppression? And what is the relationship between macro-structures of power and meso- and micro-'circuits' of power? It is impossible to attempt to analyze politics and society without asking these questions and judging between different possible answers.

Power and institutions

The very fact that a society is a society – neither a clump of atomistic individuals nor an automatic instinctive collectivity like an anthill – hinges on the phenomenon that people reflexively construct structures and institutions within and through which to interact.[4] Human society is a human *artefact*. And to the extent that these patterned structures are seen from a political perspective, such structures and institutions – not just formal political institutions like states or governments, but all forms of social organization – involve power. At a very broad level they are about distributing, controlling and influencing power in society more widely in some relatively systematic way – who has power, how much power, how power is exercised, how it is enforced, how it is legitimated, and, indeed, what are the rules of the (power) game for determining the answers to these questions in an ongoing way over time and in changing circumstances. And at an endogenous level they are themselves structures of power which are seen to have relative autonomy in terms of their own internal rules and the internal distribution of power amongst those participating within those institutions as such. Indeed, Goehler (Chapter 1 of this book) argues that any effective political system must be organized around a 'common space of action' characterized by an overarching form of what he calls 'intransitive power'. Let us take a brief look at four of the many dimensions of institutional power that have been important in discursive debates and ongoing practices – democracy, institutional bias, the technologies of power, and the impact of globalization. Globalization will also be treated in more depth in the section on theoretical issues.

Probably the most important debate about power in the modern era has been concerned with democracy. Democracy is an ongoing political project, and it is never a *fait accompli*. The modern democratic project has primarily been not about the distribution of wealth or social prestige as such but about the distribution of power through democratic political institutions. It is an attempt to construct a less unequal social playing field through giving people a *more* equal share of certain kinds of specifically political power – mainly through the vote but also through what the American Constitution calls 'the equal protection of the law'. However, as Haugaard (1997a) emphasizes, what is crucial here is how political power is defined in contrast to economic power, social power, or whatever. On the one hand, if political power is narrowly defined, then the legitimate and effective scope of action of governmental institutions will be seen to be significantly narrower (in both empirical and normative terms); on the other hand, if it is broadly defined and includes significant elements of what is thought of as economic power or whatever, then the scope of the state will be seen to be much broader. Liberals and economic conservatives will support the former, while radicals and socialists (as well as some socially conservative *étatistes*) will support the latter. Democracy is thus crucially not only about power in general but about how particular political institutions can be constructed that will establish, control and facilitate the development of a particular kind and distribution of power. Once again, empirical analysis and normative judgments are joined at the hip. The issue of power and democratic theory will be examined more closely below in the section treating some theoretical issues of power.

Another debate that has been prominent in political science and political sociology since the 1970s concerns the perception that institutions – especially those of the state – are not neutral, but biased or skewed toward the production of particular outcomes, the promotion of particular values, and the domination of particular groups. In other words, the state in and of itself can never promote the common good or the general welfare as such, but must be analyzed critically in terms of which opponents or competitors for power are systematically favored or privileged by its *underlying structural configuration* (rather than simply by the discrete or cumulative decisions of individual or group agents alone). At one level, this would be an obvious, self-evident observation. However, it emerged as a theoretical issue most recently in quite particular circumstances as a reaction to two sorts of trends at different ends of the political spectrum.

On the one hand, it arose as a reaction against the mainstream pluralist political analyses fashionable in the 1950s and 1960s that saw politics primarily in terms of a power struggle (and/or peaceful competition) among pressure and interest groups – and also saw political science as a discipline as being about a more scientific study of political behavior. In order to explain what was happening in politics, the pluralists and behavioralists of the era believed that formal political institutions had relatively little value as an independent variable, but merely constituted a dependent variable or even a neutral playing field amongst contending (and/or cooperating) groups. However, in the light of phenomena like the American Civil Rights Movement in the 1950s and 1960s, the expansion of the Vietnam War in the 1960s and the end of the postwar long economic boom in the 1970s – to name but three of many catalysts – such pluralist and behavioralist approaches were subjected to a sustained radical critique from the left in the United States as well as Western Europe.

On the other hand, at almost the same time, the crisis of the welfare state of the 1960s and 1970s also provoked an institutionalist critique from the right, blaming governments themselves for social and economic problems because they were seen to have too much autonomous political power and to encroach too far into what was said to be the private realm of economics, thus distorting the marketplace and making it inefficient. As Ronald Reagan said, 'Government is not the solution. Government is the problem.'

In the context of this critical convergence of left-wing and right-wing critiques, a whole range of institutionalist, structuralist and structurationist analyses emerged at an intellectual level mixing (if rather unevenly) neo-Marxist and neo-Weberian approaches (Cerny, 1990). In these analyses, the state was reinstated as the prime independent variable in the study of politics. It was seen as having independent power and relative autonomy from socio-economic variables, with the latter either constituting concurrent independent variables or even, for some theorists, being downgraded to the status of dependent variables.

In the 1990s, however, this focus on the structure(s) of the state to some extent gave way to two main trends. On the one hand, especially in Europe, the academic study of the state was increasingly subsumed into a more sociological approach to public policy-making – the policy networks perspective (criticized by Goverde and van Tatenhove in this book). On the other hand, especially in the United States, there was a rebirth of fundamentalist, nineteenth century economic liberalism (usually called neoliberalism) in which the neoclassical economic paradigm was imported into politics in the form of rational choice theory. The latter once again sought to reduce the state to a secondary status, as a simple payoff matrix at best, or as an inherently dysfunctional market-distorting mechanism at worst – in effect, an attempt at the depoliticization of politics. However, the issue of the structural power of political institutions was still at the heart of the reflexive dialectic of late twentieth century politics itself as well as of political science and the other social sciences.

A third debate is important for all approaches to institutional power but perhaps most of all to postmodernist theory, for which a fundamental problematic is the relationship between discourses of power and what Foucault called the *technologies* of power. The latter involve the way that both the exercise of power and the structures of power utilize and incorporate both hard and soft techniques. Probably the best known recent writing on this is Foucault's revival of Jeremy Bentham's *Panopticon*, or the nineteenth century technology of building prisons in ways which enable guards most easily to observe, monitor and control inmates at all times. Also the French state in the nineteenth century pioneered the use of secret police intelligence to monitor political activity most closely, generating records and accounts which are still crucial for historians today and which foreshadowed the twentieth century practices of totalitarian states.

Most recently, of course, the development of digital information and communications technologies enable states to monitor their citizens more closely than ever before, whether for purposes of control or in order to more efficiently provide public goods, welfare, etc. It must be remembered of course that such technologies are at the beck and call not merely of states and political actors, but also of firms, crime syndicates and other organizations. Furthermore, such hard technologies only operate through the soft technologies or structured practices of organizations and institutions themselves; they are the backbone of micro-circuits of power as much as of the macro-structures of political, social and economic institutions. Nevertheless, as the elite theorist Robert Michels famously noted, 'Who says organization says oligarchy.' Again, normative and empirical dimensions are inextricably intertwined.

Finally, another significant and, in some ways, quite new issue has increasingly been influencing and complicating such debates – that of *globalization*. Globalization is seen by many analysts as having the potential to alter the basic structural/institutional playing field of politics in much larger and more consequential ways than have previously been understood, not just at the global level but at all levels, macro, meso and micro (as debated in Arts' chapter in Part II and the four chapters in Part III of this book; see also the section on theoretical issues in this introduction). Assessing the impact of globalization on politics at this point requires informed speculation; it is too early for firm prediction. Nevertheless, whether we are in a period of fundamental continuity or of paradigmatic change, the very constitution of power may be changing as we begin the twenty-first century, with major normative consequences for notions such as the public interest or the common good.

Power and knowledge

In the first two categories of power debates discussed above, the role of power is not so different from what ordinary people might think of as power in the everyday terms of their own practical consciousnesses or 'life worlds'. Both the idea of individuals as power-seekers and that of institutions as power-bearers and power-wielders are fairly visible categories. However, the study of power in recent decades has also extended into a less apparent category, one linked with the idea of postmodernism in social analysis generally and, in particular, with the work of Foucault – the notion that power is both embedded in and effectuated through a crucial combination of knowledge and language, or what is called discourse.

Discourse in this sense is the complex mixture of ideas and expressions through which individuals both perceive and in turn try to explain social reality. Discourse therefore also defines the parameters and criteria people use to ascertain and calculate their *potential courses of action* and to choose particular courses of action in specific circumstances. It is thus the primary (or for some analysts, the only) medium of both understanding and action. Discourse in this sense has a circular quality, but it is not necessarily a closed (vicious or virtuous) circle. A combination of the internal terms of discourse itself (i.e., the way ideas and practices are defined and set out) and the interaction of different, contrasting discourses (in the plural, like competing paradigms) provide a more or less narrow or wide range of alternative perceptions and therefore of available choices. This is particularly significant, as most social theorists since Max Weber have come to the conclusion that it is impossible in an epistemological sense to actually know *the* truth. Consequently the most that people can do is individually and collectively to constitute their own truths through discourse and to act on those under-standings. Discourse (and the knowledge from which it grows) both limits and enables.

Discourse, furthermore, is the window or filter through which a whole range of *other* concepts and understandings must be mediated in human action. This is the case for all of the issues more directly concerned with power that we have identified, as well as with others mentioned earlier such as culture, justice and the like. The capacity and/or will to exercise power are mediated through discourse, as are the capacity and/or will to resist power. Both are as much (or even more) a function of people's awareness of power relations and willingness to use what they think of as their poten-tial power as they are of the distribution of, say, material power resources. The way that certain types of power – both its exercise and its underlying structures – are *legitimated* is even more directly a function of discourses of legitimation (and/or refusal of legitimation).

Political institutions and states, for example, are a product of discourses both in the sense that they are consciously constructed through formal constitutions and legal systems and also in the sense that informal conven-tions define and become embedded in their practices. What we have called the structural biases of institutions operate (and are legitimated and/or delegitimated) through discourse. Discourse is therefore the very medium through which human *reflexivity* operates. This is true as much at the meso- and micro-levels as at the macro-level.

Once again, however, we are faced not only with the inseparability of the normative and the empirical, but also with the relationship between discourse and technology. Material conditions are also real. As Marx said, 'Men make history, but not in circumstances of their own choosing.' There are tremendous potential constraints as well as enabling opportunities deeply rooted in the distribution of material resources and the technologies of power. Indeed, the potential impact of globalization too is related both to the possible redistribution of material and technological power which it might involve *and* to the way identities and discourses alter the way people see themselves in a so-called globalizing world – the perceived global realities which they believe constrain and empower them, and whether they think they have wider or at least different potential courses of action from before, including economic expansion and political and economic liberalization on the one hand or new forms of inequality and oppression on the other (as well as possible opportunities for resistance and emancipation).

Power and force

Probably the most salient set of normative and empirical debates about power, however, concern whether in essence power concerns what Clegg calls 'hierarchical structures of imperative coordination' or whether it is about raw power – force, coercion and violence. At the most obvious level, the latter has always been seen to be true of the state. As mentioned earlier, political philosophers like Machiavelli and Hobbes believed that violence and coercion were at the root of all politics, and Weber believed that foundations of the state itself are predicated upon its possession of (or claim to) a 'monopoly of legitimate violence' – i.e., that violence outside of or not sanctioned by the state has become illegitimate in the modern world, that the use of legitimate violence (against criminals and opponents of the state domestically and against other states internationally) gives the state a *direct* power crucial to its stability and effectiveness, and that people's *acquiescence* to state power because of their fear or respect of its monopoly of legitimate violence gives it a crucial kind of *indirect* power as a hierarchical structure of imperative coordination. The emergence of the modern state as a social form is usually seen (e.g., Elias, 1969, 1994; Spruyt, 1994) to be rooted in the ability of particular individuals and groups such as post-feudal monarchs and their followers and underlings to force people to acquiesce in the power of the state through battles, beheadings and brutality as well as through forced taxation, military service and the like – what Margaret Levi (1981) has called 'the predatory theory of rule'.

Thus the very *raison d'être* of the Janus-like modern state internally and of its second face, the international system of states, has generally been seen to lie in the way violence and coercion have been hierarchically integrated through state institutions and practices. The first face involves the consolidation of a single organized power structure ruling over a particular territory and population, shaping and molding them into an ostensible citizenry with a feeling of belonging and solidarity. The notion of the nation as a spontaneous social unit formed from below can thus be viewed as a facilitating myth – in contrast to the reality being that state actors and other elite power-wielders first created the state superstructure, the power of which in turn enabled a national social substructure to crystallize through people's participation in the supposedly common life of the state. The second face involves the external competition and conflict of states with each other in an anarchical world without an international sovereign and therefore without a proper Hobbesian social contract to ensure stability, peace and the progress of civilization.

These two faces are united in what many theorists and others have taken to be the most fundamental function[5] of the state, that of territorial consolidation and defense. Defense is seen even by economic liberals such as Adam Smith as the most basic and indispensable public good, without which not only modern society itself but also efficient, large-scale economic markets would not be able to exist in the first place. Furthermore, territorial defense takes on an even more central role in an anarchic world populated by potentially hostile, self-regarding nation-states concerned in a Hobbesian sense with their own physical survival. In this world, there is always the potential not only for defeat by another state or group of states, but even for a 'war of all against all' returning *both domestically and internationally* if national territorial consolidation and defense fail. The permanent threat, from this so-called realist perspective, is that the formal anarchy of the international system, i.e., its lack of a world government or sovereign power, may actually be transformed someday into real, violent, chaotic anarchy should the tenuous and fragile existing balances of power holding the ring amongst potentially hostile states deteriorate. Such a condition would undermine states from within as well as from without by destroying their integrity and stability. Nevertheless, it is possible that a number of practices (as distinct from formal institutions), mainly in the area of diplomatic discourse, can, as the English school of international relations suggests, also provide a stabilizing glue to counteract the tendency to defect.

However, such questions do not apply to the state alone, as we have seen in the earlier discussion of power and institutions. Looking at power from below, micro- and meso-level circuits of power usually involve analogous considerations on violence, coercion and force. Foucault is probably best known for his historical study of mental institutions and other sorts of micro-level social institutions – and, by implication, various agencies of the state too – within which, he argues, the issue of power is at the core of attempting to understand how they operate and how they manage the complex and essentially disharmonious relationship between the individual and society. Other dimensions of such a focus range across categories from those in which potential violence is usually (but not always) only latent, from families to neighborhoods to highway networks (including road rage, police car chases, and other highly salient elements not only of real life but of television, film and newspaper depictions), etc., to those where it is more manifest, including local gangs, criminal networks, drug rings and the like, as well as the protection of property or actions of the police themselves. The postmodern study of power as violence, therefore, like other aspects of the postmodernist intellectual project, rejects the 'grand narratives' of modern historical and social development in favor of more fragmented micro-level foci, where normative and empirical concerns intersect at the level of everyday life.

WHAT IS POWER? SOME THEORETICAL ISSUES

From the inception of the social sciences and normative political theory, debates on power have been virtually constant. Yet, in many instances, these power debates take place in relative conceptual isolation from one another. When debates do cross, it becomes obvious that the concepts of power at the center of these debates refer to different social phenomena. Over time, many strategies have been developed for coping with this, including: (a) insisting that 'your' concept of power is the 'right one'; (b) arguing that what others are analyzing constitutes a trivial aspect of power; or (c) ignoring what others are doing. In this section we will look at four theoretical issues that have been central to these strategies and debates:

1 power as a contested, family resemblance concept;
2 the problematic of structure and agency in power analysis;
3 the evolving debate on globalization and structuration, or the restructuring of power in a globalizing world; and
4 the relationship between power and democratic decision-making.

Power as a contested concept

To the outsider, the divergence of perspectives must appear bewildering. The obvious question he or she may wish to ask is why there is not just one concept of power which we can all agree upon. It would be theoretically easy and neat if we could agree that there is one concept of power. This need not entail that it would be impossible to approach power from different perspectives. We could, in effect, agree to disagree on our approaches (sociological, normative, feminist, etc.) but agree not to talk past one another by analyzing different phenomena by the same name. While this would be a better state of affairs, it is, unfortunately, not realizable. The reason is neither stubbornness nor disciplinary imperialism but, rather, deeply theoretical. There is no core concept of power because of the nature of words, concepts and academic disciplines.

Even at the level of everyday speech, power is what the philosopher Wittgenstein terms a 'family resemblance' concept. Wittgenstein developed the idea of family resemblance concepts to cover the usage of words which cannot be captured using single definitions. The particular example which he gave was the word 'game'. While most games have something in common, such as winning and losing, no single set of characteristics can be found which is common to all usages. At first sight it might appear that, for instance, all ball games involve winning and losing but, on the other hand, if we imagine a solitary child playing a game with a ball this commonality disappears (Wittgenstein, 1968: 36). This does not entail that all usages of the word 'power' are unrelated. They are related, but not by any single characteristic. Rather, their relationship is formed from a criss-crossing set of commonalities that interweave into a complex tapestry of related meanings. Just as members of a family resemble each other in a diversity of ways, so, too, the usages of power overlap in a complex interweaving of meanings with no single strand running through the entirety.

While the absence of a shared thread of meaning makes any one-line definition of a family resemblance concept impossible, this does not mean that usage of the word in question is necessarily ambiguous. As Wittgenstein has argued (and linguists, such as Chomsky, would agree with him on this) the meaning of words is not derived from definitions or any abstract usage rules they may entail. Rather, the usage of words derives from specific contexts which give relational meaning to the usage in question. Wittgenstein called these contexts 'language games'. In contemporary social theory, we can theorize language games as mutually constituting systems of meaning. All meanings, whether linguistic or semiotic, are systemic. The meaning of single words derives from their membership of a language.

Languages as a whole are the largest systems of meaning that we use and, because each language comprises a different set of relations, it is not possible to translate precisely from one language to the next by the use of exact equivalences. As the linguist de Saussure observed, it may at first sight appear that the English word 'sheep' is exactly the same as the French word *mouton*, but this is not the case because of a second word 'mutton' in English. A more pertinent example for our purposes might be the existence of two words for power in French (*pouvoir* and *puissance*); or, to take a more dramatic example, in one of the Inuit languages there are 50 different words for snow – words which simply do not have an equivalent in English. Not only are languages self-contained systems of meaning but within languages there are subsystems of language which reflect specific discursive practices.

Academics are well used to the frequent complaint that their ideas are inaccessible to the common person because they use concepts in ways that are peculiar to their discipline. The usual accusation that goes with this is that this jargon is a deliberate mode of exclusion and an attempt to make what they say appear more sophisticated than it really is. While this may be the case in certain instances, there is a deeper theoretical reason for the development of such local languages. One of the mistakes that we tend to make is to think of words as embodying absolute essences. Rather, we should think of them as tools which are crafted for specific jobs. Just as plumbers and carpenters have tools specially designed for specific tasks, so, too, disciplines develop conceptual tools that enable practitioners to do their job more efficiently. These local usages and words are mutually related in a similar manner to the way that words in a language are mutually constituting.

Possibly the easiest way of thinking of this is in terms of an analogy with games. Within a game of chess each piece gains its meaning from the other pieces in the game. It is not possible fully to comprehend the meaning of, for instance, a bishop in chess if you do not understand how it differs from and is similar to the other pieces in the game. Understanding the meanings of the pieces is inextricably tied to a knowledge of chess as a game. This includes not only that meaning is systemic but that it is constituted through a set of practices. Not only are these practices self-referential local language games but they reflect local ways of life which enable practitioners to accomplish certain tasks. These local systems of meaning form a power resource which facilitates certain tasks.

However, the other aspect of this empowering facet of local meanings is a certain incommensurability with other systems of meaning. Just as it is conceptually impossible to imagine someone finding exact equivalence between chess and some other game, so too we will discover differences in meaning between, for instance, explicitly sociological approaches to power, on the one hand, and those that are normative and based on political philosophy, on the other. The political sociologist and the political philosopher live in different local life worlds in which they use conceptual tools that have been specifically forged to accomplish specific tasks. These are local resources which gain their meaning from within the discipline itself and, as a consequence, will not have an exact equivalence external to that discipline.

Power, structure and agency

In 1963, Talcott Parsons wrote a highly influential article entitled 'On the concept of political power', in which he argued that power was a circulatory medium which gives members of a political system the type of increased capacity for action which they also derive from the economic system. While Parsons's actual account of how this process took place would no longer be accepted within sociological circles (because of its overly functionalist premises) the image is still very much with us. In contemporary sociological thought, we find this image replicated in the work of Anthony Giddens, who argues that social structures give us a capacity for action as agents. We would not otherwise have this facility, if it were not for the existence of social structures. In Giddens's theory of structuration, structures are the elementary units of social order (and thus, by definition, of structured power relations) and are characterized by a patterned recursiveness. Actors have knowledge of these structures as tacit knowledge of *rules* enabling them to order their action in a manner lending predictability to their interactions as well as tacit knowledge of the existing *distribution of power*; in other words, actors have tacit as well as discursive knowledge of the constraints and opportunities they face, and they act reflexively within that knowledge. This not only gives actors a sense of security in the outside world but also facilitates collaboration through the creation of orderedness.

To turn to the analogy with physical power, our knowledge of the physical world involves a knowledge of predictability which facilitates physical power: so, similarly, the fact that we all have a tacit knowledge that others will structure their behavior in a relatively predictable way gives us the capacity to engage in collaborative endeavors with them. This gain in predictability is also accompanied by constraint. While structures facilitate interaction, they also preclude certain modes of action and, consequently, constrain actors. Thus, structures are both enabling and constraining. While Giddens's contribution is significant in alerting us to the structural basis of power, it is also problematic in a number of ways. Significantly, it involves a relatively static, consensual portrayal of structural reproduction and there is not a sufficient link between micro-level interaction and the development of power resources, especially with regard to any potential for resistance, change and/or emancipation.

While Foucault has not, strictly speaking, been classified as a political scientist or sociologist, his work provides a fertile source for the analysis and description of structural conflicts and their relationship to power. In his work we find detailed descriptions of conflicts over meaning. He describes how systems of thought entail specific relations of domination. By systems of thought, he means systemically constituted relations of meaning which constitute agents as subjects. Within Foucault's thought, power exists at two levels: first, local power conflicts which actors are conscious of and which take place within these systems of thought, and, second, deep conflicts over those systems of thought themselves. The latter take the form of resistance to dominant modes of subjectification. While these resistances hold the promise of liberation at a local level, they do not promise total liberation in the form of a total escape from power. Rather, they are strategies without the possibility of ultimate liberation. While his account of power does explain resistances and conflict over meaning, there are theoretical problems associated with Foucault's tendency to downplay the significance of agency, paradigmatically expounded in his 'death of man' hypothesis which, in essence, amounts to a denial of meaningful agency. However, as one of the editors has argued elsewhere (Haugaard, 1997a: 41–98), when we analyze the empirical reality of Foucault's description of the creation of meaning and resistance to it (his genealogical histories), agency would seem to be present in a very real sense – even though Foucault frequently denied that this is the case.

Foucault's view of power has been highly influential on Stewart Clegg's work. In *Frameworks of Power* (1989), Clegg argued that there are three distinct 'circuits of power'. Equivalent to the local conflicts within a system of meaning is episodic power. This is power at the agency level where actors create power by reproducing structures of meaning in an interactive context; it is where agents are most directly autonomous through their reflexivity. This is theoretically equivalent to Giddens's description of the realization of power and agency through structural reproduction. However, this agency-level or micro-level exercise of power presupposes that there are already in existence those meso-level systems of meaning which the actors in question are reproducing. This, the second circuit of power, defines relations of empowerment and disempowerment. At this level, meanings are created, recreated and also contested: effective resistance or change, for example, requires collaboration, which means that interaction with others must be mediated through discursive practices that are less open and malleable. Furthermore, while this engagement with structures of meaning implies agency, the power relations are, at a deeper level, reflections of systemic forms. While actors may resist meaning as single agents, the meanings themselves are a reflection of deeper systemic forms. This deep systemic level is the third circuit of power which constitutes the general systemic set of relations which give overall systemic meaning through relational coherence and, in so doing, define power and powerlessness at the macro-level.

The relationship between individual agency resistance to (rather than mere reproduction of) meaning and systemic form lies at the heart of the concept of a second circuit of power. This is precisely the theme which Clegg develops further in Chapter 3, 'Power and Authority, Resistance and Legitimacy'. The issue for Clegg is how to conceptualize these relations between the individual relations of empowerment and disempowerment on the one hand and, on the other, systemically constituted systems of meaning which convey authority. In a manner which parallels Clegg's concern, Penttinen (Chapter 10, 'Capitalism as a System of Global Power') explores the relationship between globalization and the constitution of individuality. As traditionally conceived, globalization is ultimately a highly systemic form. However, as argued by Penttinen, the most important dimension of this systemic form lies in its implications for the constitution of individual agency.

The Foucauldian emphasis upon power as constituting reality is a central theme of Penttinen's analysis of globalization. Another area where this issue is played out is in recent feminist literature on power and identity formation. In this literature, gender is analyzed as a social construct shaped by power relations as the *conditions of possibility* which define what constitutes the 'feminine' and the 'masculine'. The work of Judith Butler (1990) and Amy Allen (1999) provide pertinent exemplars of that literature. To refer back to Clegg's conceptual scheme, on the one hand, we are at the second circuit of power at which there is an interphase between individual re-creation of and resistance to meaning and the power relations which they entail and, on the other hand, we are at the third circuit of power which in this instance is the system of globalization. Penttinen's analysis of the relationship between globalization and individual relations of empowerment and disempowerment draws not only upon Foucauldian concerns but also upon critical theory and Bauman's work on the human consequences of globalization.

The relationship between the contestation of meaning and the exercise of power is a central concern of Haugaard's work. In *The Constitution of Power*

(1997a) Haugaard argues, like Foucault, that there are two levels or types of conflict: conflict over meaning itself; and conflict which reproduces relations of meaning. Developing Giddens's characterization of structures as tacit knowledge, Haugaard argues that the tacit nature of a system of meaning is central to the maintenance of systemic relations of domination. Within this paradigm, structure is seen as synonymous with meaning. In Parsons's analysis of power as a consensual medium which exists systemically, this power is actually the consensual aspect of structural reproduction.

However, structural reproduction is an interactive phenomenon. In other words, it involves, at very least, two actors – and it is this essentially collaborative aspect of structural reproduction which constitutes a field within which both resistance to meaning (non-collaboration with structural reproduction) and the re-creation of meaning (collaboration) take place. Arguing that structural reproduction is open to contestation in this way raises the fundamental issue of the contingency of social order itself. If we theorize resistance into structural reproduction, the theorization of legitimacy becomes interestingly problematic. Legitimate structures of domination are structures which actors willingly reproduce even though they are fully aware that these contribute to the reproduction of relations of domination. Why do they do this? This is the subject of Chapter 2, 'Power, Ideology and Legitimacy'. The analysis of legitimacy and the theme of globalization in turn raise the broader issue of the development of power resources over time. The development of structures of legitimacy and their relationship to social order is one of the big themes of sociological theory going back to Max Weber. We are looking at the development of the third circuit of power over time.

Structuration and globalization

Part III of this book, indeed, looks at globalization in terms of the evolution of this third circuit of power and its problematic and possibly transformative relationship with the first and second circuits. In *The Nation-State and Violence* (1985), Giddens moved away from the more micro-level approach of his previous work and analyzed these forms of systemic changes over time. As many critics have argued, while this analysis is interesting, it is not very well integrated with his own theory of structuration. In *The Changing Architecture of Politics* (1990), Cerny expanded the notion of structuration in order to examine the evolution of power resources over time through an analysis of the modern state itself. The process of modernity has been inextricably tied up with the formation of ongoing historical patterns of structuration which have been central to the constitution of the state as a systemic form of power. At the same time, the development over time of the domestic state or internal political structure has nonetheless always been inseparable from and embedded within an international or global order, an order based on the distinction discussed earlier in this introduction between the state itself and the states system.

As the global order has changed, therefore – especially as the economic, social and political linkages *cutting across* states have increased in their density – states have not merely been passive dependent variables, nor have state actors merely focused on resisting so-called globalization. Rather, political actors have sought to capture the benefits of globalization for their domestic constituents, i.e., to make firms and economic activities located within their borders more competitive in international markets – moving, in Cerny's (1997) words, 'from the welfare state to the competition state'. Thus state actors themselves (and states in a structural sense too) are increasingly becoming key agents in the process of political globalization, and thus, in turn, of economic and social globalization too. In this book (Chapter 8, 'Globalization and the Disarticulation of Power: Towards a New Middle Ages?') and elsewhere (Cerny, 1995; 1999a; 1999b), Cerny argues that this process transforms the state and undermines or disarticulates many of its traditional functions, including that of security and defense. In contrast, Lentner (Chapter 9) argues that globalization actually reinforces state structures although at the same time causing them to evolve in a more traditionally internationalist direction and cooperating through multilateral arrangements.

If we think of globalization therefore as the development of a new global systemness, we are essentially arguing that a new third circuit of power (to use Clegg's terminology) is developing. However, this raises an interesting question. Are we witnessing the development of a new system with an internal dynamic of its own or, alternatively, the expansion of an existing system of domination? In Chapter 7 ('Globalization as Americanization'), Berndtson argues that globalization is actually the expression of American hegemony. The global system is simply the extension of US relations of domination. This hypothesis is at variance with Lentner's analysis in which globalization is seen as separate. For Lentner ('Politics, Power and States in Globalization'), the US is a very successful actor within this newly developing system of globalization and, indeed, is the primary guarantor and carrier of liberalism in the contemporary world; nevertheless, although American power may drive liberalism, liberal practices encompass more than Americanization. This is theoretically fundamentally different from arguing that globalization is Americanization even if both positions acknowledge the importance of the US as a world actor.

Furthermore, Lentner's analysis of globalization is also significantly different from Cerny's in his view of the state. For Cerny, the modern state is a phenomenon of modernity itself which is slowly being superseded by new postmodern power structures which are consistent with globalization. On the other hand, Lentner holds that modernity continues and the state simply adapts to unfolding historical circumstances. He argues, furthermore, that the liberal state has in most respects come to dominate politics at the beginning of the twenty-first century. Thus, for Lentner globalization means greater connectedness among persisting states which themselves drive globalization processes; and he denies that either the state form or the states system are in a process of transformation. In contrast, Cerny holds that the state form and the states system are probably undergoing transformation through a process of a deep historical shift from modernity to postmodernity. This difference in interpretation is, in part, tied to differences in their fundamental philosophies of history. Lentner has what can be termed a continuist view of history whereas Cerny has a discontinuous one. The debate between continuous and discontinuous views of history is fundamental to the analysis of history. Foucault, for instance, holds a discontinuous view of history. For him, modern history is characterized by radical systemic breaks which make things totally unalike on either side of a given systemic break.

To take a specific instance, in the early sixteenth century science was essentially an art of interpretation, whereas in the late sixteenth century it became a matter of empirical classification. As a consequence, if we look at an early sixteenth century text in biology we find an elaborate exegesis of signs and signatures, whereas in the latter part of the same century biology is a matter of careful empirical description. Because of this fundamental shift, the two biologies are incommensurable. That is to say, they are fundamentally unalike and, as a consequence, not comparable with each other. In the philosophy of science, the Kuhnian position also involves a discontinuous view of history. For Kuhn (1962), a scientific revolution is a fundamental reordering of modes of perception, like a *Gestalt* switch, which makes things incommensurable with each other before and after a scientific revolution.

The Foucauldian and Kuhnian views of the history of the sciences are at variance with more traditional views of scientific development. In these views, scientific advances are built upon one another in a slow and laborious manner over time. In this perspective there are no radical discontinuities but, rather, great discoveries, which move the progress of science faster than before. This debate between continuous and discontinuous interpretations of history is, of course, not unique to the history of science. Ernest Gellner, for instance, argues that nationalism is unique to the nineteenth century, whereas Hastings (1997) argues that nationalism has been with us for a very long time, even though he acknowledges that it has undergone certain important transformations during the last couple of centuries. Similarly, there are those who argue that the modern sovereign territorial state is a phenomenon which is purely associated with modernity whereas others view it as part of a continuous evolutionary process which goes back to ancient Greece and Rome.

In all these debates the issue is not simply an empirical matter but a theoretical one as well. To generalize: the discontinuists tend to hold a more systemic view of social relations than the continuists. If you hold a strongly systemic view, this entails the hypothesis that once the system undergoes transformation then incommensurability takes place. On the other hand, if you are less systemically inclined, you will view the continuous development of things on their own as a historical possibility. To take the instance of the state, for the continuist the state has a history of development on its own which progresses over time (from ancient Athens to the state in the global world) whereas, for the discontinuist, systems transform themselves and, in so doing, totally redefine the internal relations of the elements which constitute them. Hence, the sovereign territorial state is possibly only a phenomenon of modernity. In the latter view, once the system changes there are no equivalences, just as there is no equivalence between the 50 Inuit words for snow and anything which can be said in English. For example, for Lentner the liberal discourse of modernity and neoliberal discourse of globalization constitute equivalent processes, whereas for Penttinen there is no such equivalence between them despite their superficial similarities.

Power, democratic theory and decision-making

In normative political theory, power is by definition conceptualized relative to the normative concerns of the political theorists in question. The contemporary power debate began in the 1950s as a debate concerning the democraticness of the US. Under the influence of European sociology, from the 1930s to the 1950s, a number of critics of American democracy began to argue that the formal political equality, which existed institutionally, did not amount to actual political equality. By working from the bottom up, for example, community power theorists argued that, even at the very lowest, local level, the US was governed by a small clique. Given that even local issues were not in the hands of 'the locals', it made sense to argue that the US as whole was not democratic. Working from the opposite top-down end of the analytical spectrum, C. Wright Mills (1956) argued that there was a core elite of about 400 people who made all the decisions that really mattered.

It was at this stage that Robert Dahl entered the debate by arguing that the community power theorists' and Mills's critiques of American democracy were fundamentally flawed because of an inadequate concept of power. In democratic theory, he suggested, we are interested in actual rather than potential events. What is significant is who actually exercises power, not who has the potential to exercise power. What the critics of American democracy had done was to show that there was a massively unequal distribution of power resources but not of power itself. It may be that there are local and national elites who have resources which are vastly greater than others, but this is not the same as showing that power is actually exercised to the benefit of that elite. Based upon this, Dahl developed a language of power analysis which contained a number of conceptual distinctions, the most important of which included the difference between power and resources (Dahl, 1957; 1968). Money is a power resource, but that is not the same as power. One millionaire may collect paintings and the other politicians. Both may have the resources but they do not have the same power; only the latter is powerful. Based upon this (and other distinctions), Dahl argued that while the US contained highly unequal distributions of resources, this was not the same as claiming that it was not democratic because democracy concerns the power politics of actual decision-making. Power is synonymous with the exercise of power as manifest in *decision-making processes* in which identifiable actors are observed to prevail over others.

Dahl's concept of power was essentially linked to his view of democratic politics. As a democratic theorist, Dahl was concerned with describing the way in which actors realize their interests through decisions which are made within a democratic system. Democracy entails a normative commitment to political equality but in this context it is not a totalizing equality. Rather, it is an equality within a clear distinction between what is deemed political and what is private. Within liberal democratic theory, the economic sphere has always been considered predominantly (although not entirely) private and, as a consequence, beyond the normative reach of the normative democratic principles of equality. Marxists, of course, have always disputed this division between public and private and, more recently, feminists have done the same, albeit from a different perspective. The dispute between liberals and their adversaries rests upon the fundamental validity of this distinction between political practice and a private realm. Critics of the division argue that a set of political practices may guarantee formal political equality – such as an equal vote for all – but such a formal procedure will not actually deliver equal outcomes if there are biases which prevent actors from converting their formal equality in decision-making into actual equality as manifested in their ability to realize their interests and it is frequently the case that these biases arise from the private sphere. These biases thus concern both the dividing line between public and private and the structural configuration of the political structures and institutions themselves, as outlined in the discussion above in the section on normative and empirical power dimensions of the power debate involving institutions.

Furthermore, once power moves from equality in decision-making processes to equality in outcomes, the concept becomes expanded. Bachrach and Baratz (1962; 1963) argued that Dahl's analysis of power was too limited in being confined purely to overt decision-making. Power is also exercised by preventing the interests of others from reaching the decision-making forum. Since Bachrach and Baratz, like Dahl, were schooled in behavioralist political science, they insisted that the biases should be empirically observable. In order to establish that bias existed, it had to be demonstrable that someone somewhere was preventing others from having their specific interests realized. They called this exercise of power 'non-decision-making' and were insistent that this was the empirically observable act of blocking the interests of others. In this sense, a non-decision is still a decision. The attempt to limit the concept of non-decision-making to observable behavior is, from a normative perspective, entirely arbitrary – although it makes sense from the perspective of good practice within behaviorist political science. After all, if we evaluate political equality in terms of outcomes, then any biased aspect of the social system prevents certain actors from realizing their interests as effectively as others, irrespective of whether from another agent actively engaged in non-decision-making or, alternatively, from structural biases which are not reducible to the deliberate actions of others.

Steven Lukes took this line further in *Power: A Radical View* (1974), arguing that the biases of a system are sustained not simply by overt decisions and non-decisions but, equally significantly, by structural biases for which no one actor is responsible. If, from the point of view of empirical political sociology, for instance, it can be shown that social order influences the ability of actors to realize their interests within the political process, this becomes power in the normative sense. The difficulty with this position is that, from a normative point of view, if we analyze things sufficiently, virtually everything affects the principle of democratic equality. Lukes argued that the consciousness of actors was a form of power. If actors do not understand their real interests, then their capacity to make decisions is affected. Lukes called Dahl's decisional view of power the first dimension of power, Bachrach and Baratz's non-decision-making the second, and his own emphasis upon structural biases and false consciousness the third dimension.

When considering decision-making from a normative perspective, it is important to remember that the outcome of a decision is not simply made at the moment individuals decide to do one thing rather than the other, but is determined by a whole series of factors. Decision-making is often said to consist of six steps, as follows: (1) the perception of an issue over which a choice has to made; (2) the identification of a number of possibilities with regard to this issue; (3) the admission of the issue and attendant possibilities to the decision-making process; (4) the comparative assessment of these options; (5) the election of one of the possibilities as the one to be chosen; and (6) the implementation of that choice. From the perspective of a normative orientation toward political equality, all these steps are crucially important because each one has the potential to change the outcome. The first two steps may be extended right back to the socialization of the individual. As feminists argue, the patriarchal nature of education is a fundamental source of power which facilitates male domination even in circumstances in which stages 3 to 6 are essentially democratic. If women have lower aspirations than men, they may neither question existing social relations (step 1) nor realize possibilities which alternative arrangements might offer (step 2). Similarly, Marxists have argued that the Western procedural type of democracy furthers capitalist power because it gives legitimacy to a system by providing the illusion of democratic equality. In reality, actors' abilities to perceive the choices available to them have already been predetermined by socialization through ideological state apparatuses or superstructures.

Stage 3 is the stage with which Bachrach and Baratz were concerned in their second dimension of power. Here political outcomes may be affected by agenda setting, institutional biases against certain outcomes, and bureaucratic red tape. All these processes have the potential to determine an outcome, even if stage 3 is democratic. Stages 4 and 5 are focused upon by Dahl – the actual conflict between actors over decisions, who prevails and who is prevailed upon. Stage 6 is also crucial, since many factors can prevent a decision, once made, from being actualized; this is the focus of much policy analysis.

As we can see from the analysis of these six stages of decision-making, it is a complex task to evaluate the distribution of power within a political system. In public policy analysis we see an interesting process of moving back and forth between the normative and the more empirical or political sociological analysis of power. Like normative theorists, policy analysts are concerned with locating power in a conflictual situation but this is not necessarily so explicitly influenced by normative concerns over democraticness and political equality: in this regard they also share the political sociologist's concern with how power is created by the social system. However, there is a sense in which the policy focus on power is very much a development of the democratic theorists' concerns, given the strong focus on decision-making while, at the same time, their perception of context is clearly influenced by political sociology. In the policy-making chapters contained in Part II of this book, we can clearly see how power is located and operates within these six stages of decision-making.

POWER SHIFT: TOWARDS A NEOLIBERAL HEGEMONY?

The various problematics and debates discussed in the previous sections certainly do not exhaust the various ways that the concept of power is (and could conceivably be) contested. Even the list presented at the beginning of this introduction is merely indicative. The chapters contained in this book, however, focus primarily on the most salient of the current debates prevailing at the beginning of the third millennium. And one predominant theme cutting across all power debates today is the renaissance since the late 1970s of political and economic liberal ideology in a more assertive form called neoliberalism, particularly in its American manifestation. Neoliberalism, whether good or bad, true or false, is widely seen to be in the process of becoming the dominant discourse of today's world.

At a domestic level, continuists argue, modern liberal democracy originated at the end of the eighteenth century with the American Revolution of 1776 and the French Revolution of 1789. As a part of these developments, power shifted within societies from aristocracies to middle classes. In the case of the United States, the application of the ideas of Montesquieu concerning the separation of powers insured a political process of struggle for control of national policy. The invention of federalism further divided institutional power along subnational lines of authority. These arrangements, though institutionalizing channels and mechanisms for political combat among factions and parties, also afforded scope for groups to constitute themselves as political actors with power to operate *within* the political system. Moreover, by embedding ideas such as individual liberty, rights and equal protection of law both within the Constitution and within American ideology more widely, the American system also provided powerful symbolic means for exerting pressure on dominant groups by aspirants – blacks and women providing two obvious examples – who aimed to share in or oppose the dominant arrangements.

At an international level, liberalism has been associated with American power, especially visible since the United States' rejection of isolationism in the Second World War. At the beginning of the twentieth century, the expansionism of the United States was seen in the context of similar behavior by apparently even more dynamic powers, such as the imperial United Kingdom and France and the rising centers of Germany and Japan. During the First World War, Russia was overcome by revolution, which eventually brought the new model of leadership under the Communist Party which put into place a command economy. Soon thereafter, fascism and Nazism took over in Italy and Germany and military authorities assumed the helm of Japan, all three exhibiting expansionist dynamism and a threat to the international status quo. Building on their huge industrial potential, the United States and the Soviet Union produced immense quantities of arms, which not only led to victory in the Second World War itself but also set the stage both for the Cold War contest between the two superpowers and for the creation of the American-led 'embedded liberalism' international political economy of the postwar period. With the disintegration of the Soviet Union in 1991, the United States and its allies appeared to dominate the international system not only militarily and economically but discursively as well.

Thus although much of the historiography of the twentieth century renders these contests as being between ideas and ways of organizing societies such as fascism, communism and liberal democracy, the ultimate outcome has also to be explained by factors of power such as economic production, scientific and technological inventiveness, military prowess, political leadership and the increasingly consensual predominance of the discourse of neoliberalism across a growing range of geographical areas, societies and life worlds. Probably the most important ideological debate today is whether these power resources are derived principally from the ideas of economic and political liberalism as such (as represented today in the American discursive tradition and American-style practices of power) or from the material power of American and global capitalism.

Therefore, with the end of the Cold War, not only had liberal (and neoliberal) ideas become increasingly dominant in other countries too (as Berndtson points out in Chapter 7 of this book), but also the US/UK-led coalition demonstrated its military power during the Gulf War against Iraq in 1991 and again in 1999 in Kosovo. Former communist countries have also adopted liberal democratic forms; virtually all of Latin America entered transitions from authoritarian and military regimes to democracy; and such Asian countries as the Philippines and South Korea liberalized too. Neoclassical market economics, more squarely at the core of neoliberalism than of traditional political liberalism, has become the standard discourse, and increasingly the dominant practice, not just of democratic political systems but of authoritarian ones such as China as well. The international economic system has been rendered more liberal in trade and finance, as represented by the Washington Consensus and the actions of the new World

Trade Organization, the International Monetary Fund and the World Bank in promoting financial as well as trade liberalization.

This is not to claim that the United States as such is omnipotent, for other forces remain in play, including the decolonization/national-independence process that occurred across Asia and Africa in the first three-quarters of the twentieth century and its continuing aftermath in the last half of that century. The dynamic expressions of domination that spread European and North American rule across much of Asia and Africa also precipitated new resistances, including Japan's industrialization and imperial aspirations. Japan was seen by many in Asia as a successful attempt at resistance to imperial domination by the West, in part through imitation. It was these successes that demonstrated to other Asian countries that they no longer had to accept inferiority to the West. Eventually, resistance to Western domination called forth exceptional military efforts in Indochina, first against the French and then against the United States, with ultimate triumph in a unified Vietnam only in 1975. Today, paradoxically, American-style globalization processes dominate the region economically. Thus, China and other East Asian countries, including even Vietnam, for the most part participate in international trade, accept foreign direct investment and admit limited aspects of Western culture.

Much of the emphasis in modern discourse about new developments in political life has been given to transitions to democracy and market systems. However, other developments have also reshaped distributions of power within societies, from technology to social attitudes. For example, a number of trends met in the 1960s to produce a so-called counterculture in the advanced industrial countries, which contained elements of extreme self-expression as well as of more libertarian, grassroots conceptions of freedom outside and beyond the formal freedoms available through macro-level liberal democratic institutions. Today, one interpretation of the spread of personal computers and the internet, with its vast fund of information, holds that individuals are thus empowered by such technology; the prominent role of innovators who had grown up in the 1960s counterculture in places like Silicon Valley has rewritten the book on managerial hierarchy towards much looser, flatter and more diffuse forms of organization. Of course, some increases in individual autonomy reduce the social control of families, religious leaders, teachers, and other traditional sources of constraint on the individual. However, new collective identities are also emerging, based on ethnic ties and multiculturalism, gender categories, the growth of new professional and occupational groups as capitalism is transformed by new technologies, consumerism, media images and the like, and these appear to be profoundly shaping discursive change.

A discursive emphasis on individual development can also provide a catalyst for struggles for power by broader groups, especially when social and political arrangements have traditionally repressed and/or discriminated against members of identifiable groups. Two such groups are blacks and women. Black slavery throughout the western hemisphere and elsewhere lasted for 300 years until the mid nineteenth century. With emancipation, blacks in all of the countries where slavery had been a widespread institution struggled in the aftermath to attain rights, status, protection of law, economic wellbeing, education and other benefits deriving from citizenship in the polities in which they lived. The narrative of that struggle for power, and the sustained resistance to it, continues, as does the narrative of anti-imperialism in formerly colonized areas.

For women, since the mid 1970s a worldwide feminist movement has been attempting to wrest power from those who sustained repressive arrangements in many countries. Individual empowerment gained through feminist activities represents better lives with greater freedom and autonomy than such people endured under traditional, male-dominated families, social taboos and constraints, and discriminatory legal and property arrangements, although some believe that one important effect has been the breakdown of the traditional family. Another, more broadly social and political implication is the expansion of the workforce with the addition of women to the job market. The complexity of this power shift increases with the expansion of the competing labor force made available by the global rationalization of production. Thus capital, always privileged in a liberal market economic system, gains additional leverage in the contemporary world as power shifts from families and social groups to corporations and from labor to capital.

These trends growing out of the liberal emphasis on the individual are supplemented by a new political emphasis by liberal political authorities on human rights in international relations. Received practice in relations among states refrained from direct and open unfriendly interference by one government in the internal affairs of other states. In the period after the Second World War, however, the liberal states constructed norms of human rights which, at least at the level of nominal standards, provided protections to individuals against violations of those norms by their own governments. A key development was the Helsinki Agreement of 1975 which was formally accepted even by then-communist governments. Other things were at work in Eastern Europe in the 1980s, economic decline in particular, but the empowerment of citizens through their own efforts made an important contribution to the weakening of communist authority in those countries.

Unrestrained liberalism or neoliberalism in the post-Cold-War period has also provided a context in which nongovernmental organizations (NGOs) have become considerably more active than previously. Both liberal and neoliberal discourses not only allow for but actively promote the private, nongovernmental sector, in terms, respectively, of the political marketplace of interest and pressure group politics on the one hand and the expansion of market economics on the other. This attribute is particularly manifest in the case of business, for liberal economic doctrine holds that minimally encumbered free enterprise produces goods and services more efficiently than governmentally directed and owned enterprises. Liberalism does not limit its promotion of private activities to the economic sector, however. The idea that autonomous individuals and private groups comprise civil society remains an important part of liberal doctrine. Thus, neoliberalism in the post-Cold-War era claims to have provided an expanded political space for enhanced and increased nongovernmental activities and individual autonomy. Of course, many of these groups are opposed to the very agenda of neoliberalism as supported by the United States, as they see it as causing environmental degradation and the crystallization of new inequalities in a globalizing world.

In summary, a variety of developments in political life have occurred and are still occurring that shape power arrangements both within national societies and in the world at large. At the center of such developments at the beginning of the twenty-first century are the discourse and practice of neoliberalism. Just as the last centuries have proved to be very fluid, one can expect that many of these developments will continue in the future; yet others may be transformed into paradigmatic or systemic change. At the core of the concerns of social science will be the question of whether neoliberalism, seemingly so dominant in the last two decades of the twentieth century, will continue to occupy its current dominating role. Given the complexity and dynamism of the world, one can probably expect that new, perhaps unimagined political developments will arise. At other levels, too, the character of political power within national societies may be changing as well. In the policy science approach, for example, particularly in policy network analysis, the idea is gaining ground that political systems are being transformed from command polities to negotiation polities. Some argue that the state itself seems to have become less hierarchical, being required to negotiate with other power centers rather than commanding from a position of authority. However, state structures are not about to wither away. Perhaps the lion is no more the king in the jungle, but this does not mean that the lion as a species no longer exists. As always, such dynamics, the interaction of continuities and discontinuities, will involve the exercise of power, the formation of new patterns of power distribution, and resistance to coercion by many of those affected.

NOTES

1 The so-called meso-level represents a structured *intermediate* level of social, economic and/or political organization lying somewhere between the macro- (large-scale) and the micro- (small-scale) levels, partly separate and autonomous but also linking the two.
2 Kuhn (1962) argues that scientific method in the natural sciences in fact looks more like social science than is normally understood by natural scientists themselves, mainly because it too is dependent on the construction and acceptance of paradigms rather than on pure objectivity. In political and social philosophy, however, there is usually a plurality of potential paradigms available to the analyst at any one time, whereas in the natural sciences there is generally only one socially accepted 'dominant paradigm' in a particular time frame which defines the parameters of 'normal science' for a period.

3 Power itself is a highly contested concept in terms of its definition and implications
   – what is called a 'family resemblance' concept. See below, 'What Is Power? Some
   Theoretical Issues', under 'Power as a contested concept'.
4 The distinction between 'structures' and 'institutions' is a debatable and fluid one.
   Most authors tend to use 'structure' as the broader *genus*, including at one end of
   the spectrum informal but regularized patterns of social behavior constituted
   through practical consciousness ('practices'), as well as, at the other end of the
   spectrum, those more formal, organizationally distinct structures constituted
   (institutionalized) through discursive consciousness; the term 'institution' is
   normally, but not always, reserved to the latter species (compare Cerny, 1990 and
   Haugaard, 1997a).
5 The word 'function' is used here not in its sociological structural-functionalist
   sense of a necessary relationship deriving from the inherent imperatives of a social
   system but merely as denoting the *de facto* 'tasks, roles and activities' (Sorauf,
   1972) of a particular organizational unit.

1 THEORIES

Since the publication of Lukes's *Power* (1974) there has been a change of emphasis in the analysis of power. This is most obvious if we look at the authors and concepts associated with power today, as compared to then. At present references to Foucault and Nietzsche, and terms such as 'discourse' and 'practices', are inextricably tied to the concept of power. In the 1960s and 1970s references to Gramsci and Marx, and to terms such as ideology and class consciousness, abounded.[1] This move is not symptomatic of a new fashion for certain authors or concepts but, rather, a manifestation of a deeper shift in social theory.

From the Second World War up to the late 1970s, the analysis of power tended to be divided between Marxist-derived social theories and consensual perspectives based upon either Parsonian functionalism (Parsons, 1963) or (less frequently) Blau's exchange theory (Blau, 1964). In contemporary analysis, the concerns of the Marxists have remained important (power as domination still counts) but they have been retheorized within a different concept of social order. Ironically, while the consensual theorists' view of social order has fallen into disfavor, their view of power has resurfaced in current perceptions of social order.[2]

At a broad level, one of the crucial transformations which has taken place is that social theorists no longer make any normative foundational claims for their theories. Even in the most analytical (and, consequently, least prescriptive) Marxism there was always an implicit claim to the effect that the Marxist author in question enjoyed privileged access to certain absolute truths concerning what constitutes a good society. This foundational normative claim was based not only upon normative principles (privileged insights into what is right and wrong) but upon a scientific insight into a meta-narrative concerning the sociology of history. In that context, scientific meant foundational – absolutely true. The shift away from foundationalism and metanarrative is, of course, not unique to social theory. Even if we do not accept Lyotard's (1986) characterization of this social phenomenon as a move from modernity to postmodernity but prefer to think, as Beck (1992) or Giddens (1991) do, in terms of a maturing of modernity,[3] this shift is part of a wider phenomenon which characterizes a larger aspect of social life as a whole.[4]

In social theory this shift contributed not only to a redefinition of the parameters of what constitutes good practice but also changed social theory into a more self-reflective discipline. When Lukes wrote *Power* (1974), the relationship between power and knowledge was one in which power was perceived as corrupting knowledge. Knowledge which was corrupted by power was considered the opposite of truth. The task of the critical social theorist was to unmask these types of distortions using the sword of truth and metanarrative – the real interests of the proletariat (truth) and the historical inevitability of class struggle (metanarrative). This, of course, presupposes that the social theorist has a privileged position based upon 'the truth' and an understanding of social processes which others participated in but were unaware of. Lukes's third dimension of power is typical in this regard. The third dimension of power is a highly effective manifestation of power whereby those over whom power is exercised do not understand their 'real' or 'true' interests and, simultaneously, find themselves enmeshed in a historical process, inherited from the past, which is contrary to their 'real' interests.

While claims to truth and metanarrative gradually ran into disfavor during the 1980s, social theorists still concern themselves with explaining power as domination. Theorists are still interested in understanding how power relations are sustained over time but, now, the analysis has a self-reflexive aspect. Authors such as Clegg (1989) reflect upon Marxist and functionalist claims to truth and the manner in which these claims were sustained by the local social orders of the recent past. As a consequence, the problem of social order is to understand the creation and reproduction of specific discourses.

A discourse is a local social order which allows one to say certain things but prevents others from being said. A discourse is not a metanarrative, in the sense that, for instance, feudalism, capitalism, socialism or communism are part of some prescripted historical evolution or, to take two other examples, there are deep structures which determine social life (Lévi-Strauss), or there are systems with specific needs (Parsons). Rather than focusing on social forces which go on behind people's backs (as metanarrative analysis presupposes), social order is theorized in terms of the construction of meaning. Understanding social order involves understanding how individuals create and recreate meanings when they engage in social practices. These meanings form parameters within which agents can give expression to themselves. These are not simply the meanings of specific objects or things: the issues are much wider than that. Significantly, they include the creation of the meaning of self by understanding the construction of ontology, or ways of being.

Power makes the reproduction of certain meanings possible and precludes others. To use the jargon of those working within the Foucauldian tradition, it defines 'conditions of possibility'. Within discourse, power facilitates certain modes of thought and militates against others. Within this theoretical context, claims to truth are inextricably tied to strategies of power that facilitate and preclude certain modes of expression and being. Truth facilitates while its shadow, untruth, precludes the production of meaning.

Within this analysis, Marxism itself became theorized as part of a set of conditions of possibility which facilitated self-expression based upon class but, equally effectively, delegitimated ontologies of self-expression based upon excluded categories, such as sexuality and lifestyle. As a consequence of this change in orientation, social theory became tied to the rise of new social movements, or more precisely, the need to theorize them.

In Foucault's work we find a careful documentation of how discourses are formed and transformed. He used history to enable us to understand how it is that we have come to be the way we are – our ontologies. In this context the object of social theory, as social critique, rests not upon either a claim to truth or exposing falsity but rather in showing how discourse shapes the conditions of possibility within social life. Within this paradigm the claims to truth made by others are interpreted as a strategy of power which enables those who have truth on their side to speak, but renders mute those who do not.[5] As argued by Laclau and Mouffe (1985), truth becomes a way of giving discursive fixity and, in this way defining the possibilities of debate (see Clegg, Chapter 3).

In Foucault's thought power does not simply preclude, it does not simply say no, but facilitates certain modes of expression at the expense of others. Acknowledging that power not only precludes but also enables draws upon the vision of power (but not the social theory) of those who, like Parsons, argued that power is not simply 'power over' but, also, 'power to'. Discourse does not simply preclude certain modes of expression; rather, its effectiveness lies precisely in the fact that it simultaneously facilitates modes of expression other than those which are excluded.

While the work of Giddens and Foucault appear dissimilar in theoretical orientation, the theory of structuration and high modernity[6] can be analyzed as part of a similar paradigmatic shift in social theory. The theory of structuration is an explicit rejection of the type of metadiscourse associated with Marxism, structuralism and functionalism. Under the influence of Heidegger, it is an explicitly ontological theory which concerns itself with the being of social order. As the basic units of social order, structures exist through social practices. Social structures are available to social actors both as facilitators of social action and as constrainers of social action. Just as discourses do, structures constitute part of the conditions of possibility of social practices. To use Giddens's terminology, structures are both enabling and constraining. The enabling aspect of social structure is 'power to', as capacity for action (the consensual image of power). This capacity for action, 'power to', can also be exercised to dominate others and, hence, can be exercised 'over' others. Central to Giddens's theorization of contemporary society (high modernity) is the idea that in contemporary society one of the key problems for individuals is the constitution of self. In previous, more traditionally minded societies, a sense of self was given (you are born a wife or worker) whereas as today the constitution of self is an essentially reflexive project. In other words, the constitution of self is a key problematic, just as it was for Foucault. While noting this convergence it has, of course, to be acknowledged that a key difference between the two is their particular use of their own local language games and Giddens's tendency to take the constraints upon conditions of possibility less seriously than Foucault.[7]

In normative political theory, this emphasis upon the conditions of possibility and the constitution of self has strong resonances with Aristotelian and civic republican political thought. In the Aristotelian world view all living things have a telos which constitutes both their final end and their essence. To take a simple example, the telos of an acorn is to be an oak. 'Oakness' is both what makes an acorn grow and its true essence. Translated into normative theory, Aristotle's assertion that 'man'[8] is naturally a political animal is a statement to the effect that man's telos is fully realized in a political society. Only in a polis does he realize his true essence.

Within civic republicanism, the idea of a natural political telos became part of the project of political theory. Building upon this, for civic republicans a key objective of political association is to facilitate the development of human potential through the creation of a political arena which nurtures the human essence.

A key thinker in this tradition is Arendt. She argued that power should be considered not purely conflictually but, rather, as a capacity for action which individuals gain by membership of a social system (Arendt, 1970). Her analysis shows strong parallels with Parsons's concept of power but nevertheless there are fundamental differences. Arendt's view of power is not tied to functionalism but, rather, is inextricably bound up with her normative project.

At the time of her work, the field of power analysis was dominated by the three-dimensional power debate and the consensual position of Parsons. As a consequence Arendt's analysis of power did not receive the prominence that it might have at the time of publication (1970).[9] However, the Aristotelian and, consequent, ontological emphasis of her work has made her view of power particularly pertinent to the concerns of contemporary power theorists. The idea of discourses (Foucault) or structures (Giddens) shaping the conditions of possibility for human development is ideally tailored to her normative project and her concept of power is compatible with contemporary views.

While these convergences have been noted by many, Goehler's analysis (Chapter 1) is the first theorization of power to use them to construct a single comprehensive view of power. He argues that there are in fact two forms of power: 'transitive' and 'intransitive' power. Transitive power is 'power over' and is the form of power that Lukes dealt with in *Power* (1974). Intransitive power, on the other hand, is 'power to' and is theorized in terms of a coupling of Arendtian and Foucauldian views of power. The latter is accomplished by making use of insights from a number of sources in contemporary social theory, including Bourdieu and Luhmann. This theorization allows Goehler to show how all power (transitive and intransitive) presupposes the construction of social order based upon a consensus on norms and practices.

In Chapter 2, Haugaard looks at the whole issue of ideology and legitimacy. In the analysis of ideology he shows that the type of phenomenon which interested power theorists, such as Lukes, when they wrote about 'false' consciousness, has not gone away. What has changed are the theoretical premises of contemporary social theory. Consistent with the latter, Haugaard argues that we should think not in terms of 'true' and 'false' consciousness but, rather, in terms of levels of consciousness. With regard to legitimacy Haugaard takes a step further than contemporary debates concerning inclusion and exclusion of meaning. He analyzes the exact process whereby certain meanings and ontologies are legitimated and others delegitimated.

The whole issue of ideology and legitimacy (as examined by Haugaard) and the normative basis of intransitive power (Goehler) is linked to the issue of authority. In Chapter 3 Clegg analyzes the conflictual side of authority and the manner in which symbols and meanings are given an authoritative basis through the construction of a fixity of meanings. Clegg looks at the whole issue of the resistance to meaning and the strategies open to actors wishing to contest dominant discourses. This builds upon, and contributes to, Foucauldian analysis, the contributions of Laclau and Mouffe and, indeed, also his own theorization of circuits of power (Clegg, 1989).

If we look at these three chapters together and compare them to the state of the art at the time of Lukes's *Power* (1974) we can see certain continuities and discontinuities. On the one hand, on the continuous side, the perception that power is both conflictual and consensual is still present. However, on the other hand, on the discontinuous side, we see that there is a convergent focus upon the problem of social order as a problem of meaning and ontology. While it is undeniably the case that Goehler, Clegg and Haugaard view social order differently, and that each places slightly different emphasis upon the conflictual and consensual aspects of power, there is not the same radical incompatibility of perspectives as there was between, for instance, Parsons and Lukes. As stated in the general introduction, there will never be one theory of power, and nor should we wish for one, but this convergent theorization gives us new conceptual tools which enable us to understand contemporary transformations of social order with a higher degree of sophistication than was previously possible.

NOTES

1 This discontinuity is less noticeable in the analytical tradition of political theory. Authors such as Brian Barry (1991), Dowding (1991; 1996), Morriss (1987) and Wrong (1988) have generally continued with their focused analysis of the use of the word 'power' and its relationship to issues of democratic theory. This continuity is in part a consequence of the fact that their concerns are highly specific and, as a consequence, they have a certain legitimate leeway to have a relatively self-contained language game. However, in a few instances it is also (unfortunately) a consequence of the lack of dialogue between 'analytical' and 'continental' philosophy – in the eyes of analytical philosophers Foucault and Nietzsche would be continental.

2 Neither structural functionalism nor exchange theory has much currency in contemporary social theory.

3 Both authors hold that modernity was, from its very inception, anti-foundational. As argued by Kant, reason does not accept any form of authority and, according to Giddens and Beck, both foundationalism and metanarrative are a form of authority in the sense that both are an externally imposed constraint upon reason. As such, they perform the same functions as authority by, in effect, stating 'thus far and no further'. Consequently, the rejection of metanarrative and foundationalism can be theorized as implicit in the logic of modernity as a continuation of the Enlightenment project.

4 How wide this social phenomenon is has to be open to debate. It could be argued that both postmodernity and high modernity are not part of a generalized worldwide phenomenon but, rather, confined to the social milieux of a fairly confined (Western in origin) globalizing intellectual elite. Because these intellectuals tend to associate with one another on a global scale they mistakenly believe that everyone else thinks as they do. Of course, they are aware of the existence of so-called Muslim and Christian fundamentalists, but either they are theorized away as 'irrational reactionary forces', or the issue is sidestepped by focusing on the dialogue between postmodernists and high modernists and those opposing views which have certain post/high modernity characteristics – even if one party is neither 'post' nor 'high' modern.

5 For an overview of Foucault's analysis, see Haugaard (1997a: 41–97).

6 The *Constitution of Society* (1984) is Giddens's fullest statement of structuration theory and *The Consequences of Modernity* (1991) is a good starting point for understanding his theory of modernity. Haugaard (1997a: 98–115) gives a short summary of Giddens's theory of power and structuration.

7 Given Giddens's appreciation of constraint in the theory of structuration, this would appear to be an inconsistency.

8 The gendered usage is deliberate, Aristotle excluded women – a position which contemporary political theorists working in this tradition would reject.

9 Habermas did engage with it seven years later (Habermas, 1977).

1   Constitution and Use of Power

Gerhard Goehler

TOWARDS A NEW FRAMEWORK FOR CONCEPTUALIZING POWER

Any attempt to grasp the concept of power opens a variety of different and most controversial meanings. One of those oppositions in conceptualizing power is Max Weber's view on the one hand and Hannah Arendt's on the other. To start with these two not only illustrates again the difficulty of clearly understanding one of the most familiar characteristics of our society, but also helps to get some new insights into the nature of power, its constitution and its use in society.

Max Weber understands power as the *carrying out of one's will* in a social relationship, something which can also be accomplished through violence: '"Power" is the probability that one actor within a social relationship will be in a position to carry out his own will despite resistance, regardless of the basis on which this probability rests' (1978: 53). Power understood as the exertion of influence over others, either in accordance with or, even more significantly, against their will, is – in different variations – widespread throughout the social sciences. It also corresponds to our everyday understanding.

By contrast, Hannah Arendt understands power as 'speaking and acting in concert'. Power is, for her, the counterconcept to that of violence: 'power springs up between men when they act together . . . Power is what keeps the public realm, the potential space of appearance between acting and speaking men, in existence' (Arendt, 1958: 200). 'The space of appearance comes into being wherever men are together in the manner of speech and action' (1958: 199). 'Power corresponds to the human ability not just to act but to act in concert' (1970: 44).

Hannah Arendt stakes everything upon power as the human capacity for acting in common with others, and opposes to it her concept of the violence of the individual. This conception of power is both comprehensive and normatively charged. Its focus is not the exercise of power in Max Weber's sense as the carrying out of one's will. Rather, it concerns the power of a society in the sense of its ability to exist, in the sense of its self-empowerment as a community. This is what Arendt defines as the political: 'All political institutions are manifestations and materializations of power; they petrify and decay as soon as the living power of the people ceases to uphold them' (1970: 42). This emphatic view of power takes, on the one hand, the Greek polis as its model. But at the same time, it presupposes an existentially charged understanding of power prevalent ever since Nietzsche, a succinct example of which can be found in the metaphysical notion of an intensification of life understood in terms of a 'will to power'.

The concepts of power put forward by Max Weber and Hannah Arendt are completely different: the empirical concept of Max Weber and the highly normative concept of Hannnah Arendt appear not to be at all compatible with each other. Can these two conceptions, then, for purposes of normative and empirical political analysis, be understood as addressing *the same phenomenon*? Neither can be simply pushed aside with respect to our actual experiences. Yet they cannot simply be combined. What is required, then, is a systematic approach to the phenomenon of power which demonstrates that the two conceptions concern different aspects of power which cannot be reduced to one basic concept, but must be seen as coexisting in complementary relationship to each other. What is required, then, is to take seriously not only the concept of Max Weber which seems to be more familiar to our everyday understanding of power, but also the concept of Hannah Arendt which entirely ignores the empirical perspective of effectiveness, and focuses solely on power as speaking and acting in concert, through which a human community, the political sphere and the political are constituted, and through which human beings are only able to acquire their quality as human individuals.

At first glance, the difference between the power concepts of Max Weber and Hannah Arendt only reflects the distinction between 'power over' and 'power to' as formulated by Hanna Pitkin – a distinction which proved to become very authoritative in recent power discussion (Pitkin, 1972: 276–7). 'Power over' refers to power over other persons, to the carrying out of one's own intentions against the intentions of others, to the realizing of one's own options at the expense of the options of someone else. It is actual power and a social relationship *par excellence*. 'Power to', on the other hand, is not, or not primarily, directed at other persons in a social relationship. It represents rather the capacity to do or achieve something, irrespective of the intentions of others. 'Power to' refers, in the first instance, only to a single individual or group and its capacity for action. It is potential power and it does not, following Hanna Pitkin, refer to any social relationship.

In this framework, Hannah Arendt takes an extreme position, as she explicitly limits the extension of power to 'power to'. The aspect of 'power over' not only is left out, but is conceptualized as violence and opposed to the concept of power as 'power to'. But while describing the constitution of power, Arendt does not refer to a single individual. The constitution of power actualizes the community of individuals, and therefore Arendt's 'power to' is not restricted to being mere potential power. Quite the opposite: it is power actualized through joint communication. Following Arendt's view, the constitution of 'power to' blurs the distinction between potential and actual power. 'Power to' in the understanding of Hannah Arendt is a social relation as well as 'power over' in the understanding of Max Weber.

When we consider power essentially as a social relationship, it becomes clear that Max Weber and Hannah Arendt actually have two very different *types of social relationships* in mind. Max Weber understands power in terms of a relationship in which one person directs his will at another person in order to subject him to this power. As opposed to this, Hannah Arendt conceives of power as a relationship between persons that develops in the form of communication and joint action, and is not primarily directed towards people outside. We could also say: Max Weber's formulation concerns *transitive* power, while Hannah Arendt's concerns *intransitive* power. These terms are derived from grammar. Power is transitive when it refers to others (e.g., the carrying out of one's will, mentioned above). Power is intransitive when it refers back to itself.[1] Political science – and most of all, empirical political science – has up to now made little use of this way of viewing the phenomenon of power; it limits itself, on the whole, to the analysis of transitive power.[2] But it is indispensable to consider the two types of power relationships.

To this end, I attempt to structure the concept of power such that, in addition to approaches of a traditional, structuralist and post-structuralist provenance, the normative approach formulated by Hannah Arendt also receives the attention it deserves.[3] I try to formulate the two conceptions of transitive and intransitive power in a way that allows for a normative perspective of power to take account of what the members of an existing community have or must have in common. This normative perspective of power is just as important as that perspective which conceives of power in terms of its exercise over others. It even represents the basis for a polity's existence and has consequences for our understanding of certain crucial aspects of politics.

TRANSITIVE AND INTRANSITIVE POWER

Transitive power

The basic model of transitive power consists in the subordination of one person's will by the will of another. This is also the everyday understanding of power, and it is what concepts concerned with the exercise of power in relations of 'power over' refer to. When power is exercised in this way, relationships get structured as follows: through the will of actor A, the options of actor B become restricted and brought into line with the preferences of actor A. 'A social agent A has power over another agent B if and only if A strategically constrains B's action environment' (Wartenberg, 1990: 85). B is not able to act according to his or her own preferences. B must orient his or her behavior so as to fall in line with the preferences of A – either by avoiding actions that do not meet with A's approval or by engaging in those which do. Otherwise, B risks sanctions.

This power differential does not mean that B, for his or her part, is without power; B's options are not reduced to zero. Power is not possible without counterpower, otherwise it would be no different than pure force or violence. Furthermore, the more powerful action may employ the power of the less powerful. Actor A cannot, as a rule, exercise unlimited power over B, for he always risks provoking resistance and evasion strategies. That's why, if he is well advised, A will always take B's resistance into consideration. Even when one power position prevails over the other, power always runs up against counterpower.

Power and counterpower can exist in either asymmetrical or symmetrical relationships. In asymmetrical relationships, the superior power is tolerated. In symmetrical relationships, A and B exercise power reciprocally in relation to each other so that they mutually limit each other's exercise of power and produce a kind of balance of power relations. This is of particular interest for political scientists, especially when the complementary exercise of power becomes institutionalized. Such is the case in Western liberal democracies when, through the various forms of the separation of powers, state authorities, horizontally or vertically, mutually limit one another's exercise of power; or when, in the relationship between elected officials and the electorate, the latter exercises control either by re-electing incumbents or voting them out of office.

Institutionalized transitive power, just as non-institutionalized transitive power, is primarily brought about directly, that is, through actors directing their power towards others. But it can also be brought about indirectly, that is, by way of behavioral expectations, as when the addressees of power anticipate possible acts of power and act accordingly. Structures, that is, formal and informal rules of behavior, also influence the options of addressees without there necessarily having been any concrete actions undertaken (Giddens, 1984; Lukes, 1974; Offe, 1977). But structural power is fundamentally institutionalized, while indirect power is by comparison only more or less so. Against institutionalized power stands the transitive power exercised by citizens in various forms: in the form of the concrete exertion of influence by individual or corporate actors based on their own interests; in the form of general support, which can also be withheld; and finally, in the form of direct control, in so far as it is provided for by the political order and desired by the citizens. Citizens' moral expectations concerning the behavior of politicians and institutions are also a form of transitive power, since they, to a certain degree, limit citizens' political options. In the real world, all of these transitive power relationships are intertwined with one another in a variety of different ways. They are, in any case, always zero-sum games: whatever A has in terms of power, B lacks, and vice versa. The available quantum of power, one could say, is in the case of transitive power variably distributed, and it is over its distribution that political struggles are fought.

Building blocks for an understanding of intransitive power

By contrast, intransitive power is not a zero-sum game. For it refers not to the subordination of one person's will under the will of another within a community, but rather to the community itself, to the conditions for its possibility, to its constitution. To speak of 'power' in this context is to understand power as being self-referential, in the sense of the 'powerfulness' or 'self-empowerment' of a social unit. Intransitive power encompasses the ensemble of relationships constituting a group of people as a community; it exists in the common practices of actors. Viewed in this way, intransitive power, although it refers in the first instance to 'power to', is ultimately more than just the capacity underlying 'power to': it is itself actualized power, only in self-referential and not other-referential form.

The more intransitive power is 'exercised', or the more intensive the common action, the more intransitive power is increased. The game is therefore no longer a zero-sum game, but has a positive payoff. In order to demonstrate the difference between transitive and intransitive power more clearly, I will employ some of the concepts of power that have been discussed so far, and will make additions to them in order to recontextualize them in the light of the current discussion. The transition from a concept of power as a zero-sum game to a concept of power understood as productive for all participants is most clearly demonstrated by *Talcott Parsons* and *Niklas Luhmann*: in relationships of reciprocal interaction, power engages with counterpower in a way which leads not to a reduction, but rather to an increase in power for both sides. The power of A is strengthened through the power of B and vice versa. The increases in power on both sides of the relationship are mutually dependent on one another, and both are equally necessary. For Parsons (1986) power is, analogous to money, a circulating medium through which obligations are exchanged in the political system. It is in this way that the possibility of common action is generated and increased: power is 'the generalized medium of mobilizing resources for effective collective action' (1986: 108). For Luhmann (1988), power is a symbolically generalized medium of communication. By the medium of power, credit is given and performance is expected; the high performance expected of leaders by those being governed demands an 'investment' in the form of increased support. The result is a joint increase in power.

In these concepts, power is understood as an interdependent relationship. The interplay of power brings about an increase in the power of all participants simultaneously. When this perspective is now directed away from the power of individual actors and focused instead upon the collectivity – which itself receives power through the relationships of actors, and can only be constituted by those relationships in the first place – power exists mainly in the common practices of actors. This is the intransitive side of power.

Hannah Arendt provides us with the basic normative model of intransitive power: whenever people 'are together in the manner of speech and action', a 'space of appearance' – that is, the public realm or the political – comes into being (1958: 199–200). Only in this space of appearance can humans realize their humanity. Arendt is making the Aristotelian argument here that humans are essentially communitarian beings. The community takes the form of a 'praxis' that is always political, and it is only in this community that humans can realize their telos (in the Aristotelean tradition, the telos signifies the ultimate purpose derived from human essence). Power refers here to the generation of collective capabilities. It is not understood instrumentally as being directed towards the attainment of external ends, but is understood rather as an end in itself. For it is only in such social relationships that the inner nature of human beings can be fully constituted and experienced. What is convincing about this position is its claim that a political unit cannot exist for very long without a fundament of this kind of power, that is, intransitive power. This is what Arendt (1970) is getting at in distinguishing 'power' from 'violence'. Her concept of power is, however, decidedly normative. From an empirical perspective, it purports to offer only a few functional conditions for the existence of a stable political system. But exactly how intransitive power functions in modern fragmented societies, what mechanisms it develops, and how it comes about, cannot be inferred from the normative concept itself.

A completely different theoretical position, namely, that of *Michel Foucault*, provides us with some indications as to how we might begin to tackle such questions. Connecting his position with Hannah Arendt's normative concept may seem unusual at first glance, but it is actually not so far-fetched (Ball, 1988: 102). In the present context, it helps demonstrate how the concept of intransitive power may be applied empirically.[4] Foucault does not ask how citizens constitute a political unity. Quite the opposite. He is rather interested in what holds society together in its heterogeneity. This task is accomplished by a multiplicity of force relations, extending from indirect domination and discursive forms of knowledge to relations of direct repression. Taken together as a multiplicity of force relationships, however, they yield intransitive power. Societies are not in the first instance held together through repression ('violence' in Hannah Arendt's terminology). Rather, individuals are penetrated in various ways by relations of power that are considerably more subtle. In the form of 'disciplinary' or 'pastoral' power, they not only insert individuals as subjects into the dominant relationships of force, but lead to a complete, internalized integration, and thus also to a social productivity. Even though Foucault dissects our societies with critical intent, his analyses make clear that at the same time as relationships of power restrict certain opportunities for engaging in different types of action, they make others possible. Schematically speaking, the result of Foucault's analysis of power is what Arendt postulates from a normative perspective. However, a crucial dimension of intransitive power remains just as absent in Foucault's writings as in Hannah Arendt's: the representation of power through symbols. Power must not only be produced. To be capable of providing actors with orientations, it must also be visible. This occurs above all through the symbolic distinctions within a society that are much more simple and flexible than the entire systems of knowledge described by Foucault.

The symbolic aspects of power are the focus of *Pierre Bourdieu's* social theory, and in drawing our attention to the significance of symbols for understanding relationships of power, Bourdieu makes an essential contribution to the sociological grounding of the intransitive side of the concept of power.[5] The dominant symbolic order of a society generates its system of social stratification and makes this system visible. This symbolic order is the outcome of struggles in which actors attempt to raise the social value or level of distinction of their particular lifestyles. It is thus primarily through transitive power that the dominant symbolic order comes into being. Once institutionalized, however, the symbolic order comes to represent a legitimate world view, shared by all, which commonly structures the perceptions of the members of different social classes. The final result of struggles for symbolic distinction is therefore intransitive power, and thus what Hannah Arendt simply presupposes from a normative perspective is explained by Bourdieu as the outcome of symbolic struggles. His genetic perspective is also realistic in the sense that symbolic power not only is constitutive of society, but provides the basis for the legitimation of a society's system of stratification as well. However, in attempting to understand another aspect of intransitive power's role in the relationship of citizens to their institutions, Bourdieu's theory remains inadequate. Although he stresses the constitutive function of symbols, these serve solely to legitimate domination – and for Bourdieu, this means disguising domination. With the use of Bourdieu's concept of symbolic power alone, then, we cannot gain access to that normative model of intransitive power which takes the form of a political space of action that is not imposed, but rather arises out of a reservoir of shared value conceptions and is symbolically represented as such. Hannah Arendt correctly insisted on this basic condition. Without this latter normative orientation, a merely realistic, genetic perspective is not enough to ground the concept of intransitive power, even if its critique is convincing – at least not in so far as it is at the same time supposed to contribute to the legitimation of democratic systems.

There is another aspect to this problem. Intransitive power is self-referential, but this does not mean it is unstructured. Under the conditions of the modern territorial state, intransitive power requires a form of organization which, according to democratic criteria, is capable of including all participants, without their having to be always physically present. Historically, it was as an organized form of intransitive power that the state developed. Although, in the form of the nation-state, the state certainly does not represent the historical endpoint of intransitive power, it is nevertheless, from the perspective of democratic criteria, currently the most developed form in which the real participation of all participants becomes possible. Although he did not use the term specifically, the German scholar of constitutional law in the Weimar Republic (and staunch opponent of National Socialism), *Hermann Heller*, set out in his pioneering studies to explain how the state can be understood as a democratic form of organized intransitive power. In his Staatslehre of 1934, he conceptualizes the state as an 'organized unit of decision-making and effectiveness' (*organisierte Entscheidungs- und*

Wirkungseinheit). What at first looks like a conception of transitive power, in that power is understood as being exercised by the state, is actually founded upon an intransitive concept of societal power. It is implicit in the concept of the political that the state act as a decision-making unit. A precondition for this, however, is that it also act as an effective unit – which, for Heller, demands a form of organization based upon the collaboration of all those for whom decisions are to be binding. Organized societal power is the overcoming of the logic of the zero-sum game. For the collaboration of societal members constitutes a unit of power which is more than the sum of individual power shares. Organized societal power is a *Gestalt* (Heller, 1934: 99)[6] with a quality of its own. It does not refer to particular ends, and can only be actualized as a totality. As an effective unit, it is the presupposition of all political outcomes. In the democratic state, it is that 'acting in concert' which is transposed into political action, both externally and internally, by political leaders. Intransitive power is in this perspective not merely the normative presupposition of politics; it refers to the actual conditions which are constitutive of politics, that is, to the making, regulating and implementing of decisions that affect the community. The self-referential quality of intransitive power, which only finds its focused and concrete expression in the practices of political actors, is therefore the basic condition of politics. In the last analysis, the goal of political action is not only that of being effective for common ends in an instrumentalist sense. It is also to actualize, again and again, shared value conceptions and principles of political order. Without these, a political unit will in the long run lack inner strength and the capacity for self-empowerment.

Intransitive power as a common space of action

In summarizing the various building blocks of intransitive power, while avoiding their respective shortcomings, we can define intransitive power, with its self-referential character, as follows: intransitive power constitutes a community as an effective unit in the form of a common space of action which is symbolically present.

This definition of intransitive power takes account, first of all, of the commonalities existing between the members of a community, of the minimum conditions necessary, in the form of common orientations and common actions, for human coexistence. The *common* space of action which intransitive power makes possible should be distinguished from the *interlocking* space of action involved in transitive relationships of power. In common spaces of action, A and B generally act on the basis of, and within the range of, common value conceptions and principles of order. By contrast, in cases of transitive relationships of power, the space of action between A and B is only defined by the superordination and subordination of their respective wills, and consists in the interlocking of their respective options (see Figure 1.1).

The interlocking space of action brought about by transitive relationships of power exists only as long as do the acts through which power is exercised

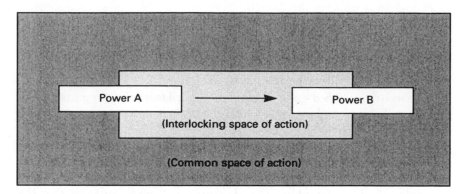

FIGURE 1.1 *Spaces of action*

or the situations which the transitive exercise of power defines. If a community is to be of lasting duration, then intransitive power must be fixed beyond changing situational contexts, and this requires additional mechanisms. The decisive mechanism is the process of institutionalization. When social relationships take place over an extended period of time, institutions develop, and intransitive power – *pace* the anarchistic hopes for its continual generation in ever new forms – becomes inconceivable in anything other than in institutionalized form. Institutionalization establishes the framework for social interaction; intransitive power, which is of lasting duration, is thus an institutionalized (i.e., both structured and structuring) common space of action (Bourdieu, 1979).

Political institutionalization occurs through commonly shared values and principles of order and is maintained through the authoritative symbols of a community which make these values and principles of order visible. The aspect of structure becomes visible through the authoritative symbols of a community, while the aspect of structuring becomes effective through them. Such symbols represent the common space of action as an organized unit of the various interlocking spaces of action and keep common values and principles of order – and thereby intransitive power – continually present. They provide citizens with orientations which are just as affective as cognitive. In this way, they make it possible for citizens to identify with the community, as well as to form ties with it in a 'softer' and longer-lasting form (since they are internalized) than material sanctions.[7] This connection will be looked at in greater detail below, under the heading 'integration'. At this point, however, it needs to be emphasized that intransitive power, in the form of an institutionalized and symbolic common space of action, to a certain extent transforms the other-reference in relationships of transitive power into a self-reference for those involved. In doing so, intransitive power thereby results in a unit of effectiveness which takes the form of an organization.

Intransitive power produces both an increase and a decrease in actors' options. On the one hand, self-empowerment generates forces which are more than the sum of individual power shares. This is the overcoming of the limits of the zero-sum game of power. On the other hand, in this community, actors can no longer do just whatever they desire. Effective intransitive power sets clear limitations upon the arbitrary exercise of transitive power. Such limitations, which are the natural result of 'acting and speaking in concert', become institutionalized – and thereby uncoupled from changing situational contexts – by means of symbols which make the common space of action orientations visible.

With regard to the community as a political entity, real (and not only simulated) intransitive power is the condition for the community's ability both to maintain its position externally and to actualize common values and principles of order internally. This does not, of course, rule out that the exercise of transitive power may play a considerable role in the historical emergence of a common space of action. The concrete form in which a common space of action is actualized and maintained, as well as the specific value conceptions and principles of order that become established in a community, are not simply matters of consensus and conviction, but first and foremost the result of social struggles (that is, of transitive relationships of power). Nevertheless, as long as a community is able to maintain its existence, such conflicts will, again and again, lead to intransitive power.

The characteristics of transitive and intransitive power are summarized in Table 1.1.

TABLE 1.1   *Main characteristics of transitive and intransitive power*

Transitive power	Intransitive power
Other-reference	Self-reference
Relationship of wills	Symbolic relationships
Brings something about	Represents something
Regulation	Integration
Realization	(Self-)empowerment
Exercises power	Generates power
Interlocking spaces of action	Common space of action
Instrumental	End in itself

INTRANSITIVE POWER AND POLITICS

Conceiving relationships of power in terms of transitive and intransitive power gives us a better understanding of some crucial aspects of politics which are frequently overlooked. The concept of intransitive power helps us better to understand the presuppositions of domination or authority, and to bring out more clearly the significance of normative integration in politics as opposed to the more technical, regulative role of politics. This also provides a context for analyzing the symbolic dimension of politics.

Authority

Intransitive power is not merely the normative foundation of a community, it is also its actual empirical foundation – for there is no surrogate for intransitive power that could provide for anything more than a limited and temporary basis for a community. The same applies with regard to intransitive power's role in enabling a polity to acquire and maintain legitimation. To be sure, for legitimation to occur, an explicit and durable consensus on the part of citizens is not all that is required; historically, success has also provided a basis for legitimation. Legitimation can also be tied to transitive power – to the outcome of social struggles and to the achievement of particular interests, if these manage to establish themselves in the long term and to integrate the population. Sometimes, ideology can be substituted for legitimation. In the end, however (and this is a fact which no realistic political philosophy can get around), legitimation has to be based on the intransitive power of citizens, in whatever of its possible forms. This is the phenomenon of domination or, more precisely, of authority, which, in contrast to isolated phenomena of power, is always both transitive and intransitive. It is important to keep this connection in mind. Max Weber understands authority as the institutionalized and legitimate exercise of power. Directly after defining power, Weber continues: 'Domination [*Herrschaft*] is the probability that a command with a given specific content will be obeyed by a given group of persons' (1978: 53).

As opposed to power, authority does not include just any mode of carrying out one's will. Rather, it describes the relationship between command and obedience in clearly defined social settings. Authority thus presupposes a solid and empirically effective scheme of control sustained over time. Social relationships which fulfill this condition are institutionalized. At the same time, they must also be legitimate. For the probability that a command will be obeyed rests upon the fundamental willingness of addressees to comply, that is, upon an 'interest in obedience' (1978: 212). Obedience will occur if a political order is accepted – and therein lies its legitimacy. The validity of claims to legitimacy, as Weber argues, can rest upon a belief in the legality of an impersonal legal order, upon a belief in the sanctity of inherited traditions, or upon devotion to charismatic leaders. These are the 'pure types of legitimate domination': legal, traditional and charismatic authority (1978: 215).

Authority is thus, in the first instance, a transitive relationship of power, since commands are given with the expectation that they will be carried out. It also rests, however, on intransitive power. For authority can only take place in a common space of action in which the respective relationship of command and obedience is fundamentally accepted (notwithstanding the fact that commands are also sometimes carried out against a background of conflicting interests and accompanied by the threat or actual use of sanctions). Thus, in the words of Max Weber, authority is based upon subjects' 'belief in legitimacy' (1978: 213). Authority, as institutionalized power, requires legitimation. The claims to legitimacy accompanying the exercise of power must correspond to the beliefs which the addressees of power have concerning its legitimacy. This is intransitive power as a common space of action, and without it, the relationship of command and obedience would not be one of authority but one of oppression. Because the correspondence between a claim to legitimacy and the belief in legitimacy is only a normative postulate, or ideal condition, frictions always exist which we repeatedly experience as legitimation crises, and which can never be resolved, if only temporarily, without the support of intransitive power.

Integration

Corresponding to the two types of transitive and intransitive power are the two basic functions of politics: regulation and integration. A political community requires, on the one hand, *authorities* that can make binding decisions, and, on the other hand, effective mechanisms which hold the community together. The performance of regulation and of integration is the ancient as well as contemporary demand made of politics. And even if politics does not always successfully meet this demand, these functions are still required.

The connection between regulation and transitive power is obvious. Regulation includes all forms of goal-directed controls over actors' options in a political unit. When the goal is that of channeling and restricting the options of individual and corporative actors, regulation works negatively through commands and prohibitions. When the goal is that of making certain options appear attractive, regulation works positively through incentives, especially through financial ones. With regard to our discussion of power, we can leave aside the question of whether or not politics really performs this kind of regulation successfully, as well as the extent to which – under the conditions of highly differentiated, modern societies – it is even capable of doing so. But even these societies require regulation, which only politics has the potential of delivering. Regulation follows the basic model of transitive power. When A has the intention of controlling B's behavior, A can attempt to carry out his or her will either by restricting B's options or by making certain options appear desirable. Both have the effect of pre-structuring B's space for action. In the first case, the costs for B in following options which through law or other forms of regulations are forbidden rise drastically. In the second case, it is advantageous for B to pursue certain offers, since all the alternatives make him worse off.

Less evident than the connection between regulation and transitive power is the connection between intransitive power and *integration*. This latter connection only becomes apparent when we understand integration in a non-technical sense as 'normative integration' (Parsons) or as 'social integration' (Habermas, 1981; Lockwood, 1964). What is being investigated with the concept of integration is the question as to what holds a society or community together (Peters, 1993). Politically speaking, normative integration can be understood as the process and result of citizens' permanently renewed orientations towards the basic values and principles of a political order. It brings about the requisite identification and collective identity.

The requirement of such political integration has been convincingly argued for by *Rudolf Smend* – a German scholar of constitutional law in the Weimar Republic, whose work has up to now received little attention in the social sciences. In his writings on political constitutions, Smend stresses that the state and its political constitution are to be evaluated above all for the contribution they make towards the task of integration (Smend, 1968; 1956). What is considered to be decisive is their role in integrating citizens in a way that points beyond citizens' rationally conceived goals. The reason for this is quite simple. Societal cohesion rests less upon rational discourse than upon intersubjective acts of experience, imagination and feeling. The political constitution plays an integrative role in society not only by providing a procedure for rational will formation and decision-making, but also, and significantly, by enabling citizens to share in an 'experience of community'. Since, in modern territorial states, social unity can no longer be experienced directly through participation, it must instead be experienced through the symbolic representation of the shared values of the community. The constitution above all has this symbolically integrative function, and Smend thematizes all of its various aspects from this perspective. This is the dynamic and expressive version of Max Weber's claim, described above, that legitimate authority rests upon a belief in legitimacy.

In Smend's writings, the aspect of normative or social integration is undoubtedly overdrawn; constitutions are significant for other reasons as well. However, from his analysis we gain the insight that politics must perform the task of integration – that is, that it should generate out of a social plurality a social unity without destroying that plurality, and that it should do so, namely, in two distinct ways. First, from a technical perspective, a social unity is generated through the coordination and organization of action: people must act according to the same rules and are subject to decisions which are commonly binding. The process of European integration, for example, is supposed to achieve such a unity through member states giving up some of their national sovereignty rights. Just as in the case of political regulation, then, technical integration concerns the exercise of transitive power. But integration also takes place through common *orientations*. This is the second function of integration that politics must play. It occurs when citizens orient their actions – as far as these actions affect the community – towards a reservoir of shared values. This is how collective identity, a 'we-identity' (Elias, 1987), in the polity is formed. Within a common culture, tradition, language, etc. (some but not all of which are required for a 'we-identity' to develop), a collective identity emerges in a political sense through common orientations towards the community's basic values and principles of political order (cf. Heller, 1971). But for these orientations to do their work in generating such a we-consciousness, they must be visible, ever present, and capable of being continually experienced by citizens. Common orientations must, in other words, find *symbolic* expression – publicly available signs which visibly represent orientations for common action. The kinds of signs which provide for symbolic integration are those core symbols of a community such as flags and anthems. No less important are texts and documents, such as political constitutions, which, while having a regulative function, at the same time stand for the value orientations of the citizens. Most decisive are the visible actions of political leaders and officials in political institutions. As such actions draw the citizen's attention to how political power is exercised, they are highly symbolic and have an immediately integrating or disintegrating effect.

Intransitive power and the symbolic dimension of politics

When we consider many of these issues more closely, however, it becomes clear that we cannot simply leave matters where they are. For intransitive power is, in the end, as we have seen, a normative category. Intransitive power is not simply a functional prerequisite for the continued existence of a community. It is, above all, the normative basis – to use the old European expression – for a 'well-established polity', that is, in communitarian terms, for a good society. From this normative perspective, then, symbolic integration and the orientations provided by politics have still other specific requirements to fulfill – even if the issue is a bit complex.

As both historical and current experience shows, the role of politics in providing common orientations neither can nor should be one of producing real guidance for citizens. Today, politics cannot perform the task of providing society with a general source of meaning in the way that religion once did. The modern constitutional state – for good reasons, and as the result of painful historical experiences – refrains from providing a *Weltanschauung*. In the twentieth century, the experience of totalitarianism has clearly demonstrated just what kinds of catastrophes result when politics is given the role of enforcing ideologies or when it is misused as a substitute for religion. Politics must primarily, and in a quite instrumental sense, take care of those regulative mechanisms which enable and maintain human coexistence. What tasks are there left, then, for normative integration and orientation?

Since a reservoir of commonly shared values is restricted in modern, complex societies, first of all a consensus is needed regarding, on the one hand, the values which must be held in common for the continued existence of the community and, on the other hand, those values which are *not* and should not be the business of the community, since they concern only citizens' private life conduct. These common value conceptions give rise to principles of political order by means of which politics is able to regulate social life in the community. When intransitive power is framed in this way, the concept of normative and symbolic integration, as developed by Smend, turns out to be quite helpful in dealing with the issue of citizens' orientations. Viewed from a normative perspective, the foundation of common values and principles of political order is first and foremost something which citizens themselves must reach a consensus about. However, this does not release politics from the task of playing an active role with regard to citizens' orientations. All the more, it must be continuously experienced by citizens that the polity is based upon common values, and that means that these values must be made visible for them. Otherwise, citizens will not have the sense of belonging to the community in which they live, they will not have the feeling that it is their community. In this respect, the polity must provide orientations representing the values upon which it is based: it must demonstrate that it is these values, and only these values, that have a common validity. Only by providing such an orientation can the polity maintain its existence as a community of citizens. Providing this kind of orientation is a necessary political function of normative integration.

This is, then, the concept of *symbolic representation*, a concept which is directly related to intransitive power. The concept of symbolic representation has its origins in the German *Geisteswissenschaften* of the first half of the twentieth century.[8] It emphasizes that a polity must visibly express the values upon which it is based. Generally speaking, representation means making something present which is absent, something visible which is invisible. It is also in this sense that the values of a community must be represented symbolically. Eric Voegelin (1952) argues that every kind of political representation is based upon the 'self-articulation' or 'self-expression' which a society needs in order to exist. A community 'has' its existence only when its values are visibly present. Intransitive power always has an expressive side (Taylor).[9] In this way, common values appear *vis-à-vis* citizens in the form of the symbols of the community itself and in the form of political texts or actions which have a symbolic effect that points beyond the immediate intentions with which they were originally written or carried out.

This is the symbolic dimension of politics. It transcends those various symbolic uses of politics which are merely derivative of the underlying symbolic dimension.[10] Symbolically represented values do not provide citizens with orientations that give them direct instructions on how to act.[11] Rather, they provide citizens with orientations which operate more in terms of indicators, signaling to citizens what kind of community they live in, and what kinds of options they have in this community. When the symbols resonate with citizens, when they are able to activate the participation of citizens, we can make the normative assumption that these citizens consider the represented values to be theirs, and that they consider the community to be theirs. When the symbols do not resonate with citizens, or have a negative resonance, the polity will find itself in a legitimation crisis. This is especially the case in democracies. From a normative point of view, politics or political institutions are only legitimate when they correspond to intransitive power – to citizens' fundamental value conceptions of social life in their society. Only then can we be said to be dealing with 'good' politics, or 'good' political institutions. This correspondence is expressed and made visible through symbolic representation. On the other hand, those symbols make visibly obvious that politics, political institutions or political actions do not correspond to citizens' intransitive power. This is the indicator of legitimation crises. In both cases, symbolically represented intransitive power is the standard of legitimation for all democratic communities which are founded upon the people's sovereignty, however the process of political representation may specifically take place.

CONCLUSION

The basic idea of this chapter is that power is best understood by making a distinction between transitive and intransitive power in social relationships. This new way of structuring the concept of power has several advantages. It helps us to understand better the variety of power aspects discussed in the social sciences today. Moreover, it contributes to a better understanding of the normative dimension of power and to its direct inclusion into the analysis of power.

The systematics of the concept of power I have discussed refers in particular to *political* power. Here, what becomes especially clear is the requirement of a concept of power which is both analytical and normative. The political order of a community – and this is something which can be learned from the long history of political thought, and not least from Hannah Arendt – must be based upon a normatively understood power which generates a minimum level of common ground between the members of a community, and without which the political order would not be in a position to maintain its existence. In this way, intransitive power is tied closely together with the process of *integration*, namely with social and normative integration, and both integration and intransitive power require the continual *symbolic* expression of the values they stand for to be effective and maintained. Thus analyzing power remains defective without referring to intransitive power, and analyzing intransitive power remains incomplete without paying attention to the symbolic dimension. As to the first, we have to go beyond the scope of mainstream empirical analyses; as to the latter, we have to complete Hannah Arendt's normative concept.

NOTES

1 The concepts 'transitive/intransitive' are used in philology to describe the behavior of verbs. In Latin, *transire* means 'to pass by'. Philologically speaking, a verb is considered transitive when the action it describes refers to another object (example: 'I like ice cream'). By contrast, a verb is considered intransitive when the action it describes does not refer to a direct object (examples: 'Nations exist' or 'Birds fly'). Intransitive verbs lack objects which might be the target of a particular activity. Whatever is being expressed in a sentence with the use of an

intransitive verb can be defined as a self-referential system in that the goal of the action is the subject itself.

2 The distinction between transitive and intransitive power is not capable of being conceptualized in the 'two faces of power' (Bachrach and Baratz, 1962), in the 'three dimensions of power' (Lukes, 1974), or in the 'three faces of power' (Boulding, 1989). Clegg (1989) unfolds a framework for conceptualizing power in which relationships of power are modeled upon *circuits of power*. In so far as they stretch beyond *episodic agency power*, e.g., the '"normal" power of social science' (1989: 211), they are determined through social integration and system integration. However, following Lockwood (1964), Clegg stresses system integration, whereas I, from a much stronger normative perspective, and following Hannah Arendt, emphasize the constitutive significance of intransitive power in the sense of social integration.

3 In discussions concerning power, Hannah Arendt, to the extent that she is even mentioned, is mostly criticized for not including the aspect of 'power over' in her concept of power. From this it is generally concluded – with a certain sense of relief, it seems – that her work does not therefore need to be included in any further reflections on the question of power (Ball, 1988: 92–7; Haugaard, 1997a: 146–7; Lukes, 1974: 31; Wartenberg, 1990: 50). This applies as well to Jürgen Habermas's (1976) reception of her work, in which he very subtly and precisely elucidates her communicative understanding of power. In the end, he too arrives at the conclusion that while Arendt's concept of power is important for conceptualizing the production or generation of power, it is not very useful for purposes of analyzing the exercise of power. Thus, one will not find anything more than hints of Arendt's thought in Habermas' social philosophy of communicative action or his political philosophy of facticity and validity (Habermas, 1981; 1992), for her concept is not really compatible with Habermas' universalistic approach.

4 Foucault's complex work is only being drawn upon here in so far as it contributes to an understanding of intransitive power (see Foucault 1978, 1980, 1983 and 1986). For a comprehensive analysis of Foucault's concept of power, see Clegg (1989) and Haugaard (1997a and 1999).

5 See Bourdieu 1985, 1986 and 1989; cf. Goehler and Speth 1998.

6 Heller is clearly referring here to *Gestalt* theory in psychology, which stresses that entities appear to humans as wholes, and that they cannot simply be broken down into discrete parts. It is in this sense that the modern Western state is to be considered a *Gestalt* (Heller, 1934: 63). Remarkably, Heller anticipated much later approaches which view organizations in general in this way. Organizations are closely bound up with power (Clegg, 1989: 18, 187–98, 226); they not only generate transitive power, but themselves rest upon intransitive power.

7 The connection between intransitive power and symbolic expression is not often seen when intransitive power is thematized. This applies to Hannah Arendt as well, whose concept of intransitive power remains nevertheless the most useful. A more precise and detailed analysis of this connection would have to explain how symbols – as opposed to relatively unambiguous signs – are hermeneutically interpreted. I have attempted to provide such an explanation elsewhere (Goehler, 1997: 28–37; 1998).

8 See Carl Schmitt (1989/1928), Landshut (1968/1964) and, above all, Voegelin (1952). With respect to symbolic representation, see Pitkin (1967: 92–111). For a critique, see Pitkin (1967: 107–11).

9 Hints of this are found in Taylor (1975). A more developed version exists in Taylor (1989: Chapter 21, 'The Turn towards Expressivism').

10 The separation between more factual, substantial politics on the one hand, and mere symbolic politics on the other (Edelman, 1964; 1971; Sarcinelli, 1987), underestimates the degree to which politics, just as every social reality, is

symbolically constituted (Berger and Luckmann, 1966; Cassirer, 1923–9; also, Goehler, 1997: 32–7; 1998).

11 Symbols are not denotative, they are rather connotative. They are not unambiguous, and therefore must continually be interpreted. Their effect is not causally determined, but is dependent upon the degree of resonance they are able to find. For more on this, see Goehler (1998).

2 Power, Ideology and Legitimacy

Mark Haugaard

This chapter analyzes two processes whereby relations of domination are sustained through the perceptions of social actors. We shall examine how systemic structures are routinely sustained by an actor's knowledge of social life, often despite the fact that these structures confer differential power resources upon these self-same actors. We want to analyze how this takes place both when the individuals involved are not fully aware that the structures in question entail relations of domination which disadvantage them and when they are aware that this is the case. In particular, we will analyze the phenomenon which, in the Marxist tradition, has variously been called 'false consciousness' and ideology, and we shall analyze the process by which legitimacy reinforces power – a Weberian theme. The focus upon social knowledge leads to methodologically bracketing forms of domination which are not built upon social knowledge. In particular, the chapter does not include any extended analysis of coercion or violence.

The structure of the argument encompasses a number of conceptual moves. The chapter begins with a context-defining section, which includes the analysis of power as a scalar phenomenon and a short theorization of agency and structure. This leads us into our analysis of ideology and 'false consciousness' – also contained in the first section. The second section analyzes the concept of legitimacy which is, of course, a project which social theorists have inherited from Weber.

CONTEXT

Power and structure

In *The Constitution of Power* (1997a: 136–62), I argued that power relations are usually neither entirely conflictual nor consensual. In this respect power should be considered as a scalar concept where, at one end of the scale, there exists pure conflict and, at the other, absolute consensus. While it is conceptually possible that an interaction can be characterized by either of these extremes, the empirical reality is that most interactions fall somewhere between two opposite ends of the spectrum. There are two reasons for this.

The first is, rather straightforwardly, that actors are usually not totally unambiguous in their attitudes to either the content or the outcomes of an exercise of power. The second reason is a theoretical one having to do with the nature of social interaction. While actors do not tend to think explicitly of their social actions in these terms, it is the case that all social interaction has both a goal-oriented and a structural aspect. If, for instance, a lecturer tells a student to write an essay, the outcome of the interaction is that the latter either writes, or does not write, an essay. In this instance the goal of the interaction is the writing of an essay while the structured aspect of the interaction includes, amongst others, the authority structures of the university. If the interaction results in an essay, not only has a specific goal been realized but the structures of the university system have been reproduced. This dual aspect of social interaction entails the possibility of conflict and consensus at two levels. Let us imagine that an actor A with traditional authority *a* tells B to do *x*: the interaction has the potential to be either conflictual or consensual with regard to *either* authority *a* or goal *x*. Authority is a structural systemic quality and *x* is a goal. Hence, in order to analyze the conflictual or consensual nature of the interaction we must analyze both structure and goal and, when we do so, we may well find that a single social act may simultaneously contain both consensual and conflictual elements.

The most obvious instance of conflictual interaction with a consensual base is the democratic process. Political parties are continually in conflict with regard to goals but, in well-established democracies, the structures of the system have a consensual base which constrains and orders conflict. This is despite the fact that, to the participants involved, the practice of politics may appear intensely conflictual. The most obvious instance of this is in adversarial parliamentary systems, such as the British one, where conflict is structured into the process of decision-making and, yet, democratic procedure is a deeply internalized source of overlapping consensus between conflicting parties. In the British case, it is an overlapping consensus which has been built up over hundreds of years and is internalized into British political culture, not only through the parliamentary system, but also through a myriad of other processes of socialization, including college and school debating societies.

According to the theoretical position developed here, the structural consensual element, which is central to the management of ordered conflict, is the very same consensual element which both Parsons and Arendt observe as associated with power. Both theorists argue that power is not the same as coercion but, rather, presupposes some form of consensus. In the theoretical context of this chapter, the consensus which they observe as central to political power is actually consensus on structural reproduction. This theorization applies not only to the democratic process but to any exercise of power which is socially structured. The example of traditional authority represents a structured exercise of power. Similarly, what makes Parsons's analogy between money and power[1] effective is the fact that money is the ultimate example of pure social structure. The pieces of paper used as money have no intrinsic use value but receive their exchange value from the fact that they are carriers of meaning. Structure is the basic unit of social order and, as such, is pure embodied meaning. After all, the perception of order is nothing other than an act of interpretation which, in turn, presupposes a process whereby we impose meaning upon things. When we speak, sounds are carriers of structure, and when we pay for things with banknotes, bits of paper are carriers of meaning and, as such, structure. Structure, as meaning, is what makes social order possible.

It is important to understand that structure is not simply reproduced by a single act of structuration, as argued by Giddens (see, for instance, Giddens, 1984). If one understands structuration as ordered action according to rules (Giddens's conceptualization), structuration, in itself, is not a sufficient act (albeit a necessary one) for a social structure to be reproduced. Systemic structures are reproduced only when others recognize and validate the implicit structural content of the action in question. After all, we do not create meaning simply by intending to mean something. We do so in situations where others interpret our intended meanings as we intended: in other words, when there is a convergence of interpretation of meaning between two actors through a merging of interpretative horizons concerning social reproduction. This entails that structural reproduction presupposes both an act of structuration by one actor and a second act of 'confirming structuration' in which the second actor confirms the intended meanings of the first actor.[2] Obviously, when confirmation takes place, it does not have to be an absolutely perfect convergence. Rather, all that is required is that the actors involved believe that they have been understood and their intended meanings accepted.

There are many instances in which actors structure their action but others fail to recognize the validity of the structuration practice. In a sense Garfinkel's (1984) breaching experiments imitated some of the processes of unsuccessful structuration practice which we find in everyday life. When the participants in the experiments are asked to interpret 'Hello, how are you?' as a literal request concerning their wellbeing, or when students use a formal mode of language register to their parents, their actions are not random, they are ordered according to rules – but inappropriately so. It is an inappropriateness which is defined by interacting others who have internalized existing social norms. As a consequence, those with whom they interact refuse to validate the structuration practice and structure is not reproduced. This type of phenomenon is not restricted to the artificial confines of Garfinkel's experiments but frequently occurs in everyday life. In everyday social life, 'Hello, how are you?' is not always an unambiguously phatic communion. If a close friend asks us this question we may decide to tell them our troubles and then regret having done so when their response makes it clear that they intended only phatic communion. Similarly, when students write essays they are frequently penalized for failing to use the appropriate language register. When we commit a *faux pas*, when we find ourselves in unfamiliar social surroundings, when we miscommunicate, or when others challenge the taken-for-granted premises of our actions, we are, in essence, in precisely the same type of situation which Garfinkel simulated in his experiments. We find ourselves structuring our actions in ways which others refuse, or fail, to legitimate or confirm. The frequency of failure or partial failure (individuals frequently let it pass that they have been 'taken up' slightly differently than they intended) is highly significant for our understanding of the relative (but not absolute) stability of social order. Non-confirmation of structuration practices represents the mechanism of structural constraint at work in everyday interaction. As such, structural constraint is not some mysterious systemic process but, rather, a characteristic of everyday social practices.

When we say that an act of structuration has failed to reproduce structure, what is meant by this is that the structuration practice is not admitted to the social system. Social systems are not things which, in some reified form, have the capacity to reject structures; rather, it is other actors who make judgments that particular acts done by others fail to conform with what (in their judgment) are the accepted or acceptable norms. In this sense 'miscommunication', or the rejection of others' intended meanings, is a highly significant phenomenon in the explanation of the reproduction of social order. If structural constraint were not there and we could intend and, consequently, create new meanings at will, social order would collapse into praxiological chaos. On the other hand, it is equally important to remember that individuals are not totally trapped within existing systems of meaning. There is always the potential to find others who are willing to confirm new meanings. In this way actors can find like-minded others and, with their help, reproduce new local meanings which may take the form of counterculture which, in essence, becomes a subsystem within existing systems of meaning.

Structural constraint works through the agency of others because of the need for collaborative others in order to reproduce social structure. It is this need for collaboration which is the consensual aspect of structured interaction, which Parsons and Arendt are observing when they claim that power is consensual at a deep level; and I would argue that what Goehler describes (in Chapter 1) as 'intransitive power' is, in part, the structural basis of political power.[3]

If we look at the work of Foucault, we also find observations concerning the collaborative aspects of power. The way Foucault expresses it is that power is the opposite of war because power and politics involve the reinscription of the rules of war. To place this within our terminology, power involves the ordering of conflict through the establishment of structured rules of interaction. In this sense, war represents the absence of social order and, consequently, is the opposite of political power because the latter presupposes structured interaction.[4] It is only in war that conflict is conflictual all the way down. Individuals are not simply conflicting over certain goals, or outcomes, but there is no structural consensus upon which they can build their conflict. In such a situation compliance takes place only because of violence, the threat of negative sanction or the use of positive inducements.

The reproduction of structure is not a solipsistic event but many acts of structuration are solipsistic in that the intended meaning of an utterance, or act, remains just that – only intended meaning, not structure. In contrast to the situation in which social structure is reproduced because both actors converge with regard to the structured content of an interaction, the intended meaning is, in essence, excluded from the structural content of the social system. In this sense, Weber's image of social action simply as action which is oriented toward others has taken social theory along the wrong path – to the conclusion that all action which takes account of others entails structural and systemic reproduction. To reiterate, structure is not reproduced simply when a single actor takes account of others and orders their action in a manner which they consider appropriate. If we return to our stylized A and B example of traditional authority, the structures of authority which A holds are reproduced only at the moment that B actually does x and not before. When A tells B to do x, A is structuring his or her action but these structures only publicly (non-solipsistically) exists at the moment that B responds appropriately. This aspect of structural reproduction is clearly demonstrated when actors lose power. They may continue to issue whatever orders they wish (structuring) but the structures which empower them only really exist so long as others are willing to respond appropriately as co-reproducers of the structures in question. This means that the question 'Why is it that structures of domination are reproduced?' involves, in part, understanding why it is, or how it is, that less powerful actors in interaction consent to be co-producers of structures of domination which constitute them as less powerful.

Inducements and coercion

The most straightforward, but theoretically least interesting, answers to this question are cast in terms of internal or external positive or negative inducements. Inducements are intrinsic to the interaction if they follow directly from either the goal realized or the structure reproduced and extrinsic if they have been artificially linked to the interaction. If the extrinsic consequences are of a negative situational nature then we speak of coercion. Much more may be said on this but, for the moment, let us bracket any deep analysis of this type of answer and move on to the more complex problem of the reproduction of relations of domination which cannot be explained through outcome-oriented consequentialist answers.

Ideology and levels of social knowledge

The second type of answer to this problem concerns the practical conscious-ness knowledge of social structure. This is an explanation that covers the type of phenomena which Marxists have in mind when they write about 'false consciousness' and/or ideology and Lukes (1974) was thinking of when he introduced the concept of three-dimensional power. However, this explanation does so without any foundational claims to 'true consciousness'. The objective is not simply to defend a particular tradition in Marxism but to accept that these terms do correspond to an important aspect of social power and domination while jettisoning much of the baggage usually associated with them.

The concept of ideology has two related usages: one within political theory and the other in social theory. For the political theorist, ideology is political doctrine which mobilizes people into political activity of a particular form. This covers the use of the word 'ideology' in the type of context in which 'socialism', 'liberalism' and 'conservatism' are described as ideologies. In this context what distinguishes 'ideologies' from political theories is that they are more popularly based, less rigorously theorized and contain higher levels of tacit knowledge. In social theory, ideology has a slightly different connotation. Marx did not use the term 'ideologies' but 'ideology' (singular). What he, and subsequent social theorists, had in mind is a general system of social knowledge which reinforces relations of domination.[5] For instance, as a system of social relations of domination, capitalism is sustained not solely by the economic and military resources of those who benefit most from the system but also by the fact that those who are most dominated by the system have internalized values and perceptions which reinforce capitalism as a legitimate system of relations of domination. To take a different example, patriarchal relations of domination are sustained not simply by the abilities of men to mobilize material resources but also by the general prevalence and acceptance of patriarchal interpretative horizons as ways of seeing the world. In both cases, these ideologies are ways of conducting social life and interpreting reality which are inextricably linked to specific relations of domination. While the political theory and social theory use of the term 'ideology' can be shown to be related in interesting ways, we will methodologically bracket such an analysis and continue with the social theory use of 'ideology'.

Although relations of domination are frequently sustained by a broad body of beliefs and perceptions, the traditional explanatory theorization of this is fundamentally flawed. Lukes's (1974) concept of three-dimensional power is typical in this regard. Lukes argues that relations of domination are sustained through structural reproduction which takes place partly because actors have certain beliefs and perceptions, which is consistent with the premises of the argument developed here. However, in the traditional manner, Lukes then goes on to argue that this takes place because certain actors do know what their 'real interests' are. They are suffering from 'false consciousness'. The object of social critique, as a critique of relations of domination, is, in essence, an act of disseminating the 'truth' by informing the dominated of their 'real interests'. Within the frameworks of most high modern and postmodern social theory, such claims are untenably elitist, unacceptably unfalsifiable and too foundational. They also have ethnocentric implications when applied in cross-cultural contexts. For instance, it may appear to liberated Western women that certain Muslim women are suffering from 'false' consciousness but it can be argued that such an interpretation is ethnocentric. However, these critical observations do not entail that ideology does not sustain relations of domination; rather, they entail that the 'false consciousness' or 'real interests' argument is an unacceptable solution. So, what is the alternative? In showing that there is a theoretically acceptable alternative, we will demonstrate that the concept of ideology is a useful one in the world of high modernity or postmodernity and that 'postmodern' theorists, such as Foucault, are, in essence, engaged in a critique of ideology.

The ideology argument which we intend to rescue revolves around the claim that relations of domination are sustained by the social perceptions, or social knowledge, of the dominated. This knowledge involves knowledge of how to reproduce social structure – structures which, in assembled form, constitute a system of domination.

Social structure does not exist materially outside its moment of reproduction. What gives structure its permanence is the fact that there exists a system of ideas and beliefs which actors use to reproduce those social structures as a matter of routine. In Giddens's (1984) terminology, these beliefs are carried in two parts of our consciousness: our tacit knowledge (practical consciousness knowledge) and the part of our consciousness of which we are discursively aware (discursive consciousness). As phenomenologists point out, the vast majority of our social knowledge is actually practical consciousness knowledge. Speech is possibly the paradigmatic instance of this. As we speak, we use tacit knowledge of the rules of the language to order our actions with the unintended consequence that the structures of language are reproduced. Similarly, when we engage in interaction with others, we routinely reproduce a complex set of structural practices of which we are only tacitly conscious. Structural reproduction is not a solipsistic act but, rather, involves active collaboration between actors. What makes speech, and other forms of meaningful action, possible is the coming together of intended meaning with convergent interpretation by others. The knowledge which makes this collaboration possible is largely, but not solely, practical consciousness knowledge. This is of necessity the case because when we interact there is so much 'going on' in terms of the reproduction of meaning that it simply is not physically possible for the human mind to handle all this information at the level of discursive consciousness. Even the simplest interaction involves vastly complex linguistic structures and, simultaneously, complex rules concerning turn talking, posture, facial expression, etc., etc. However, this does not entail the conclusion that some of these cannot be discursively conscious. There is a continual flow of information back and forth between practical and discursive consciousness and what pertains to practical consciousness in one set of circumstances may be discursive consciousness in another. When we learn a language, or when we take a job which involves a set of social circumstances with which we were not previously familiar, we are learning discursively what others (native speakers or colleagues) know at the level of practical consciousness knowledge. Over time we may become competent speakers or 'professional at the job' with the result that discursive consciousness knowledge becomes practical consciousness. We are reminded of the 'old days' of discursive knowledge of these practices only when we hear the hesitation or 'mistakes' of someone else acquiring these practices for the first time. We may experience this as a moment of recognition and empathy or, alternatively, we may have so deeply internalized our social knowledge into practical consciousness knowledge that recognition is absent. Not only does social knowledge move from discursive to practical consciousness, but the reverse also takes place. If a stranger asks 'How are things done around here?' (in other words, what are the social structures which order social interaction?) we may hesitate but, given some time to reflect, we do have the capacity to convert our practical consciousness knowledge into discursive consciousness knowledge. In so doing, we describe local structural practices.

Because of its tacit nature, practical consciousness knowledge is immune from critical reflection. In order for our knowledge of structural reproduction to be subject to critique it must be converted into discursive consciousness knowledge. Owing to the fact that all interaction presupposes practical consciousness knowledge, it is inevitably the case that all social actors collaborate in the reproduction of social structures which they have not subjected to critique. Critique, in this instance, entails understanding how specific structures pertain to a system of domination. Structures do not exist in isolation. Meaning is relational and, consequently, systemic. Critique entails a dual process of converting practical consciousness into discursive consciousness and, following that, the ability to place these structures in a system of social relations. From this perspective, social critique does not entail telling people what their 'real interests' are but (and possibly more mundanely) entails facilitating the conversion of practical consciousness into discursive consciousness and explaining how specific social structures are relationally constituted and supportive of a specific mode of domination.

For years no one questioned the use of gendered language. However, what feminists did was to make people discursively conscious of the fact that their speech was gendered and, as a consequence, demonstrated to the satisfaction of many, but not all, that these gendered usages were part of the overall system of patriarchal relations of domination. The use of the word 'chairman' becomes unacceptable only once people are discursively aware of this gendered aspect of their speech patterns and how this relates to a specific set of relations of domination. Once this is understood, otherwise unconnected structured acts suddenly become connected. The use of the word 'chairman', the practice of opening doors for women, the assignment of lower pay for women, the infliction of violence upon women and the act of rape suddenly stand within a set of systemic relations. This is not, of course, to say that these are in any way morally equivalent, but simply to observe that they all are structural practices which characterize a particular set of relations of domination.

The woman who has been socialized in a society where patriarchal social practices are the norm will, in many instances, internalize practical knowledge and use it to reproduce patriarchal structures of domination. In this instance, it is not the case that she does not know her 'real interests'. Rather, she is not aware that her practical consciousness knowledge is integral to the maintenance of relations of domination which are contrary to her interests – interests as defined by herself. Hence, in a context such as this, feminism does not represent 'true consciousness' as defined by an 'enlightened elite'. Rather, the concepts of 'true consciousness' and 'false consciousness' are entirely inappropriate. Feminism facilitates the transformation of practical consciousness into discursive consciousness and, in so doing, undermines patriarchal relations of domination.

While practical and discursive consciousness knowledges are analytically separate, there is a continual flow of information from one to the other and, consequently, actors who routinely reproduce structural patterns which entail their relative powerlessness are not trapped into doing so forever. They may convert their practical consciousness knowledge into discursive consciousness knowledge and, as a consequence of this act, reject that part of their practical consciousness knowledge. If they do so, they may refuse to cooperate in the reproduction of social structures which they previously reproduced as part of an unreflective routine.

The fact that much of social knowledge is practical, as opposed to discursive, consciousness knowledge is a source of systemic stability which frequently contributes to the maintenance of structured relations of domination by making a confirming structuration routine possible even in instances where the structures reproduced entail asymmetries of power.

It is not that this form of power obscures actors' 'true interests'. Rather, it is the case that the majority of acts of structural reproduction take place based upon practical consciousness knowledge and some of this is knowledge of how to collaborate in the reproduction of structures which are integral to relations of domination or which disadvantage the collaborating actors. In such instances, it is not the case that the individuals involved do not know what their 'true interests' are; rather, they are not aware that their practical consciousness knowledge contributes to relations of domination which are contrary to their interests. When Marxists, or feminists, explain how certain taken-for-granted world views contribute to relations of domination, they are not dispensing the 'truth' but, rather, helping individuals or groups to convert practical consciousness knowledge into discursive consciousness knowledge (by telling them what they already know albeit in a different form) and showing how these structures are integral to the perpetuation of total systems of domination which structurally disadvantage the realization of their interests as perceived by themselves.

The effectiveness of Foucault's histories works precisely upon this level. The historical detail of his work may even be wrong (as historians point out) but this is not the point. What he does is to make us confront our taken-for-granted reality, or practical consciousness knowledge, and, in so doing, enables us to resist the system of thought and meaning (structure) which defines who we are and what we can do. When we read his analysis of the

Panopticon in *Discipline and Punish*, the image works, not because we already know the historical details of Bentham's designs, but because we already know tacitly, at the level of practical consciousness, how discipline works to reinforce relations of domination. In the design of the Panopticon, we do not recognize certain historical facts, nor are we informed about 'truths' which Foucault has unearthed. Rather, we recognize the schools which we attended, the examinations which we have taken and the hospitals which we have been to. The Panopticon image systematizes what we already know at the level of practical consciousness while leaving us the dignity of defining our own interests. We do not come to know the 'truth' or our 'real interests' but come to recognize ourselves; and, in so doing, we are given the possibility of reflexively reconstituting ourselves,[6] and the society which surrounds us, through social critique.

Unlike the 'false consciousness' argument, this form of social critique is open to falsification. For the social theorist practicing this form of social critique there are two immediately obvious levels at which their analysis can be falsified. On the one hand, their description of structuration practices may not be recognized by others. The dominated (and the dominators) may reject the description of their practical consciousness knowledge. The second source of falsification concerns the validity of the systemic analysis of the structural relations in question. The issue here is simply: how good is the description of social relations? This may be judged according to the usual criteria used to test any sociological or political science framework: does it enable us to make sense of phenomena which we could not previously? Is it open to falsification? Does it facilitate predictability? Is it explanatorily more economical and neater than competing theories?

LEGITIMACY

The previous section concluded by arguing that structures of domination may be sustained and continually reproduced because our knowledge of structure is carried at the level of practical consciousness. The argument moves to a different level, and we will now examine some of the possible sources of structural stability which exist once the structures in question are discursive and coercion is not part of the picture. In other words, if it is the case that individuals are discursively aware that particular structures of domination contribute to relations of domination which disadvantage them, why might they still collaborate with the reproduction of such structures? There are many aspects of this which could be explored but this chapter deals with just one: legitimacy. The others include: trade-offs between structure and outcome (see Haugaard, 1997a: 136–66), unintentional effects, coercion and organizational outflanking (for the latter see Clegg, 1989). However, for the moment, the chapter revisits the terrain once trodden by Max Weber.

As has been argued by Beetham in *The Legitimation of Power* (1991), there are two broad traditions of analysis of the phenomenon of legitimacy. Political theorists concern themselves with the normative justification of legitimacy and, consequently, tend to be prescriptive, while the sociological tradition is primarily descriptive. The sociological tradition has largely been shaped by Weber's famous analysis of three forms of legitimate authority.

Weber classifies legitimate authority into three types – legal, traditional and charismatic. Legal authoritative resources rest upon a 'belief in the legality of enacted rules and the right of those elevated to authority under such rules to issue commands'; traditional authority rests 'on an established belief in the sanctity of immemorial traditions and the legitimacy of those exercising authority under them'; while charismatic authority rests 'on devotion to the exceptional sanctity, heroism or exemplary character of an individual person, and of the normative patterns or order revealed or ordained by him' (Weber, 1978: 215).

These three forms of domination are considered legitimate because they are consistent with four modes of meaningful action – two of which are rational and two irrational. These are: instrumental rationality, that is a form of action based upon a teleological, means–ends rational logic; value rationality, that is action rationally oriented towards ultimate values; affective action, that is emotionally based irrational action; and traditional action, that is irrational action based upon routine. The connection between these modes of thought and domination is as follows: instrumental rationality is the ultimate basis for bureaucratic authority; traditional rationality is the source of traditional authority; and charismatic domination has its basis in value rationality and affective irrationality.

Aside from noting the consistency between these forms of rationality and these modes of domination, Weber does not go on to explain what happens in an interaction when a form of thought corresponds to a mode of domination. To return to the earlier schematic A–B example, if A has traditionally based authority, what precisely is the process by which B obeys A (if they are both traditionally minded) or not so (if B is, for instance, instrumentally rational)? In order to answer this question, Apel's and Habermas's theorization of communicative action proves useful. Apel and Habermas argue that communicative action is basic to all forms of social interaction. Even so-called instrumental action is actually parasitic upon communicative action. The latter is fundamental because of its basis in mutual understanding (see Cooke, 1994: 1–27). In communicative action others are treated as an end in themselves. It is action which is broadly ethically based as theorized according to the Kantian tradition.

In communicative interaction the speaker asserts validity claims and the hearer can respond either affirmatively or negatively and, if challenged, both participants in the interaction can supply a reason for the validity claims presupposed by their speech act (1994: 12). These validity claims presuppose both truth and rightness. The actual form which this takes is as follows:

> The speaker must choose a comprehensible expression so that the speaker and hearer can understand one another. The speaker must have the intention of communicating a true proposition . . . so that the hearer can share the knowledge of the speaker. The speaker must want to express his intentions truthfully so that the hearer can believe the utterance of the speaker (can trust him). Finally, the speaker must choose an utterance that is right so that the hearer can accept the utterance with respect to a recognized normative background. Moreover, communicative action can continue undisturbed only as long as participants suppose that the validity claims they reciprocally raise are justified. (Habermas, 1979: 2–3)

The object of communicative action is to reach agreement based upon shared comprehensibility, truthfulness and rightness (1979: 3). Because communicative interaction is the ultimate basis of communication, both instrumental action and coercion (positive or negative inducements) may be facilitators in the reproduction of social interaction but the meaningfulness of the interaction derives neither from the logic of instrumentality nor the inducements. Rather controversially, and without much justification in my opinion, Habermas argues that communicative interaction will always lead to convergence: there will always be agreement in the end. However, this proposition would be theoretically warranted only if one presupposed inevitable convergence in situations in which there is a shared system of meaning, logical reasoning and a normative framework. It is the absence of all, or some, of these three elements which makes intercultural communication so problematic.

If communicative action presupposes shared validity claims of either truth or rightness, the question has to be: when do the participants decide that convergence has been reached? In other words: when does the communication stop? The obvious and somewhat frivolous answer (which actually applies in a significant number of contexts) might be when one of the participants gives up from fatigue or lack of motivation. Based upon Wittgenstein (and also conversational analysis), the more serious answer is that both participants reach a position where further mutual interrogation is pointless, or involves some form of logical contradiction, because they have reached a shared foundation of some kind. The idea that a foundation is a point of convergence is brought out by Wittgenstein in the example of an imaginary conversation in which a speaker is trying to explain to a hearer what is meant by a toothache:

> When we learnt the use of the phrase 'so-and-so has a toothache' we were pointed out certain kinds of behaviour of those who were said to have a toothache. As an instance of this behaviour let us take holding your cheek. Suppose that by observation I found that in certain cases whenever these first criteria told me a person had a toothache, a red patch appeared on the person's cheek. Supposing I now said to someone, 'I see A has a toothache, he's got a red patch on his cheek.' He may ask me, 'How do you know A has a toothache when you see a red patch?' I should then point out that certain phenomena had always coincided with the appearance of the red patch.

Now one may go on and ask: 'How do you know that he has got a toothache when he holds his cheek?' The answer to this might be, 'I say, he has toothache when he holds his cheek because I hold my cheek when I have a toothache.' But what if we went on asking: 'And why do you suppose that toothache corresponds to holding your cheek?' You will be at a loss to answer this question, and find that here we strike rock bottom, that is we have come down to conventions. (1969: 24)

From our perspective, Wittgenstein is making two significant points here: first, that convergence will not always be achieved if the appropriate conventions are not in place (which is contrary to Habermas's assumption concerning the inevitability of convergence); and, second, that any communicative interaction presupposes a shared set of assumptions, derived from a common way of life, beyond which further interrogation is impossible.

The link between forms of action and modes of domination is created by a shared moment of convergence derived from a commonality of assumptions. To return to an archetypal example: if A, in the capacity of holder of traditional authority, tells B to do x, in a situation of communicative interaction (i.e. non-coercive interaction), A's traditional authority presupposes that B accepts the validity claims of traditional authority and, as a consequence, demands no further reasons once tradition is evoked. In other words, if interaction is to be successful, then if B were to challenge A's authority, B would accept that A's appeal to tradition is valid, right and appropriate under the given circumstances and, as a consequence, B would confirm A's act of structuration.

Once A and B have reached a shared foundation, this entails that B would be either in a position of logical self-contradiction if he or she were not to be compliant with A's wishes, or engaged in pointless time-wasting. The self, referred to as contradicting itself, is the self as constituted by a social interpretative framework which includes norms and meanings, as manifest in their interactive behavior. In other words, convergence takes place because non-compliance would contradict the premises of an actor's interpretative horizon – the way in which they make sense of the world. This interpretative horizon involves not only a way of seeing the world but, as Heidegger would have argued, a particular ontology or sense of being-in-the-world. This sense of ontology involves not only a sense of self relative to the external world of objects and things but, more significantly for social theory, a sense of being-in-the-social-world. Within this ontology social others constitute an external horizon which defines the self.

The basis of legitimacy is found at a point of convergence where further justification would appear pointless and non-acceptance would entail logical self-contradiction. The moment of convergence, which is fundamental to the concept of legitimacy, is rooted in the human logical predisposition to avoid self-contradiction. This avoidance of logical self-contradiction comes not from some strong commitment to a particular form of reasoning but, rather, from a desire to avoid ontological insecurity. As Giddens argues (1984:

51–64) in his analysis of structural reproduction, the insecurity which individuals feel when they break social norms derives from a need for ontological security rather than from some form of reasoned commitment to the validity of conventional social norms. Contradictoriness is defined relative to a shared way of life involving a set of meanings, truths and norms which are in themselves not necessarily derived according to reasoned principles. While this position does not commit one to some form of social determinacy by reason, it does entail that all legitimacy is, to some extent, reflexive and reasoned, or at least potentially so, in the sense of resting upon the avoidance of self-contradiction. This would be contrary to Weber's perception of traditional and affective action as irrational. This is, of course, only in the minimal sense that these types of action are based upon the avoidance of self-contradiction but not in the stronger sense of a commitment to rigorous reasoning. What distinguishes forms of legitimate action is the type of assertion which gives rise to convergence derived from the avoidance of self-contradiction. If A justifies order x by an appeal to tradition, this appeal presupposes the hope that B will be satisfied with that answer and not wish to dig deeper. Obviously, if B is a non-traditionally minded actor this appeal will fail. B may say: 'So what if we have always done things this way?' Alternatively, if A is instrumentally rational and assumes that B is similarly so, then A's legitimate authority will rest on a presumed convergence based upon utility if A's act of structuration is to result in a successful outcome. When B confirms A's action, B contributes both to the reproduction of a shared interpretative horizon and to common ontologies. If it is the case that both A's and B's actions are based upon respect for tradition or instrumental rationality this entails alternative highly specific ways of being-in-the-social-world. It is a being-in-the-social-world which is mutually constituting and, as a consequence, would involve a denial of self if the interaction were not successfully completed. The denial of self involved in non-confirmation of A's traditional structuration practice involves ontological insecurity if it is the case that B is still traditionally minded but, obviously, not so if they have made the decision to reject the traditional world view. When B chooses the path of ontological insecurity the choice is a trade-off between guilt or shame on the one hand and the intrinsic desirability or undesirability of the resultant outcome of the interaction in question on the other. In a traditional society, where it might be customary for children to care for their elders, the children may 'shirk their responsibility', preferring guilt to the 'onerous' task of caring. Over time they may also overcome their guilt by rejecting the traditional world view into which they were socialized. This may entail a conversion of practical consciousness knowledge into discursive consciousness knowledge along the lines described in our analysis of ideology.

One can see the process of legitimacy at work in an analysis of the democratic process as a legitimate system of domination. If A and B are both democrats, then the legitimate authority of A derives from the fact that denial of this would involve logical self-contradiction with respect to a set of democratic principles and practices which constitutes part of B's interpretative horizon. As Dahl has argued in *Democracy and its Critics* (1989: 280–98), liberal democracy does involve a common good but it is not a common good of outcomes, as Rousseau and some contemporary communitarians would argue. This common good which Dahl writes of is, I would argue, the willingness of B to confirm A's structuration practice because both actors share a common ontology as democrats. This argument also has an affinity with Rawls's later position as outlined in *Political Liberalism* (1993). In *A Theory of Justice* (1971), Rawls grounded his principles upon a type of Kantian foundationalism but, in the former work, this was replaced by the idea of overlapping consensus. Overlapping consensus is a point of convergence between interpretative horizons (what he called comprehensive world views) which can be otherwise quite dissimilar. The problem which the hypothesis of overlapping consensus solved for Rawls was not simply the issue of getting away from foundationalism but also that of constructing a political order which would be considered legitimate by those who were not necessarily liberal. As Rawls' critics pointed out, a theory of justice which could be subscribed to only by those holding a liberal interpretative horizon would in itself not be liberal. However, overlapping consensus presupposes not a comprehensive liberal doctrine but, rather, a fairly minimal ontological commitment to being a democrat. Hence, convergence is found in the perception of self as a democrat. It is important to remember that democracy entails the willingness to let procedure override outcome. If two parties A and B contest an election, when one party loses it is self-contradictory not to consent to defeat. Of course, in real politics, not all parties do consent to their defeat, and by not doing so they expose themselves to the accusation of being non-democrats. However, such an accusation entails the claim not that they do not respect the democratic process at all but, simply, that they do not do so sufficiently to let that commitment override their desire not to be defeated. Interestingly, relative to the analysis of levels of consciousness and power, there are few, if any, instances of democracy being dissolved in societies in which democratic procedure has been established for more than 20 years (Dahl, 1989: 315). In other words, over time, the gradual internalization of democratic procedure and ontology into practical consciousness knowledge strongly reinforces democratic structures, as one would expect according to the present theoretical perspective.

Affective action is no different from the other forms of action just outlined. Justifying an action based upon love, for instance, does involve invoking principles of non-self-contradiction through an appeal to shared presumptions concerning the appropriateness of love as a basis of convergence. 'You should do *x* if you love me' entails the assertion that not doing *x* means that actor B does not love A – an assertion which is only effective if B has, at some other point, said or done something, or occupies a position with ontological commitments (e.g., father, mother, husband or wife, etc.) which entails that B loves A. If B does not do *x*, he or she is in a position of self-contradiction with respect to their love of A. In most Western cultures, if B is a father but does not love his children, he would be considered falling short of the conventional image of 'a real father'. In other words, he would violate the ontological essence of fatherhood. Of course, he may choose to do so but frequently at the cost of suffering ontological insecurity (unless he develops an alternative morality as a rationalization of his position). Even affective action is not irrational action in the sense of being self-contradictory.[7]

Following the logic of some of my previous arguments concerning Foucault (see *The Constitution of Power*: 41–98), Foucault's observations concerning the beginnings of modern regimes of truth production may be theorized as an account of the establishment of new points of convergence whereby non-compliance involves new forms of self-contradiction. From a sociological point of view, the power of truth lies specifically in the fact that its non-affirmation points to self-contradiction. We cannot deny what is true, even if it suits us to do so, without our actions being perceived as illogical. Hence, the effectiveness of the use of truth as a power resource is precisely that non-compliance is a form of contradiction of self as a logical being. To Weber's threefold classification of modes of legitimate domination can be added domination by experts as a fourth type of legitimate authority. As described by Foucault in his histories, this form of domination is as central to modernity as bureaucratic/legal legitimacy. In the case of expert domination, the source of legitimacy is scientific truth.

Much more research should be done and much more can be said but, in this context, the claim that we are in a process of transition from modernity to postmodernity is, in essence, a claim to the effect that a new set of convergence points is developing. So, for instance, if there is skepticism toward metadiscourses, essentialism or 'truth', this entails that, in an instance of communicative interaction, an appeal to any of these will not give the closure it might have done some years ago. In other words, the basis of expert domination seems to be changing or, much more likely, a new (fifth) form of legitimate domination is emerging. Given the strong links between postmodernity and countercultures or alternative lifestyles, it would appear that this new form of domination is also replacing legal/bureaucratic domination. However, countercultures have a logic and systemic quality of their own and, as a consequence, there are local rules of structuration and confirming structuration. In other words, there are new points of convergence which constitute a foundation. Much as Foucault argued that there was no escape from power, I would argue that there is no escape from structure.

The establishment of new points of convergence is one of the tasks of those who wish to create new power resources. Consistent with most contemporary (postmodern?) skepticism toward grand narrative, no theoretical reasons suggest themselves for arguing that there is a limited set of legitimate forms of domination. In short, Weber's threefold typology appears too limited. Authority based upon truth and postmodernity do not seem to fit neatly into the Weberian threefold classification of authority and the fourfold schema of ir/rationality. However, it can be argued that Weber's categories were simply an organizing device derived from empirical observations – not a theoretical imperative. As a consequence, there is no inconsistency what-soever between Weber's ideas and the hypothesis that there is a theoretically open number of classes of logic justifying different forms of legitimacy. We are simply moving on from where Weber left off. Similarly, the theorization of ideology in terms of practical consciousness knowledge should be viewed not as a rejection of Marxism but, rather, as a move beyond it.

NOTES

1   Parsons (1963) argued that power and money are to be understood as analogous to each other. Money performs the function of a circulating medium in the economy. Similarly, power is theorized as the circulating medium of the polity. What gives money its value is the confidence which we all share in it. This becomes a self-fulfilling prophecy whereby, for instance, one accepts a five pound note in exchange for a commodity because one feels confident that others will do the same. Similarly, most people accept the authority of official institutions because they are aware that others do so. Of course, it is the case that these institutions have violence (police, jails and armies) to ensure compliance but, in sophisticated and complex power systems, official power vastly exceeds coercive resources. See Barnes (1988: 12–44) and Giddens (1968).

2   In a previous work (Haugaard, 1992) I called this act of confirmation 'restructuration' but since then I have come to recognize that this was an infelicitous choice of term. 'Confirming structuration' captures the convergence more accurately.

3   It is not entirely the same as what we mean by structure here because of the particular normative language game in which he constructs his terminology. Intransitive power presupposes more than the simple tacit knowledge consent of structural reproduction. It entails a normative commitment to practices and, as such, is a particular subset of social structures.

4   In this instance war is characterized as an ideal type. Actual wars do have structural form but they are substantially less structured than everyday social interaction. The ideal type image of war approximates to Hobbes's state of nature – a state of affairs where anything goes.

5   Marx also argued that ideology entailed 'inversions'. However, I use the term 'ideology' more loosely than that – as is current in most contemporary social theory.

6   In this regard there is a certain parallel between our account of ideology and Giddens's and Beck's account of modernity (Beck, 1992; Giddens, 1991). However, unlike these authors, I do not think that society as a whole can become more reflexive because this presupposes the hypothesis that societies in general can become more discursively conscious. This is implausible. What happens rather is that societies become differently discursively conscious and this has implications for the way in which they transform themselves into new social forms.

7   Not only is the idea that non-contradiction is central to legitimacy contrary to Weber's distinction between rationality and irrationality, but it might be contrary to any view of historical evolution whereby legitimacy is based upon higher and higher levels of reason and the related idea that so-called primitive societies are prereflexive. On these points, empirical anthropological evidence would be pertinent but, from a purely theoretical point of view, there does not appear to be any prima facie case for assuming that social evolution entails movement from

prereflexivity toward high reflexivity. Rather, social change would entail changes in the map of convergence points which govern local perceptions of contradiction. Such a theoretical position is consistent with the general observation (which is an anthropological commonplace) that primitive societies are primitive only technologically but not culturally or linguistically.

3 Power and Authority, Resistance and Legitimacy

Stewart Clegg

TWO TRADITIONS IN THE ANALYSIS OF POWER

When one examines the two main traditions in the analysis of power in organization analysis they bear evident, and opposite, historical traces. First, in conventional organization theory (as argued in Hardy and Clegg, 1996) the emphasis has been very much on power as an aspect of informal and illegitimate organization, a tendency that achieves its strongest expression in Mintzberg (1983). In this tradition power employs illegitimate resources to coerce others into the attainment of illegitimate ends by the exercisers of power; in contrast, where there is legitimacy there is authority. The reasons for this treatment go back to Parsons's and Henderson's translation of Weber (1948), where *Herrschaft* (literally 'domination') was always translated as authority. Supporting this tendency towards overemphasizing legitimacy, one may recall March and Simon's (1958) notion of organization membership being the result of a balance of 'inducements' offered by the organization that are accepted as legitimate by the member. In this formula, membership carries the obligation to accept the legitimacy of the 'contribution' required. To join an organization is thus to accept its legitimacy at the outset. Hence, in these orthodox traditions that constituted the contemporary sociology of organizations, the legitimacy of hierarchical structures of imperative coordination was established by definitional fiat. Thus, power was by definition illegitimate and coercive – in the familiar way of power being the capacity to get others to do what they would not otherwise do. Later, in both resource dependency and strategic contingencies theory (Clegg and Rura-Polley, 1998), it was also quite natural to stress the legitimacy of authority. Consequently, power as a variant from authority was already predefined as more or less implicitly illegitimate, being dependent upon members having control of some strategic resources outside of the imperatives of formal authority. The most famous articulation of this is Crozier's (1963) account of the maintenance workers in a French tobacco monopoly.

From the reception of Braverman (1974) into labor process theory, an opposite set of assumptions came to predominate. Here the assumption was that any structure of imperative coordination would always be exploitative. Hence, resistance to it, rather than its acceptance as legitimate authority, would be normal. The concept of real interests was central to this debate. It was expressed in the following terms: capitalists control the labor process in the interest of exploitation; proletarians resist this exploitation in defense of their essential interest in autonomy. The 'romance' of labor that informed this position derived from Marx and Engels's (1970) 'German Ideology', and its celebration of craft labor, a position that spoke directly to Braverman's biography.

In the 'labor process debate' in British sociology the crucial criticism of Braverman (1974) came to be that he had neglected resistance and overstated power as control (Littler and Salaman, 1982); meanwhile, ever more subtle forms of resistance were identified (Clegg, 1994). In these, people asserted their interests against structures of labor process control based on an objective interest in 'exploitation'. Sometimes the category of resistance became broad enough to accommodate almost any kind of 'escape attempt' from everyday organizational life. In the post-Braverman debates, resistance was only to be expected and should be seen as legitimate as well as justified. In the labor process literature there is an overstatement of the concept of resistance that parallels, exactly, the overstatement of legitimacy in the more orthodox literature. What is required is a theoretical framework that seeks to understand the dynamics of legitimate power and resistance not as necessary but as contingent and conditional.

Any political theory of power, to be adequate, requires an organization analysis to bridge the gap between the sovereign subject and the sovereign state (see Flyvberg, 1998 for a case in point). Each of these sovereign sites has been occasion for an overdetermining liberalism and an overdetermining structuralism, respectively. Neither leaves much space for the organizational. Equally, organization theories not embedded in social theory are at risk of being impoverished. Important debates will simply pass them by: there needs to be a reciprocal enrichment of organization and political theories. The non-recognition by the majority of orthodox contributions (with significant exceptions such as Walsh et al., 1981) of social theoretical work developed from Lukes (1974) onwards is an unfortunate sign of the selective inattention that has bred this situation. Not only Lukes's but also Foucault's contributions to the power debate have largely gone unrecorded.[1]

Foucault (1977) increasingly became enlisted to the labor process debate in which the chief criticism was that Braverman (1974) had neglected resistance (Littler and Salaman, 1982). Foucault (1977), it seemed, held the key to a more appropriate understanding of resistance in the labor process (Knights and Vurdubakis, 1993) through stressing power as always exercised on free bodies whose vitalism gave rise to resistance.

RADICAL DIMENSIONS

Steven Lukes's (1974) *Power: A Radical View* argued that power not only operates through one person or agency getting another to do something that they would not otherwise do but also by structuring the thoughts of the other, the concepts and categories they use, so that they already think through dominated terms. This radical view of power played out through the concept of hegemony, a key term of Western Marxism (Gramsci, 1971). Initially, hegemony was conceptualized as a form of control or rule through the contents of knowledge, especially popular culture. The concept of hegemony as a form of power that operated on and through the consciousness of the oppressed, such that they were unaware of their oppression, became less stable as debate developed in the 1980s. It was Laclau and Mouffe's (1985) work, in particular, that did most to deconstruct, and reconstruct, the concept – in a manner that, as Geras (1987; 1988) noted, required renovation of the Western Marxist frame that had housed hegemony. The new design proposed by Laclau and Mouffe owed a great deal, implicitly, to the work of Foucault (1977).

From 'real interests' to 'post-structuralism'

Some time after Lukes's (1974) work was published the concept of hegemony came under sustained revision, most notably in the work of Laclau and Mouffe (1985), in a reversal of the dominant interpretation of Gramsci's (1971) themes. While hitherto the focus had been on the content of ideas as a characteristic of hegemony, they proposed instead that emphasis should be on the form. Their argument was that hegemony reigns wherever there is discursive fixity, clarity in assembly and ascription, floating signifiers rather than fixed ones that are pinned down, ordering the form of debate, irrespective of the content.

Laclau and Mouffe's (1985) ideas were related to the themes of what was known, theoretically, as post-structuralism. Lukes, with his layered dimensions of power, was clearly using a structural frame where at root was a conception of power thought of in terms of a characteristic model of random mechanical intervention – one that had marked mainstream power debates since Hobbes (Clegg, 1989; Hindess, 1996). In post-structuralism new terms and approaches were developing that stood in marked contrast to classical mechanical conceptions of power as a causal relation. Chief amongst these was the notion of discourse.

Behind Laclau and Mouffe's (1985) endorsement of post-structuralism were some big implications. At the core of both recent post-structuralist debates and the classical conception of the relation between consciousness and interests is some conception of a significant relation between power and language. In classical socialism, and radical views of power, the relation was always one of masking, of appearances, of falsehood – one in which language distorted or misrepresented reality. Hence derived the centrality of vocabularies of 'false consciousness'.

In post-structuralism the relationship of language to consciousness is not one of falsehood. Reality cannot be assumed to be known unequivocally: it can be known only through its representation in language, as the horizon of its being; hence language cannot mask anything, as it is depicted as doing in traditional concepts of ideology and hegemony. What it can do is to represent possibilities and position possibilities in relation to each other. In the broadest terms, language defines the possibilities of meaningful existence at the same time as it limits them. Language constitutes our sense of ourselves as a distinct subjectivity. Subjectivity is constituted through myriad 'discursive practices' of talk, text, writing, cognition and argumentation, of representation generally. The meanings of and membership within the categories of discursive practice become a constant site of struggle over power. Forging individuality is the expression of an active process.

Post-structuralism admits of no rational unified subject as the locus or source of the expression of identity. Identity is contingent, provisional, achieved rather than given. Identity is always in process, as always subject to reproduction or transformation through discursive practices that secure or refuse particular posited identities. Identities are not absolute but are always relational. Difference defines identity, rather than its being something intrinsic to a particular person or category of experience, such as worker, wife, woman or whore. Each of these is a possible signifier of self, carrying complex, shifting and frequently ambiguous and contradictory meaning. Foucault (1977) sketches some of the identity-shaping disciplines that have been constituted through practices of power and knowledge. Knowledge used to structure and fix representations in historical forms is thus the accomplishment of power.[2] Following on from Foucault, in a move reminiscent of the Frankfurt school of critical theory (albeit expressed through elements of post-structuralism), Laclau and Mouffe (1985) argue that hegemonic power exists neither in specific individuals (as in Lukes) nor in concrete practices (as in Foucault). Instead, they would locate hegemony in the way in which agents and practices articulate in a particular fixed ensemble of representations. No fixed, real, hidden or excluded term or dimension exists except in its representation. To the extent that meanings become fixed or reified on certain forms, and these then articulate particular practices, agents and relations, then this fixity is what achieves hegemonic power. Power is the apparent order of taken-for-granted categories of existence fixed and represented in a myriad discursive forms and practices. Power is neither ethical nor micro-political: above all it is textual, semiotic, inherent in the very possibility of textuality, meaning and signification in the social world. The central feature of power consists in this fixing of the terrain for its own expression.

Within postmodern discourse there are no 'real' interests with the potential to function as a holy grail for analysis. Claims to know the real interests of any group, other than through techniques of representation that one uses to assert them, do not survive the post-structural reconceptualization of power. The demise of certain types of essentialist conceptualization of real, but unrealized, interests signifies a decline of 'class politics' and leads to calls for a new politics. One of these calls is for a greater transparency, for a politics attuned to 'real' bases of moral life such as religion, gender and the ecology. Parties and movements may be able to present themselves as advocates of more or less unequivocal and neglected 'goods'. The most salient of these will be, in ascending order of abstraction and consequent inverse simplification: the politics of one earth, one body, one nation and one institution. These correspond to the interests of the ecology, to the interests of women, to the interests of communitarian aspirations to statehood inscribed on the basis of whatever markers of difference – be they cultural, linguistic or ethnic – and the subordination of all interests to those that find expression through the market. It should be clear that reduction of politics to single-issue moralities does not present a very flexible basis for actual conduct, with all of its specific complexities, fudges and ambiguity, however appealing it is as a ground for the pronouncement of moral judgments. Note an absence from this list. Today, in the advanced societies, no party would seem to want to take on the role of defending the state. Some commentators conclude from this a requirement for a more encompassing theory of citizenship to reflect postmodern times (Barbalet, 1987; Roche, 1992). The globalization of capitalist economics and culture (Robertson, 1992) transforms the nature of citizenship in relation to sovereignty and the nation-state (Mann, 1986; Rose and Miller, 1992). The socialist project, in its various Marxist forms, was one that made sense only within a restricted conception of the relation between the state and the economy. States were sovereign; economies were not. Global institutions have transformed that relation: while it is evident that some states retain more sovereign powers than others do, the basic calibration that framed the earlier assumptions has shifted. National economic space is no longer the sole project of sovereign national subjects.

RESISTANCE

Foucault, Laclau and Mouffe all write from a tradition of Nietzschean-influenced 'social theory'. Foucault's work around the time of *Discipline and Punish* (1977) not only placed a relational and strategic conception of power in central focus but also did much to promote the idea that wherever power was to be found one would also find resistance.

Resistance may be defined as the 'efficacious influence of those subordinate to power' (Barbalet, 1985: 542). In Foucault, power and resistance seemed almost inescapably and dialectically linked. In part, it was the notion of an inherent opposition existing naturally against power that has allowed Foucault's ideas, especially on surveillance and resistance to it, to be absorbed, relatively seamlessly, into contemporary labor process debates (see, for example, Sewell and Wilkinson, 1992). Power and resistance stand in a specific relationship to each other (Knights and Vurdubakis, 1993), where one rarely has one without the other.

Late in his life Foucault proposed that the relations between the organized and those organizing might be better captured through the concept of government rather than through the concept of resistance (van Krieken,

1996).[3] Foucault means both the strategies of organizational governance, in a broad sense, as well as those of self-governance by those who are subjects and objects of organizational governance. The point of Foucault's argument is not to refer to two different 'levels' – organizational and individual – of government but to capture what is said to be novel about liberal forms of governance, namely that the two levels get linked together. The concept of government has some advantages for organization theorists. It does not presume *a priori* that organizations are always legitimate or, conversely, that they will always be characterized by resistance. The focus is on the constitution of both legitimacy and resistance.

Foucault saw both kinds of governance (legitimacy and resistance) as presupposing the basis of free human agency: an agency whose freedom is always circumscribed within what is known. What is known includes not only that which is known differentially, and with differential value attached to it, but also that which is known in common, often as a result of its translation by experts of various kinds, into what, after Haugaard (1997a), one can address as 'practical consciousness'.[4] The effects of practical consciousness need not necessarily be seen as purposively achieved projects. 'We do not live in a governed world so much as a world traversed by the "will to govern", fuelled by the constant registration of "failure", the discrepancy between ambition and outcome, and the constant injunction to do better next time' (Rose and Miller, 1992: 191). Much of the power of this government resides in the remorseless project it unleashes on those subjected to it – both those managing and those managed.

Government refers to the projects of the organizational elites in seeking to align the interests of organization members. But there are also these other subjects to consider. Van Krieken (1996) coins the term 'proto-governmentalization' to address the process by which the initiatives, projects and strategies of individuals and groups become mutually aligned and coordinated with those of elites – the process through which existing forms of government are addressed by the governed. Such a focus involves the many small ways in which the personal projects of ordinary people become aligned with authoritative images of the social order, not always in their support, but sometimes in their transformation.

What is crucial to both the concepts of government and proto-governmentalization is what people know. The power/knowledge relation is thus central to the relations of power. A concrete example may make this clearer. Protogovernmentalization in a transforming mode is rarely as evident as it was during the week of 31 August to 6 September 1997, between the death and the funeral of the Princess of Wales. In Britain in this space the celebration of the 'People's Princess' as a 'Queen of Hearts' became a popular, if not universal, movement. However, it was one born of no single purposive project. It arose from the awful randomness with which circuits of celebrity became entangled in a twisted heap of armored metal and broken bodies, shattered dreams and ruptured wish fulfillment, disrupted tales and unscripted stories. From this contingency grew a popular power that resisted so many circuits of governmental power, programmed by constitutional monarchy, that, while it presaged no dramatic or revolutionary institutional upheaval, seemed to transform the popular perception of the House and Family of Windsor. It would be inappropriate to term the grief and sense of loss that achieved this as 'resistance'. The movement was born out of a collective experience of personal loss of someone known intimately through the texts of everyday life that celebrity, drama and virtuality provide. There was an intimacy experienced through narrative traditions of love and death, of betrayal and bereavement, of sisterhood and motherhood, that most could identify with. Sovereign majesty, with so many circuits of power at its disposal, was powerless to control or channel the responses these events unleashed. In the face of a motherless child, a grieving family, and a people stripped of their dreaming, their stories, their grace, momentarily united in a culture of loss, something happened to rewrite the scripts of governance and legitimacy. Waves of applause swept through the Cathedral from the masses outside as the brother of the dead princess spoke. The extraordinariness of the events of that week signals their sociological rarity, however.

POWER, RESISTANCE AND GOVERNMENT

Given the continuing centrality of the power/knowledge nexus through Foucault's work it would seem that a conception of knowledge would be the most promising fulcrum around which to articulate the relation of power, resistance and government. Government and resistance work on and through knowledge and the forms of social relations that embed and constitute such knowledge. The forms of social relations can be conceived of in terms of an ever-widening circle from self through significant others, to solidaristic others, to generalized others, to adopt terminology from symbolic interaction. Each of these may be thought of as constitutive of aspects of the identity of the subject. One can identify at least four 'subject positions' that differ precisely in terms of the extensiveness of organization.

The most intensive is self-organization: the acquisition of more or less disciplined and coherent self-capacities. How coherently organized is the individual, in terms of subjectivity, as a reflexive agent in power relations? How coherently organized is the individual as one who seeks to enrol, translate, interest or oppose others in projects? Does the individual subject have sufficient self-cognizance to be able to exercise this agency?

Second is social organization that implicates significant others, usually known in and through face-to-face relations. To what extent is the subject able to draw upon resources of social organization greater than the self, such as familial networks or ecologies of local community networks?

Third is solidaristic organization, involving the more extensive organization of others known only at a distance. To what extent can the subject draw upon the consciously organized resources of a social movement or collective organization in the pursuit of their agency? To what extent does power constitute the resources of human agency in terms of self, and significant and generalized others?

Fourth, there is generalized organization, involving the organizational capacities of generalized agencies, known only remotely and virtually, through their representations rather than mediated in terms of their representatives. To what extent is subject relevance enrolled into the organizational resources of pre-existing agencies, such as media organizations? The agendas of generalized organizations, such as media organizations, might interconnect with the circuits of power that one seeks to construct. Such generalized organizations have capacities to plug into one's circuitry, if they so choose, and one may seek to enrol them to one's cause. Does the subject articulate a story that connects with specific 'news values' as reporters and their editors constitute them, for instance?[5]

Following Laclau and Mouffe (1985), one may note that knowledge also has formal relations, irrespective of its content. The appropriate dimension for conceptualizing the formal qualities of knowledge is that of its framing. Knowledge may be more or less socially framed. At the most, it will be codified knowledge. Codified knowledge, such as a system of scientific propositions or of rational law, is highly abstract and thus translates across contexts easily. At the furthest remove from this is private knowledge, where what is known is not shared at all in the public sphere. For all intents and purposes it does not exist discursively (Wittgenstein, 1968). Mediating that which is most framed, through codification, and that which is not known at all (because it is not in the public sphere), is knowledge that is only imperfectly socially framed for translatability: it may be highly situationally embedded, for instance. Thinking of the matter in this way yields a table (with the residual category of non-public, or private, knowledge) where government will proceed through one or other of several major rationalities (see Table 3.1).

Organizations exist in and around power relations among people who have differential subjectivity, different identities. Different identities and the subjectivity that they make relevant can be postulated as offering differential resources for accommodating to or resisting organizational power relations. Within organizations an elite typically seeks compliance through the accommodation of others to their will, perhaps imperatively, more usually perhaps governmentally. Yet, power does not routinely produce consent (although some tendencies that always relate power with authority, such as Parsons, 1963, assume that it does).

TABLE 3.1 *Rationalities of government: social framing of available knowledge*

Subject constitution	More framed	Less framed
Self	Reflexive self-organization	Isolation
Significant others	Cultural organization	Confusion
Solidaristic others	Coordinated actions	Division
Generalized others	Available relevancy	Irrelevancy

Any codification of the types of resistant consciousness must testify to a remarkable ingenuity and creativity. What is crucial is consciousness: without it no resistance is possible. However, the consciousness in question may be in the subjectivity of either A or B, or even in the intersubjectivity that connects them. Hence, it is necessary, first, to discuss those strategies of outflanking that can render resistance redundant. (Mann, 1986 is the source for the notion of 'organizational outflanking'.) That is not to say that, empirically, outflanking will always precede resistance and that resistance will have to unfetter whatever the chains of outflanking are, but it is to acknowledge that resistance requires consciousness. Whether the consciousness is that of A or B, or shared intersubjectively, makes a difference. When the actions being constituted as resistance by B are unknown to A then A will be unlikely to seek to outflank the resistance that is offered. However, where B is unaware that the action engaged in is constituted as resistance by A it matters little: A is still able to mount a campaign of outflanking against B, even despite B's lack of knowledge of what is occurring. Hence, the problematic of the third dimension of power, focused on the 'unconsciousness' of B, is analytically prior. Before B is resistant, consciousness must exist in either A or B; outflanking, however, requires, at the minimum, consciousness by A. In terms of Lukes's problematic we require an understanding of how a consciousness of power is possible by B before we are able to discuss resistance. Thus, resistance as a form of power will first be explained in its absence, or at least its minimization, before considering its presence and those conditions conducive to its amplification.

The presentation is ideal typical; in reality one would expect that the social framing of available knowledge would have more of a variable rather than a binary character, but this presentation is intended for illustrative purposes only. In future research applications, one would anticipate that the ideal typical model might be used as a tool for generating likely hypotheses for the analysis of power, legitimacy and resistance. Resistance would be lower, one would hypothesize, the less framed the subject constitution. The legitimacy of resistance would be higher the more framed the subject constitution. The overall conditions for organization legitimacy would require empirical research to be specified in particular cases. Generally, we may note that it is difficult to address issues of organization legitimacy purely from the elite side: that is why recourse to 'strong' corporate culture is an insufficient basis for legitimacy. Legitimacy, in organization terms, depends on the variety and difference of subject positions that it seeks to organize, as well as the degree of organization of the subject constitution of these.

REFLEXIVE SELF-ORGANIZATION/ISOLATION

Where the individual actor exists under conditions of less framed knowledge, their reflexivity will be limited. For instance, at the individual level, one may simply not know or understand how power relations constitute one's own identity. Many 'coming out' accounts of the experience of sexual liberation from the assumptions of 'normal' heterosexuality often have the character of an individual overcoming his or her isolation. Such isolation is due to a lack of reflexivity about the possibilities of one's self. Subjects simply were isolated from the possibilities of sexual identity other than the one dimension proffered as 'normal', in the confines of the family, the small town, or whatever conditions had to be breached so that other forms of identity could be seen and resistance to 'normalcy' organized. Isolation contributes to resistance to change at the same time that it facilitates the acceptance of the established order. Isolation is a factor that can facilitate or restrict the imposition of a specific kind of power from one subject to others. It depends on the context.

Any act of resistance requires some degree of framed knowledge. At the very minimum it requires reflexive self-organization of one's self as a 'resistant subject'. To be a resistant subject is to be someone who knows enough about who he or she is and what he or she could, and should be, that one chooses to make a stand. One does that even if that stand is a seemingly idiosyncratic act of outrage or rebellion, or an existential gesture. Some cinematic examples are useful: the minor act of vandalism that landed the eponymous hero in *Cool Hand Luke* (directed by Stuart Rosenberg, 1967) in jail; McMurphy's attempt to watch the World Series ball game in *One Flew Over The Cuckoo's Nest* (directed by Milos Forman in 1975). In the latter Nurse Ratchett exercised classic non-decision-making power. Yet, this kind of personal resistance, the first step against the defeat of any tyranny, hegemony or regime of normalcy, is the most vulnerable to defeat. At the very simplest, snuff out the person (or in McMurphy's case lobotomize him) and one might also defeat resistance. Courage, conviction and a consciousness that is reflexively self-organized are no guarantee of success. However, they are a more probable basis for it than the isolation in which people exist in the absence of that reflexive self-organization such as characterized the inmates of the institution before the arrival of McMurphy. At the level of individual organization one might experience as a situational snub, slight or handicap a form of power whose systemic quality remains obscure because one lacks or has not yet developed the reflexive capacities to organize oneself coherently across the multiple scenes of one's individual life. One lacks a coherent framing account of oneself and sees as particular misfortunes what others might see as systematic oppression, varying only in its locales.

CULTURAL ORGANIZATION/CONFUSION

The individual's self-organization constructs divided life worlds in which one manages the trials and tribulations of relative powerlessness in one sphere by hermetically sealing experience in situational specificity. Subject compartmentalization into segmented and thus psychically protected spheres may be seen as a form of resistance in itself, as witness the 'instrumental' worker (Goldthorpe et al., 1969). Time and space may be ordered and arranged to minimize the possibilities for networks of kin or kith, or other social organization, emerging. Complex divisions of labor, anti-union prohibitions and the extreme experience of competition are examples. Other, more macro-historical examples include the use of armies from elsewhere for the business of intra-imperial subordination, a strategy that has a long history, reaching to Tiananmen Square in recent times.

Where one might anticipate solidaristic organization, time and space can be ordered and arranged to minimize the interaction and mutual awareness of subordinates, or even to render one group of subordinates invisible to another (Barnes, 1988: 101). Division can affect the stories that the subjects of power want to tell: what may be a complex of ethnic or organizational politics plays in the media as a story that focuses only on the dramatic sound-bites, or dramatic television footage. An example of the role that division can play in the outflanking of potential resistance occurs in the example that Collinson (1994) cites of the multinational corporation, where division into separate profit centers reinforces 'insecurities and barriers to resistance'. Solidaristic organization in multinational corporations always suffers from the potential risk of isolation. (In fact, isolation and division are, as it were, two sides of the same coin.) One might achieve solidaristic organization and a successful strike in one country against an employing organization that is a multinational. Yet, one is relatively powerless where the multinational can isolate and substitute for that national production with an increase from elsewhere outside the national basis of solidarism, where competing national solidarisms come into play. Coordination across the boundaries of division can provide a basis for resistance, but one that is much harder to achieve than the power that it resists. The latter is, ostensibly, a relatively unified and highly strategic locus of organizational calculation, while the resistance is much more fragmented, lacks centralization, and does not share a quantifiable strategic objective. Government can involve not only the self but also significant others whose support can nourish and sustain individually resistant self-consciousness through the building and sharing of a common culture. Where it is possible to marshal significant others, such as are provided by a family or kin network or an informal social organization within one that is formal, this will be the case. Hence, resistance, like the practice of democracy (Pateman, 1970), can thrive on its experience, at least where knowledge is more framed.

Where government is less framed, where few symbols or other signs cohere, then solidaristic organization invariably will founder on confusion. Those who are somewhat powerless remain so because they are confused or unaware of the social organization of power, of informal conduits as well as formal protocols, the style and substance of power, its shared culture embedded in a distinct social organization. It is not that they do not have a precise understanding of the rules of the game so much as that they might not recognize what game is in play, let alone know the rules. They may well be playing another game altogether. Of course, this is a particular problem where an overwhelmingly technologically superior form of life meets one that is by contrast less developed in technical terms. Historically the vast majority of cross-cultural contact has occurred on this basis: consequently it has been the force of arms that has settled the outcomes. In this context resistance usually occurs through a clash of strongly held cultural systems.

COORDINATED ACTIONS/DIVISION

An interesting contrast between recourse to more and less framed bodies of knowledge is available by contrasting two seemingly similar 'total institutions' (Goffman, 1961) – prisoner of war camps and concentration death camps. In either, at the individual level, existential resistance by individuals is always possible, where the sense of self remains intact through techniques of 'mental distancing'. At the existential extreme, individual acts of resistance, including the defiance explicit in one's own suicide, are always possible. Yet, resistance through solidaristic organization is much more difficult in the circumstances of the concentration camp than in the prisoner of war camp. Existing in severe deprivation under a regime of brutality, terror and horror is not conducive to closely organized ranks of relatively undisciplined individuals. The aggregate impact of individual acts of resistance may be effective but it is easy for the individual will to power to be broken, by death, if necessary. Without organization, resistance will not survive the individuals' death. In addition, disparate acts of recalcitrance by people exposed to certain terror if the uncertain enterprise of resistance is exposed make the achievement of collective organized resistance more fragile and precarious a probability. While little or no chance of organizing for success may exist, probabilities suggest that the attempt at organization will lead to certain failure and death. Even if breaching the confines of the camp is successful one may be picked out as part of the fleeing mob of inmates at the leisure of the authorities that command the environs of the camp. For these reasons opportunism will always be a problem. Few may be willing to sacrifice themselves for the altruistic good of the others by initiating a charge on the armed guards. Some may hope to save their skins by exposing others to the authorities. Within such a camp the thousands of inmates might succeed in concerted action against the relatively few armed guards. It would depend upon the vulnerability of the watch towers, the security of the perimeter and the strength of arms. One might object that, with sufficient sacrifice, the inmates might resist and overcome the obstacles. Yet, achieving concertation remains a technical difficulty among the inmates when they are unable to organize explicitly. Implicit organization is possible, perhaps, based on contained subunit social organization such as dormitories, but exceedingly difficult with neither mechanisms nor arena of organization. In prisoner of war camps, by contrast to death camps, the existence of a recognized command structure, its disciplines and rules, frames organization. An extensive organization functions as a resource around which resistance can function more effectively, even if it is frequently outflanked by the force of superior arms and technology.

Organizational outflanking may operate on the basis of a knowledge of objective conditions whose existence renders resistant knowledge useless. One knows that one is an exploited wage earner but the routines of everyday living and life or the identity of one as a 'man' (or some other category meaningful for existence) have greater salience than 'exploitation'. Freedom is defined by constraint. Free subjects have a necessity to 'earn' their living in dull compulsion, busy work, arduous exertion, ceaseless activity, routinely deadening, compulsory and invariable. Such techniques of power may easily discipline the most blithe of theoretically free spirits when the conditions of that freedom become evident. The most resistant of wills may bend when it realizes that it has no chance of increasing freedom to maneuver, through recourse to some alternative.

Time is double-edged here: both using the time of an agent on the routine performance of routine tasks, as well as the habituation that this produces over time as personal and intersubjective routines take on a ritual nature as bulwarks against the encroaching meaninglessness of externally imposed routine. Such rituals may be both informal and formal, the former a kind of resistance to the meaning of the latter, as Burawoy (1979) charts.

Formal rituals, myth and ceremony serve to reinforce and make meaningful the routines of everyday subordination just as resistance may seek to make these routines ironic or distant or to undercut them in some way. Thus, one endures the formal rituals of power.

AVAILABLE RELEVANCY/IRRELEVANCY

Subjects seeking to build alliances with generalized others may have a story to tell. Reaching an audience potentially interested is another matter. Such subjects can enhance their resources considerably, if they know how to connect with media organizations, or know how to construct their story in such a way that it taps into the relevance of 'news values'. But not if they are ignorant of what constitutes relevance. In the context of solidaristic organization under less framed knowledge, often there is a simple lack of awareness of the organizational agencies with whom one might construct an alliance. In terms of solidaristic organization one may, simply, be without ready access to potential allies. Though one might easily outweigh one's protagonists if one could only connect with networks, one cannot because one cannot readily access them. Here resistance cannot be part of a concerted action. It remains unframed defiance, easily surmounted and overcome even when its irruption is not infrequent across the whole scope of power. Since the outbreaks remain uncoordinated, defeat, exile or incorporation threatens their survival.

One's experience of particular conditions in their emergence and state of becoming defines one's interests in overcoming or avoiding what one takes, at that time, their implications to be. Under such conditions, where one decides to avoid or overcome such implications, theoretically, one may be said to have an interest in not being subject to such interests as one conceives there to be. Such a conception of interest is phenomenologically valid rather than premised on the theoreticians' privilege that attaches to the discredited notion of 'real interests' (Haugaard, 1997a: 141). If we understand autonomy as a capacity for self-reflection, the maintenance of large bodies of knowledge as practical consciousness is inextricably bound up with the reproduction of certain relations of domination. Once an actor reflects upon his or her practical consciousness knowledge then he or she is realizing relative autonomy.

The social relations that constitute the expression of this relative autonomy make a considerable difference to it. Such relative autonomy is essentially discursive. Self-reflection can only take place through the medium of the categorization devices that members have available to them as part of the language games that they encounter with others, through others, in others, about others and selves alike and unlike their conceptions of their self. Hence, conceptions of interests form discursively: even to the extent that one can persuade some people that they have real but unrealized interests, the expression of which their present conditions of existence block. Such discursive realities shape their actions as resistance towards the sources of domination identified.

CONCLUSIONS

Neither resistance nor legitimacy is endemic, nor can they be taken for granted: for they occur through the discursive expressions of existing conditions of existence that are socially framed. Each depends on the relation of the practical consciousness of people through those categorical devices with which they lead their everyday lives, with the discursive consciousness that various media of representation proffer. As one would expect these media of representation to be extraordinarily plural and diverse in their concerns it will only be in rare moments that such diversity is represented or resisted in the name of some great unifying narrative or theme. Most probably these will be those relatively rare moments where a privileged identity is posited as a historical subject, such as moments of nationalism. In each case, to achieve the identity being posited requires capacities that overcome individual isolation, divisions between putative subjects, the knowledge that frames the practical consciousness of these putative subjects, and the objective conditions that sustain that knowledge.

The theorization of subjectivity in terms of moves between interpretative horizons means that the ability of actors to transcend their social environments and structured context does not presuppose an ability to 'escape' the processes of socialization by adopting a neutral, culturally unbiased, position. Subjective autonomy does not involve a flight into any transcendental realism of absolute truth, nor does it involve the transcending of 'false' consciousness. Critical faculty does not imply the objectivity of truth, nor does it entail an undersocialized concept of agency whereby autonomy is gained by transcending the basis of social culture. It requires only relative reflexivity on the part of subjects.

Other than through contingent individual actions, it is only access to organizational resources greater than those of the self that can overcome situations of stratified life-chances. It is the absence of these resources of social organization, or their ineffectiveness, which leads to resignation and acceptance.

The application of Foucault's work requires analysis of resistance, not merely as a vitalist principle but as a rationality of power sometimes used by those subject to power, where government fails to align their projects with those of the governing. Thus, government should not be considered some kind of functionalist device that renders resistance impossible. On the contrary: both the will to power and the will to resistance require failure as their warrant.

NOTES

Thekla Rura-Polley gave me many valuable comments on early drafts of this chapter although, as always, we failed to agree on theology! Ian Palmer read an early draft of the chapter and gave me pause for thought over some aspects of its development. Another person who aided me in overcoming some of that bounded rationality before public presentation was Robert van Krieken; I also want to thank him greatly for his 'vigorous' and excellent comments on an earlier version of this chapter, many of which are incorporated herein. Cynthia Hardy also made criticisms while John Gray pointed out a number of typographical errors and infelicities. Dirk Bunzel encouraged me greatly with his response to earlier drafts of the chapter. Jens Bekert and Uwe Schimank made some critical observations on the chapter as discussants at the 'Mach und Organisation' Conference of the German Sociological Association Sociological Theory Section at which it was presented on 9 October 1997. Additionally, I would like to thank Claus Offe and Steven Lukes for remarks made during the same conference. Howard Lentner made useful comments on a later presentation of the chapter at an International Political Science Association (IPSA) Research Committee 36 Workshop on 'Power' held in Nijmegen in May 1998, as did some of the other participants, including Mark Haugaard and Henri Goverde.

1 Outside unreconstructed functionalist circles, few would dispute the advances unleashed by Foucauldian-influenced analyses such as those of Callon (1980; 1986; Callon and Latour, 1981; Callon and Law, 1982; Callon et al., 1986; 1983) and Laclau and Mouffe (Laclau, 1980; 1983a; 1983b; Laclau and Mouffe, 1985; 1987). These researchers made important contributions to organization analysis,

that, with few exceptions (e.g., Law, 1996; McKinley and Starkey, 1998), have gone largely unremarked. Although Scott (1987) admits Foucault to the broad church of institutionalism's adolescence, this aspect of institutional theory has been somewhat neglected in organization theory.

2 In constructing knowledge/power relations as the object of analysis some of Foucault's critics, such as Perry Anderson (1983; also see 1985), insist that it is a relativism in which any fixed point dissolves.

3 Although a number of writers have written about Foucault's later work on power, with the exception of van Krieken (1996), they do not explicitly address organizational issues (Burchell, Gordon and Miller, 1991; Greco, 1993; Hindess, 1996; Hunter, 1993; Miller, 1994).

4 Foucault stressed intellectual experts: too narrowly, one thinks. One should include also more purposive forms of agency such as talk back radio announcers and popular journalists, agents with far more efficacy than most intellectuals. In Bauman's (1988) argument, in postmodernity the interpreters have overwhelmed the legislators.

5 Alternatively one might ask to what extent we, as subjects, find ourselves in the stories that these agencies construct.

▌▌ PRACTICES

Above all, the contributions in this part share an orientation in the policy sciences. In different ways, all three chapters consider power relations involving both private and public actors. They address a common research question: how has the 'balance of power' shifted among state institutions, civil society and markets? This question aims to achieve a better understanding of the contents of policies as well as the process of policy formation. In addition, each author is concerned with both theoretical and empirical matters; and each focuses on power in political and policy processes. In principle, the practices studied cover a range from the global to the local scale, but the different contributions are not, strictly speaking, oriented to territorial issues and configurations.

The study of power is a rather classical theme in policy sciences. It was Harold D. Lasswell (1902–78), one of the founding fathers of the policy sciences, who in 1950 published, together with Abraham Kaplan, a reader entitled *Power and Society*. These authors argued (1950: 82) that 'the doctrine of power is a political doctrine and science of power (in the narrowest sense) is political science'. Of course, Lasswell and Kaplan do not give a definition of power here. They know perfectly well that power is a relevant value not only in politics but in other sectors of social life as well. Neither is power the only important value for people. In his famous book *Politics: Who Gets What, When and How?* (1936) Lasswell argued that people are interested in values like prosperity (income), respect, welfare (security, health), morality/rectitude, professional skills, knowledge and affection, but above all power. Political influence in politics and in policy processes is, according to Lasswell, only partly derived from power. In contrast, the amount of power that a person can mobilize is in great part derived from the amount of control one exercises over the other seven distinct values. A democratic personality is a person who has a balanced interest in the eight values and he or she is also willing to share this interest with other people. Although Lasswell did not believe in the rationality of life, he argued that in politics the irrationality of social life comes to the open, public realm. From a normative perspective, it is good that the rationality of policy processes facilitates openness, responsibility and accountability in political life as well as the full deployment of the democratic personality.

Another dimension of political life to which Lasswell paid attention is the idea that prevention is better than cure. Policy sciences – i.e., all sciences which provide support to human dignity – should sustain the capacity not only to understand, to explain and to solve social problems, but also to prevent the rise of these problems. This task requires sharp attention in policy analysis to the context of policy formation.

Goverde and van Tatenhove (Chapter 4) unravel the question of why power is still a rather underexposed phenomenon in the policy network approach, which claims great relevance in the contextualization of policy formation. However, this approach, which is particularly popular in Anglo-Saxon and Western European policy studies, has not paid enough attention to social change in the context of policy processes in order to be able to incorporate insights concerning the exercise of power as well as structural and systemic power. Therefore, this kind of policy analysis is often not able to fulfill the task Lasswell formulated for policy scientists. On the one hand, the policy network approach overestimates the possibility of solving problems. On the other, it does not produce the insights needed to prevent social problems.

Concretely, in Chapter 4, the authors conceptualize how public and private actors are interwoven in processes of policy-making through dynamic policy networks. In policy networks, public and private actors interact in a process of multilevel governance. Goverde and van Tatenhove discuss the methodological gap between different forms of policy network management, particularly the prescriptive variant, on the one hand, and social change as a form of dynamics in the context of networks, on the other. They claim that this gap can be bridged by a three-layered conceptualization of power: power as a capacity, power as a relational phenomenon, and structural power. In their treatment, they refer to Goehler's transitive and intransitive power and to Clegg's three circuits of power. Furthermore, they invoke power in 'figuration sociology' (Norbert Elias) and power in 'structuration theory' (Anthony Giddens) to support the claim. Although the chapter offers mainly a theoretical discussion of power in different network approaches as a scientific tool to study multilevel governance, the authors refer briefly to empirical research as well. They describe policy processes of mostly rural and environmental issues in which regional and local actors compete from the bottom up with national and European actors for dominance in policy networks.

While the field of power analysis has changed in many respects, the types of issues which interested C. Wright Mills, Robert Dahl, and Peter Bachrach and Morton Baratz are still important to power theorists. Whatever the perception of policy formation or the political arena, it is still interesting and important to know who makes and who vetoes decisions (Dahl), how specific institutions determine the types of decisions made (Bachrach and Baratz), and the extent to which resources shape the possibilities of decision-making (Mills). Rommetvedt (Chapter 5) concentrates on power shifts at the national level in the Norwegian political system, but he also reflects on comparisons with other Western democracies such as Sweden, Denmark, Austria and the Netherlands.

As argued in the general introduction, policy formation and decision-making can be broken into six moments, and each one of these is crucial to the final outcome. Rommetvedt concentrates on stages 3 to 5 (admission of the issue; comparative assessment of the options; and election of one of the possibilities). In processes of agenda setting, the institutional biases which influence the outcome seem to have changed from corporatism to pluralism. In stages 4 and 5 this implies a shift in the balance of power from the executive to an increased role for national parliaments. Thus, Rommetvedt introduces his readers to key debates within political science concerning the distribution of power in contemporary democracies. It was precisely this issue which started the whole power debate going over 50 years ago.

The chapters by Rommetvedt and by Arts are mainly based on empirical research. Both chapters consider multilevel governance in which the diffusion of power between public and private actors is made plausible. Both researchers emphasize the influence of nongovernmental actors.

Chapter 6, contributed by Arts, participates also in the debate over the measurement of power, which has formed part of the tradition of power studies since the 1950s. The chapter focuses on agent power rather than on structural power. The author claims that the actor-oriented and empirical focus of the old community power debate has been revalued, for scholars now recognize that 'power measurement' cannot be known in objective terms. Instead, Arts has developed a specific methodology to 'assess' the political influence of private, nongovernmental actors in complex, global decision-making on environmental issues. The proposed EAR instrument has three dimensions: ego perception (E), alter perception (A) and researcher's analysis (R). This EAR instrument is a revitalized combination of Hunter's reputation method and Dahl's decision-making method.

In summary, these three chapters demonstrate that the analysis and the explanation of processes of policy-making in multilevel governance require attention to different dimensions of power. In policy networks research, structural power is stressed. Both relational and structural power are emphasized, whether in Foucauldian-oriented analysis, when the impact of social change on the individual is understood and explained, or in more conventional analysis. Furthermore, shifts in power between public and private actors lead to a quest for new methods. Nevertheless, the case studies used in this part illustrate the continued utility of that tried-and-true approach. The ongoing trend away from corporatism and toward pluralism presents an interesting hypothesis for further comparative research. On the global level of governance a contrary trend seems to be imaginable. For example, in environmental affairs, hunger, education and telecommunication, a type of sectored corporatism between international public institutions and international organized nongovernmental actors can develop as long as a real global governance system is not available.

4 Power and Policy Networks

Henri Goverde and Jan van Tatenhove

This chapter is about the limited use of power in policy network approaches. In public administration science, policy networks are defined as 'more or less stable patterns of social relations between interdependent actors, which take shape around policy problems and/or policy programmes' (Kickert et al., 1997: 6). Characteristic for policy network analysis is its focus on the improvement of policy-making by concentrating on governance and management within constructed policy networks. The goal is to find solutions for policy problems by changing relations of interactions, by formulating new definitions of problems and by introducing new policy instruments. In general, policy network analyses embody attempts to understand and to explain new ways of governance in the context of changing interrelations between state, civil society and market (Benson, 1975; Hanf and Scharpf, 1978; Marin and Mayntz, 1991; Marsh and Rhodes, 1992; Scharpf et al., 1976; van Waarden, 1992). Although power is an element of analysis, the accent is on power relations in interaction, particularly oriented to resource dependency. The social engineering character of some of the policy network approaches, however, does no justice to structural power, inequality and the unintentional consequences of social change. In this chapter we try to overcome the shortcomings of the policy network approach by introducing a more sophisticated concept of networks: networks as a result of change. These networks are not constructed, but are the result of the unintended consequences of processes of social transformation and change in contemporary society. The direction and nature of social and political changes are one of the central themes in social and political science today. Although labels such as 'post-traditional', 'post-industrial', 'reflexive', and 'late modernity' reflect the diversity in the social sciences, in general theorists like Giddens, Beck and Castells redefine the idea and the discourse of the 'manageable society', in which the central idea is people's capability to shape both the social and the physical world. This redefinition is based on the supposed consequences of processes such as globalization, the information technology revolution and individualization. Characteristic for the basic structure of the new society is its networking logic, undermining the rationalities of and the relations between modernist institutions like state, civil society and market. In particular the dominance of the nation-state model seems to fade away.

In the following section we discuss both kinds of network analysis: 'change within policy networks' and 'networks as a result of change'. In the section after that we elaborate on the concept of power. Because the concept of power in policy network approaches is underexposed, *the policy network analysis fits only partly* to explain changes of policy-making and governance in a context in which the nation-state model is in transformation. Our discussion attempts to overcome the shortcomings of the so-called prescriptive policy network approach, by introducing a three-layered conception of power inspired by several scholars. This discussion on power will provide us with the tools to elaborate on power in different kinds of networks, focusing on the dimensions horizontal–vertical and inclusion–exclusion in the last section. The aim of this chapter is a more sophisticated approach to power within processes of policy-making and governance, particularly if these processes are perceived by a policy network analysis.

NETWORKS: ROOTS FROM DIFFERENT SOCIAL SCIENCES

Change within policy networks

The concept of policy networks has become very popular in political and policy sciences, because it refers to the fact 'that policy making involves a large number and wide variety of public and private actors from the different levels and functional areas of government and society' (Hanf, 1978: 12). Central elements are interdependencies among actors – a variety of actors each with its own goals and preferences and more or less stable patterns of interaction between them. In the debate on policy networks a distinction can be made between the heuristic analytical approach and a prescriptive management approach.

In heuristic policy network approaches the accent is on interactions, interdependencies between actors, the structural and institutional dimensions and the driving forces for the dynamics within and between policy networks (see Godfroij, 1989; Rhodes and Marsh, 1992; van Waarden, 1992; Wilks and Wright, 1987). Examples of policy network typologies are given by, among others, Jordan and Schubert (1992), van Waarden (1992). Rhodes and Marsh (1992) for instance distinguish five types of policy networks, ranging along a continuum from highly integrated policy communities to loosely integrated issue networks.

According to Klijn (1997) *policy science, political science* and *(inter)-organizational science* are the theoretical roots of policy network approaches. The contribution of *policy science* is the idea that policy-making is a multi-actor process. By stressing that policy-making takes place in interorganizational networks of a more lasting nature, the policy network approach takes up where the process approach leaves off. From *political science* the idea of policy-making in closed communities, such as neocorporatism and policy communities, is incorporated. The idea of power (resource dependency) and exchange processes between organizations is based on interorganization theory. Central in *interorganization theory* (Levine and White, 1961) is the resource dependency model. In this model power is related to the possession of resources (Aldrich, 1979; Benson, 1975) or with the asymmetry of the dependency relations between actors (Crozier and Friedberg, 1977; Scharpf, 1978). Being focused so strongly on resources, the interorganization theory takes less account of the existence of the norms and structures of meaning. A positive exception on this point is the work of Crozier and Friedberg (1977), which underlines a dialectical relation between the discretion of actors resulting in new structural arrangements and the institutional context which limits the actors' discretion. Most policy network analyses, however, do not incorporate the dialectic relation between the network and the institutional context, or are too optimistic about the possibilities of changing the institutional context from outside the policy network. According to Klijn (1997: 33) it is relevant to understand and, where necessary, to change this institutional context (i.e., a stable pattern between organizations), because the organizational arrangements included are a precondition for coordinating complex interaction between the various actors.

Besides the heuristic approach, the concept of policy networks is used in a *prescriptive way*, as a management instrument. Here there is a reference to 'deliberately sought interactions among individual organizations for the purposes of effective policy coordination' (Hanf, 1978: 12). Representatives of this approach are for example 'the governance group' of the Universities of Rotterdam and Delft in the Netherlands. Characteristic of this approach is the optimism about the problem solving and steering capacity of policy networks. To tackle policy problems or policy programs, a policy network should be constructed around it. Network management (Kickert et al., 1997: 10) implies influencing the type and amount of actors involved, the strategies of actors, their mutual relationships and patterns of interaction, as well as the rules of the game. In the prescriptive policy network approach, it is supposed to be possible to create consensus (common perception of the problem) among the participating actors and to create opportunities to solve the policy problem (van Tatenhove and Leroy, 1995) by managing the constituent elements and relations of the network.

The optimism that leads to seeking to manage social problems within the network is probably based on the main assumption that society, nowadays, functions in essence on horizontal relations between individuals, groups, organizations and institutions. Since in policy science the ineffectiveness of instrumentalism has been proved (Baakman, 1993), the vertical relations among actors became dubious as a fruitful concept in social and political analysis. The classical instruments – like regulation, subsidies and retributions – were thought to be blunt in a civil society dominated by the political principles of freedom and equity. It was supposed that well-educated people, under social-economic conditions of welfare, could no longer be pressed to obey governmental rules and order. Authority was no longer based on power positions, but should be earned permanently by stimulating positive actions in the electorate and by effective policies for different target groups. For many social scientists the supposed existence of horizontal relations became the guideline in developing new research programs and proposals. Not only did Habermas's thesis – namely that innovations in a society presuppose conditions for a *Herrschaftsfreie Dialog* – seem to be accepted, but such conditions were also supposed to exist in reality.

Networks as a result of change

Whether we characterize the contemporary period as late, post- or reflexive modern, it is clear that processes such as globalization, individualization, spread of information technology, etc., have deeply affected the relations among state, civil society and market. In fact, the nation-state model seems to have lost its exclusiveness, as it is parallelled by a whole series of local, regional and global networks or arrangements, set up by actors from different domains, crossing traditional borders of nation-states and their divisions (van Tatenhove et al., 2000). At the same time, the relations among state, civil society and market become less clear, revealing transboundary co-operation of localities, the rise of mega-cities, the competition of cities with regions, the clustering of nation-states, and the network enterprise. These examples are a general expression of new structures of organization and power on local, national, regional and the global levels, as a result of homogeneous and heterogeneous tendencies of globalization and new ways of building identity.

Characteristic for the institutional analyses of authors like Castells (1996; 1997; 1998), Albrow (1996) and Beck (1994; 1996a; 1996b; 1998) is that they try to understand the nature of social and political transformations and the way these transformations have been translated in the organization of contemporary society. They all conclude – although quite differently – with the erosion and transition of the nation-state model into flexible networks on a global scale. According to Castells, in the network society 'dominant functions are organized in networks pertaining to a space of flows that links them up around the world, while fragmenting subordinate functions, and people, in the multiple space of places, made of locales increasingly segregated and disconnected from each other' (1996: 476). Networks – defined as a set of interconnected nodes[1] – are open structures, able to expand without limits, integrating new nodes as long as they share the same communication codes. These networks are the result of fundamental transformations of societies. In the network society power is no longer concentrated in modern institutions (such as the state, capitalist firms, corporate media), but is diffused in global networks of wealth, power, information and images, which circulate and transmute in a system of variable geometry and dematerialized geography.

A postmodern explanation of contemporary transformations is Albrow's *Global Age* (1996). He believes the 'modern project' has ended and has been transformed into the 'global age', which involves the supplanting of modernity with globality: an overall change in the basis of action and social organization for individuals and groups. 'Globality is a new level of organization, to which any agent can relate, but which has no organizing agent' (1996: 121). The consequence of globality is the emergence of a new political order and requires a reconceptualization of the state. In the global age the nation-state loses control of the forces it previously contained, while the delinkages of culture, community and relationships and their escape from the frame of the nation-state are constant sources of concern for politicians and commentators. Because Albrow presupposes the total dissolution of the modern project he unfolds a utopian analysis. By using concepts like *free sociality* and the *global state*, he introduces a diversity of global coalitions. The global state, existing at 'every moment when the individual takes account of and seeks to perform in the interests of a common interest spanning the globe' (1996: 178), is constructed from below and relies on the global consciousness of countless individuals. In this context Albrow accentuates *performative citizenship*: the expression of concern for public good in new constellations (depending on constructed identities beyond the nation-state) which are gradually coming to challenge nation-states for the loyalties of their citizens.

Unlike Albrow, the sociologist Beck believes we are in a stage of radicalized modernity 'where the dynamics of individualization, globalization and risk undermine modernity and its foundations. Whatever happens, modernity gets reflexive, that means concerned with its unintended consequences, risks and foundations' (1998: 20). According to Beck the project of modernity resulted in the *risk society*, a phase of development of modern society in which the social, political, ecological and individual risks created by the momentum of innovation increasingly elude the control and protection of institutions of industrial society. It is essential that the transition from modern industrial society to risk society has been unintentional and unseen. In the age of risk, society becomes a laboratory, 'with nobody responsible for the outcomes of experiments. The private sphere's creation of risks means that it can no longer be considered apolitical. Indeed, a whole arena of hybrid subpolitics emerges in the realms of investment decisions, product development, plant management and scientific research priorities. In this situation, the conventional political forces and representations of industrial society have been sidelined' (1998: 10). Subpolitics refers to shaping society *from below*. It implies a decrease of central rule and growing opportunities for citizens, social movements, expert groups, etc. to have a voice and a share in the arrangement of society (Beck, 1994: 23). To understand subpolitics, that is politics outside and beyond the representative institutions of the political system of nation-states, Beck makes a distinction between politics of the first and second modernity. *Subpolitics* (second modernity) refers to politics outside and beyond the representative institutions of the political system of nation-states (first modernity) (Beck, 1996b: 18). It concerns the constitution of a global civil society of *ad hoc* 'coalitions of opposites' in opposition to modern political institutions.

The 'network society', 'globality' and 'subpolitics' are examples of networks as a result of structural transformations in contemporary societies. In interaction the structural properties of these networks are reproduced and conditions for activities are changed. From these macro-sociological theories can be deduced that, in order to understand the dynamics of networks and particularly the relations of power within (policy) networks, it is urgent to analyse the context and the structures of power in which these networks change.

Differences between network approaches

Three main differences between the two types of network analysis can be distinguished. First, there is a difference in the way horizontal relations within the network and vertical relations within the network and with other networks are taken into account. Furthermore, there is a difference in how the context is supposed to influence developments within the network: this concerns the distinction between inclusion and exclusion. Third, as a result of the first two differences, the concept of power is differently conceptualized.

In policy network approaches, particularly those focusing on management and governance, the main orientation is on horizontal relations. By considering these horizontal relations as the basis for societal development and social change, theoretical problems will arise that impede the development of an adequate theory of policy processes. In policy network approaches it is unclear how vertical relations – not only between actors within the network, but also between network actors and (more powerful) actors outside the network – influence the (horizontal) relations between actors within the network (van Tatenhove and Leroy, 1995). Vertical relations are only taken into account in so far as they influence relations of interactions (horizontal relations) within policy networks. In policy network approaches efforts are made to incorporate issues related to vertical relations, such as the position of the state, rules of democracy, representation and juridical guarantees. However, only in a network analysis as a result of social transformations are the interrelations between vertical (the context) and horizontal relations (patterns of interaction) inherently taken into account. From the context point of view, one can see the development of the new cross-points in the network ('power-brokers'), which can operate as spiders in new webs. In fact, changing relations among state, civil society and market in a global order create new networks or arrangements which interfere with existing networks (see Leroy and van Tatenhove, 2000). Via 'discourse development' based on the formation of new 'discourse coalitions' (Hajer, 1995) new developing networks compete with the older ones. The domination of a new network implies new vertical relations from the outside to the existing network.

Second, exclusion and inclusion. Exclusion refers to an analysis in which relations and patterns of the 'context of networks' are excluded, while inclusion refers to an analysis in which the formation and transformation of networks are explained from the structural context of networks. Although in policy network analysis the accent is on exclusion, with the concept of 'closedness' they try also to include elements of the context in the analysis. The closedness of networks, however, is identified on the level of interaction, by 'the veto power of the actors' (Schaap and van Twist, 1997: 66–7). Actors can deploy their veto power to exclude certain actors (conscious social exclusion at actor level), or they can deploy their veto power to ban certain points of view (actors' conscious cognitive closedness). At network level a network can be closed by veto power to actors outside the network. This type of exclusion by veto power is based on common frames of reference and discourses. Despite these attempts to incorporate contextual variables or driving forces (for example social-economic development) into analysis, network management theorists do not seriously discuss the institutional context of policy networks, while 'horizontal relations' are being over-emphasized. In network analysis as a result of change, the accent is on the interrelation between inclusion and exclusion so that the policy processes can be contextualized. Because, in network analysis as a result of change, the changing relations among state, civil society and market are the starting point of analysis, it is possible to analyze the relation between 'interdependence', the strategies and interactions between actors and structural developments dialectically.

Third, in the policy network approach, by accentuating horizontal relations and exclusion the structural patterns and mechanisms of power are underexposed, while the approach is mainly ahistorical and apolitical (van Tatenhove and Leroy, 1995). Rhodes (1997) seems to underline these omissions in his foreword to the book *Managing Complex Networks* (Kickert et al., 1997: xiii):

> They focus on steering networks, adopting a managerial perspective, and discuss only briefly the topic of the accountability of networks in representative democracies. There is even less discussion of how to open networks to citizens. There is a need to adopt a political perspective on policy networks; to explore ways of democratizing functional domains.

To summarize, the premise of the dichotomy between horizontal and vertical social relations, together with the assumption of the dominance of horizontal relations in policy networks, give rise to the theoretical question of how to incorporate in network analysis concepts which generally attend to relations of power, inequality and dominance. It is rather obvious that as soon as the mechanisms of dominance and suppression, of insecurity and violence, of influence and power, of competencies and reluctance, etc., are under-valued, the theoretical construction seems to be unrealistic, or at least artificial. To overcome this theoretical pitfall, theorists of the prescriptive approach of network analysis have to put much energy into the theoretical incorporation of concepts like 'instruments', 'norms', '(veto) power', 'responsibility', 'liability', 'control' (Kickert et al., 1997: Part II). In fact all these concepts attend to the relevance of vertical social relations in groups, organizations and institutions as well as in policy networks.

CONCEPTIONS OF POWER

In this section we will elaborate on those theoretical positions in the debate on power which deal with power as a multilayered concept. In this analysis we rely on scholars such as Giddens, Elias, Held, Goehler and Clegg. To study power relations within policy networks, we need a theoretical framework that makes it possible to acknowledge both the influence of actors on the development of policies in networks and the impact of the structural context in which the actors operate. Both 'figurational sociology' and 'structuration theory' offer such a conceptual framework to understand the link between structure and agency. In both theories power is conceived as an integral element of social life. As a structural property of all human relations, power is understood as both a relational and a structural phenomenon (Elias, 1971; Giddens, 1984). In this section we present our conception of power, based on the duality of structure and agency, to understand processes of transformation within and outside policy networks.

Power: the link between structure and agency

The projects of Elias and Giddens bear remarkable affinity with each other (for an extensive analysis, see Bauman, 1989). The central categories of 'figuration' and 'structuration' are meant to grasp the link between the individual and society. According to Elias (1971) people are interdependent and form figurations. During history these figurations change, but these changes are unplanned. Structuration refers to the ways in which a social system is produced and reproduced in interaction, via the application of generative rules and resources, and in the context of unintended outcomes (Giddens, 1979; 1984). According to Giddens, agents and structures are not two independently given sets of phenomena, a dualism, but represent a duality (Giddens, 1984: 25). With the concept of 'the duality of structure', agency is connected with the reproduction of structures. Although there are differences, both theories try to give a solution for the actor–structure dilemma in the social sciences. In addition, the way power is studied in figuration theory corresponds with the analysis of power in structuration theory. In both theories power is an integral element of social life. Power is not an amulet one actor can possess and the other not, but is a structural property of all human relations (Elias, 1971: 81; Giddens, 1984). Power refers to the capacity of agents, agencies or institutions to maintain or transform their environment, social or physical; and it concerns the resources which underpin this capacity and the forces that shape and influence its exercise (Held, 1995: 170).

POWER IN FIGURATIONAL SOCIOLOGY   In the power theory of the figuration-sociological approach the concepts of figuration and balances of power are central elements. Society is interpreted as a collectivity of actors who are interdependent. As a result of mutual dependencies between actors figurations are formed, consisting of more or less unstable 'balances of power'. A balance of power is the result of competition among actors for resources. The interdependencies among actors in a figuration reflect their control over resources, but because the access and control over resources change, interdependencies change. In other words, the balance of power reflects the actors' control over resources, while at the same time the balance of power is a reflection of forces being practiced to control resources (Elias, 1971; Goudsblom, 1974; Goverde, 1987). Figuration sociology, however, not only focuses on resource dependencies in figurations (networks), but also stresses concepts of structural power and the way structural power influences the resource dependency in networks (figurations).

This multilayered conception of power is elaborated in different studies like 'the process of civilization' (Elias, 1969) and the 'established and outsiders' (Elias and Scotson, 1965). In those studies power is a structural characteristic of every social relation generated by the social figuration, and as such this structural aspect is neither bad nor good. In a figuration people are mutually dependent upon each other, either by violence, or by their need for affection, or by their need for money, social status, career or pleasures. This interdependency will often threaten these people to operate in a way they would not have chosen without this coercion. Therefore, it is important to distinguish between the coercion which is produced by every possible interdependency between people – even in figuration in which all positions are equipped with equal chances of power – and the coercion which is caused by an unequal distribution of opportunities (resources) of power to societal positions.

From Elias's point of view, the relation between structural power and resource dependency is founded in the interplay of factors between the collectivity and the individual (Mennell and Goudsblom, 1998). The more differentiated the societal functions are, the more people are mutually interrelated and the more dense the interwovenness is concerning the network of interdependent relations. This implies that every individual has a limited discretion. So, even the most powerful individuals are conscious that their actions should be according to these limits in order not to endanger several links in the network. Crucial is the level of social cohesion, formed in dynamic historical processes, embedded in unintended networks of interdependence and figurations. In this way a severe coherent (low-class) minority can exercise more power than a group of loosely coupled individuals (Elias and Scotson, 1965). Mutual dependency could lead to mutual acceptance and more equality, as well as to a pluriform execution of power. More and more it is not easy to imagine that one person or a very small group takes all the power and controls everything. Elias foresaw a process of functional democratization, on the one hand, while, on the other hand, growing chains of interdependence and the increasing differentiation of functions that ask for more mutual coordination and integration. This often causes new creative forms of inequality, for example the inequality between the governors and the governed, between the coordinators and administrators on the one side and the coordinated and administrated people on the other side (de Jong, 1997).

POWER IN STRUCTURATION THEORY   In structuration theory structure is analyzed as rules and resources, resources being drawn upon in the constitution of power relations. An important aspect of Giddens's concept of power is that power must be analyzed not only in the use of power resources, but also in the links between the communication of meanings and the use of norms and sanctions (Giddens, 1979: 82). Following Giddens's concept of 'duality of structure' (1984: 25), interaction and structure are not two independently given sets of phenomena; instead, the structural properties of social systems (signification, domination and legitimation) are both medium and outcome of the practices they recursively organize. The relationship between interaction and structure in structuration theory must be interpreted as follows. In order to communicate, actors draw upon interpretative schemes in the course of their interaction. These interpretative schemes are organized at the level of structure in symbolic systems of signification. When actors apply sanctions, they make use of norms, which can be analyzed at the level of structure as moral rules or systems of legitimization. Power in interaction involves employing facilities which are asymmetrically divided within the present structures of domination. Giddens stresses that the distinction between these three dimensions is only analytical.

Essential for structuration theory is the idea that in the light of the duality of structure, domination and power are complementary:

> Resources treated as structural elements of social systems are drawn upon by actors in the instantiation of interaction. The power relations sustained in the regularised practices constituting social systems can be considered *as reproduced relations of autonomy and dependence in interaction. Domination* refers to structured asymmetries of resources drawn upon and reconstituted in such power relations. (Giddens, 1981: 50)

The capacity to achieve political outcomes in networks is dependent on the relations of autonomy and dependency among actors. In the constitution of power relations, agents are able to mobilize authoritative and allocative resources in policy domains. It is obvious that these resources are seldom equally divided among and accessible to all the policy players. In other words, the asymmetrical division of resources (structural phenomenon) reveals itself in relations of autonomy and dependency between actors (relational phenomenon). Power is exercised in the context of the relative capabilities of parties. For example, when positions or status (competence) are an element of the institutional order (see Frouws, 1994), structures of domination can be so obvious in relations of power that it seems that there is no visible exercise of power. The more relations of power are 'objectified' in normatively sanctioned, institutional mechanisms and routines, the more domination appears to be natural and reified and thus difficult to change. Although all social systems of any duration involve an 'institutional mediation of power', domination is also expressed as modes and 'strategies of control'. According to Giddens, no matter how great the scope or intensity of control super-ordinates possess, subordinates can bear to bring strategies of their own: 'All strategies of control employed by superordinate individuals or groups call forth counter-strategies on the part of subordinates. This phenomenon represents what I call the *dialectic of control* in social systems' (1985: 10–11).[2]

Power: three interconnected layers

In figurational sociology and structuration theory, power is considered as a multilayered concept. Power both refers to the capacity of agents and is understood as a relational and structural phenomenon. In this section we present these three interconnected layers of power to study social and political transformations in and through (policy) networks in an integrated way. By this we want to develop a dynamic conception of power by dealing with the duality of agency and structure. At this starting point of analysis are the conceptions of power in structuration theory and figuration sociology, but with the views of Goehler and Clegg we want to bring the analysis one step further.

The first layer is *power as capacity*. Power as capacity of social agents, agencies and institutions refers to the way the social and physical environment is maintained or transformed, 'and it concerns the resources which underpin this capacity and the forces that shape and influence its exercise' (Held, 1995: 170). 'Power as capacity' is the most apparent and visible type of power. It concerns 'power over' and consists in the subordination of one person's will by the will of another. This is what Goehler in this volume calls transitive power: a zero-sum game, restricting the possibilities of actor B by the will of actor A. Characteristic for transitive power is that power and counterpower are primarily brought directly to bear, that is, through actors directing their power towards others, either in asymmetrical or in symmetrical relationships.

However, power is always located and never exists in isolation. The second layer, *power as a relational phenomenon*, refers to the fact that power is always exercised in the context of the relative capabilities of actors in interaction (see Giddens, 1984; Held, 1995). Power as a relational phenomenon accentuates relations of autonomy and dependence among actors within an institutional context. Examples of this type of power are the concepts of the intransitive power of Goehler and of the circuit of social integration of Clegg. According to Goehler, power becomes normative, in the sense of generating collective capabilities, by changing the focus from individual actors to collectivities, figurations or practices: 'Intransitive power encompasses the ensemble of relationships constituting a group of people as a community; it exists in the joint practices of actors' (Chapter 1 in this book). In other words, 'intransitive power constitutes a community as an effective body in the form of a common space of action which is symbolically present'. In intransitive relations of power actors act on the basis of shared value conceptions and principles of order in the same common space. In contrast, in cases of transitive relationships of power, the space of action between A and B is only defined by the superordination and subordination of their respective wills, and which interlocks their possibilities for action.

The third layer, *power as a structural phenomenon*, refers to the fact that power cannot simply be conceived in terms of what agents or agencies do or do not do. Power is shaped by and in turn shapes the socially structured and culturally patterned behavior of groups and the practices of organizations (Held, 1995; Lukes, 1974).

When viewing these theories on power, it becomes clear that power has to be studied on three levels to understand power and social change in contemporary societies. Clegg for example connects these layers with the concept of circuits:

> Power viewed episodically, may move through circuits in which rules, relations and resources that are constitutive of power are translated, fixed and reproduced or transformed. These other circuits of power, which will be termed the circuits of social and system integration in which are implicated dispositional and facilitative power respectively, constitute the field of force in which episodic agency conceptions of power are articulated. (1989: 211–12)[3]

The networks, which can be distinguished as a result of these changes (see above), show a complex interweaving of vertical and horizontal interrelations, on the one hand, and the influence of the context and structural aspects (inclusion and exclusion), on the other. Therefore, to study power within and between policy networks *a conception of power is needed that makes it possible to acknowledge both the influence of actors on the development of policies in networks and the impact of the structural context in which the actors operate*. To understand the development of these networks we have *to grasp the link between structure and agency* on three interconnected levels of analysis. First, on the level of agency, actor A has the capacity to enforce its will on actor B. In this conception of 'power over' agents have the access and possibility to mobilize resources. On this level horizontal and vertical relations are emphasized in an interlocking space of action, in which the context is excluded (transitive power). Second, on the level of networks, figurations or practices, power is a relational phenomenon and refers to the fact that power is always exercised in interaction by actors, with relative capabilities, within the context of unintended or even unknown chains of interdependency. Power on this level is dispositional and intransitive in nature; as a result of interactions in the context of existing or created relations of interdependence, collective capabilities are generated, by a shared normative commitment, shared symbols, and a common sense of identity. With the third level of power, structural power, it is possible to incorporate the problem of inclusion and exclusion into analysis. Structural power refers to the structured asymmetries of resources as a result of specific structures of signification, domination and legitimation in a certain context and period.

LESSONS FOR THE POWER AND POLICY NETWORK DEBATE

How can we improve policy network analyses by introducing the insights of networks as a result of change and the three-layered conceptualization of power? Figure 4.1 is an attempt to summarize the findings of the previous two sections. By making a distinction between the dimensions 'horizontal–vertical' and exclusion–inclusion' we distinguish four types of networks.

In policy networks analysis, especially the prescriptive variant, the accent is on horizontal relations, while the context is mainly excluded. In this *autonomous network* the focus is on interaction within the network. Power

| | | Context | |
		Exclusion	Inclusion
Character of relations	Horizontal	*Autonomous network* Focus on interaction within policy networks; resource dependency and relational power within policy network *(transitive; episodic power)*	*From network to context* Focus on interaction within policy networks; resource dependency and relational power within a community having its own identity based on shared values, concepts and principles of order in a common space *(intransitive; episodic and dispositional power)*
	Vertical	*From network to network* Focus on interaction within policy networks; limited discretion of actors, partly as a result of interdependencies with actors in other (hierarchical/powerful) networks; resource dependency and relational power between policy networks *(transitive; episodic and dispositional power)*	*From context to network* Focus on networks as a result of change; resource dependency and relational power in the context of structural power *(transitive; intransitive power, episodic, dispositional and facilitative power)*

FIGURE 4.1 *Policy networks: perceived character of relation, context and power*

is conceived as episodic and transitive, while structural power is insufficiently perceived and understood. In the prescriptive policy network approach the power of one actor over another actor is the result of the accessibility and control of resources. Of course, the actors within a network do not have equal power. In fact, the shortage in specific resources determines the character of the mutual interdependence between actors. The logic of policy network management is based on making resources accessible to solve the policy problem. It is often recognized in policy network management that the 'vertical relations' with other networks can be an obstacle to realization of the solution of the problem. That is why vertical relations (rules, regulations) are supposed to be relevant for managing policy networks. In such a *network to network* relation not only episodic or transitive power, but also dispositional and relational power become relevant. When a network manager has the knowledge that a specific policy network has to be created to formulate a common definition of the policy problem or to find consensus for an innovative solution, the network to network relationship is relevant.

In for example the ROM project[4] 'de Gelderse Vallei' in the Netherlands, ministries and provinces constructed a policy network to improve agricultural development, and to overcome environmental and spatial problems caused by agricultural production. A historical analysis (Frouws and van Tatenhove, 1993; van Tatenhove, 1993), however, showed that the 'Gelderse Vallei' was more than just a rural area. Reducing the project to its agro-environmental dimension by the national and regional governments resulted indeed in solutions for these problems. However, many new problems such as environmental problems of industry and the planning of housing and industry were excluded from the policy network. During the policy process many conflicts arose because relevant network to network relationships were neglected. Another example is offered by SGPs (rural area pilot projects). In their study, Goverde et al. (1997) showed that initially these projects were constructed policy networks to realize nature conservation. However, as a result of negotiations with local actors, who mobilized knowledge and expertise, policy plans were modified. In addition to nature development, agriculture, recreation and sometimes housing were integrated in the policy-making process. Both of these examples demonstrate that constructed policy networks do not have enough scope to find a solution within the horizontal settings alone. Only by paying attention to the network context can the entrance of new actors from parallel networks, with common values and principles of order in a common space, create a positive impetus to realize relevant solutions. This is reflected in Figure 4.1 in the cell *from network to context*.

However, our claim goes farther. It is our conviction that the construction of policy networks is only useful to solve problems when a network is constructed on the basis of an analysis in which both the institutional context and strategic interaction are starting points, in other words, the combination of policy network analysis with approaches in which networks are considered as the result of change. In Figure 4.1 this is the column of inclusion of the context. An essential element of networks as a result of change is that they are the unplanned and uncontrolled outcome of social change. They are produced and reproduced in the course of interaction in the context of structural properties of social systems. In a combined analysis it is possible to include the institutional context, while horizontal and vertical relations are discussed as interrelated.

This kind of analysis has its consequences for the analysis of power in policy networks. By combining agency and structure in a conception of power, the accent is not on resource dependency only, but also on structural power or domination. In other words, power has to be based on the notion of duality of structure. For the analysis of power in policy networks we can conclude that in interactions actors are always confronted with an asymmetrical distribution of resources, and therefore networks exhibit some degree of political inequality. These structures of domination or structural power in networks produce specific dependencies, which enable or constrain interactions. At the same time, as a result of interaction between mutually dependent actors, the distribution of resources can change, resulting in other dependencies among actors. In other words, the structural power or domination is in itself dynamic as well. Conceptions of power, which combine structural and relational power, provide a framework to analyze and understand change within policy networks, not only as a result of developments within the network, but also as the result of general processes of economic, political and social change. When resource dependency, the mobilization of resources in interactions and structural power are all elements of the same analysis of power, it is possible to develop a policy network approach which not only is appropriate to manage complex policy problems, but also provides the tools to understand directions of political modernization in contemporary societies. What is needed is a 'change of focus' from an instrumentalist analysis of developments within networks, to reflection and explanation of changes and developments in society in general. This argument is reflected in Figure 4.1 as *from context to network*.

NOTES

1 A node is the point at which a curve intersects itself. Nodes are 'stock exchange markets . . . national councils of ministers and European Commissioners . . . coca fields and poppy fields . . . television systems etc.' (Castells, 1996: 470).
2 The dialectic of control refers to this universal presence of unbalanced degrees of autonomy and dependence that constitute power relations in social systems of all kinds. In other words it is about the two-way character of the distributive aspect of power: how the less powerful manage resources in such a way as to exert control over the more powerful in established power relationships (Cohen, 1989: 152; Giddens, 1981: 63; 1984: 16, 374).
3 In his extensive review of the relevant literature Clegg (1989) distinguishes three conceptions (circuits) of power: episodic, dispositional and facilitative. The episodic conception of power is the mainstream conception based on an agency's

'power over' (Dahl 1961; Bachrach and Baratz 1962). It involves 'a focus on behaviour in the making of decisions on issues over which there is an observable conflict of (subjective) interests, seen as expressed policy preferences, revealed by political participation'. In the dispositional circuit power is equated with a set of capacities; power is the capacity of some persons to produce intended and foreseen effects on others. The difference between the episodic and the dispositional conceptions of power is based on the idea that some authors hold that 'intentionality' is endemic to conceptions of agency and power. 'On the one hand, there is the episodic exercise of power which is initiated by an agency, while, on the other hand, there is dispositional power which is said to structure that agency's capacity to act' (1989: 84) The facilitative conception sees power as productive (Parsons, Foucault). Power has the 'ability to achieve goals, to get things done'. This facilitative conception urges power as a positive phenomenon against episodic power, which is implicitly based on conflict.

4 This policy concept of the Ministry of Environment is aimed at overcoming severe environmental and spatial problems, caused by for example farmers or industry (van Tatenhove, 1993).

5 Private and Public Power at the National Level

Hilmar Rommetvedt

The relationship between private interests and government has been described in numerous ways. Pluralism and (neo)corporatism, segmentation and iron triangles, issue networks and policy communities, are some of the key phrases used to characterize the relations between organized interests and public authorities. In this analysis of private and public power at the national level, I will use the case of Norway as an illustrative example of how private interests operate in order to influence public authorities. My theoretical point of departure, however, is a more general one, and the general framework presented in this chapter should be relevant to other polities as well.

There are, of course, many aspects of power relations in society. Here I will concentrate the discussion on three elements: (1) the concentration of private as well as public power in different types of government systems, (2) the changing power relations between executives and legislatures, and (3) parliamentary and administrative corporatism and lobbyism as types of relations between public authorities and organized interests. Within this framework, I assume that the actions taken by organized interests in order to exert influence on public policy-making are based on ideological as well as strategic assessments.

The theoretical framework of this chapter facilitates a comparative perspective, although the data are limited to the Norwegian case. Therefore, the empirical analysis will concentrate on comparisons between different types of interest organizations and on changes over time.

POWER RELATIONS: A GENERAL FRAMEWORK

In a study of 18 Western countries, Lijphart and Crepaz (1991) constructed a 'composite measure of corporatism' based on the 'combined wisdom' of 'twelve neo-corporatist scholars'. According to their calculations, the degree of corporatism in Norway is very high, surpassed only by Austria. Phillippe Schmitter, in his well-known and stimulating works on corporatism, distinguishes between state corporatism and societal corporatism (in addition to pluralism).[1] Norway, together with Sweden, Switzerland, the Netherlands and Denmark, is characterized as one of the best empirical examples of societal corporatism (Schmitter, 1979: 21).

According to Schmitter, societal corporatism is found in countries with 'singular, noncompetitive, hierarchically ordered, sectorally compartmentalized, interest associations exercising representational monopolies and accepting (*de jure* or *de facto*) governmentally imposed or negotiated limitations on the type of leaders they elect and on the scope and intensity of demands they routinely make upon the state'. Such interest associations have attained a quasi-legal status and a prescriptive right to speak for their segments of the population. They influence the process of government directly, bypassing the parliament (1979: 18).

As underlined by Schmitter (1982: 264ff), corporatism 'is clearly not something a polity has or does not have'. Practices that resemble the corporatist model are unevenly distributed across issue areas, and differences emerge and persist across countries. During the last decades, important changes have occurred in the relationship between organized interests and political authorities in Norway and, probably, in other 'corporatist' countries as well. In order to cope with these changes the chapter will focus on three interrelated aspects of power: (1) the concentration of private and public power, (2) executive–legislative relations, and (3) corporatism versus lobbyism.

Private and public power

The relationship between the degree of concentration of private and government power and types of governmental systems is an interesting element in the study of private interests in national policy-making published by Heinz et al. (1993: 395ff). They emphasize that the concentration of government power varies from situation to situation, as does the power of private interests. Combining these two dimensions of power concentration, they get a fourfold typology of government systems. *Corporatism* is characterized by high concentrations of government power as well as private power. *Pluralism*, on the other hand, is based on low concentrations of government and private power. A *state-directed* system is characterized by a high concentration of government power and a low concentration of private power. And finally, a high concentration of private power and a low concentration of government power condition *private government*.

As I have argued elsewhere (Rommetvedt, 1997a), we may distinguish between two types of concentration of power. Public as well as private power may be concentrated in a monolithic or a segmented way. The extreme version of corporatism, or state corporatism in Schmitter's terminology, is characterized by monolithic concentration of power. Schmitter's concept of societal corporatism, and Stein Rokkan's (1966) concept of corporate pluralism, indicate that there is 'something' in between corporatism and pluralism. In the 1970s, Norwegian political scientists introduced the concept of a *segmented state* in order to described this 'something' or intermediate category (Egeberg et al., 1978).

A political segment has been described as 'a set of micro linkages ... characterized by related selections as regards participants, problems, and solutions'. Such segments may be found within particular economic areas such as agriculture, fisheries and industry, or around functions like health care, communications, education and defense. Participants may come from various institutions. Thus, a segment may include representatives of interest organizations, ministries, parliamentarians, representatives of research institutions, the mass media, etc. The participants within one segment 'are assumed to share certain basic values and perceptions, such that their models of the world coincide more with one another than with those of representatives of other segments' (Christensen and Egeberg, 1979: 253).

Adding the segmented state to the typology of Heinz et al. produces five types of governmental systems, as described in Figure 5.1 (Rommetvedt, 1997a: 135).

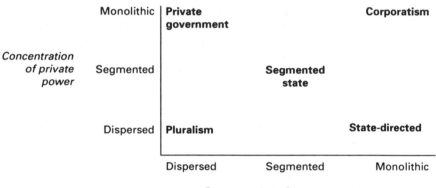

FIGURE 5.1 *Concentration of power and government systems*

It is quite obvious that neither the state-directed nor the private government 'label' is adequate in relation to the Norwegian governmental system. The Norwegian system is characterized by a certain balance between private and public power. The degree of concentration of power, however, has changed over time. The concept of corporatism seems to give a relatively good description of the Norwegian system in the 1950s and 1960s. The characterization of Norway as a segmented state was based on observations made in the 1970s. During the 1980s and 1990s Norway developed more pluralist traits.

The number of interest organizations has increased markedly, from 1100 in 1976 to almost 2400 in 1993 (Andersen and Lauritsen, 1990; Hallenstvedt and Trollvik, 1993). On the other hand, the number of corporatist arrangements like public councils, boards and committees with interest representation has been considerably reduced, from 1155 in 1977 to fewer than 600 by the end of 1995 (Christiansen and Rommetvedt, 1999). The pattern of contact between various lobbyists and the members of parliamentary committees seems to indicate that the degree of segmentation is rather low (Rommetvedt, 1998).

It should be added that the Norwegian system is a mixture of elements of corporatism, segmentation and pluralism. However, the center of gravity has moved in the pluralist direction. A certain decline of corporatism has been observed in other governmental systems as well, including countries like Austria, Brazil, the Netherlands and Sweden (Boschi, 1997; Crepaz, 1994; Lewin, 1994; Visser and Hemerrijck, 1998).

Executive–legislative relations

Researchers within the corporatist tradition tend to ignore legislatures and focus on the relationship between organized interests and the executive. As mentioned already, in corporatist systems organized interests are supposed to influence government directly, bypassing parliament. Or, as Rokkan (1966) formulated it in his analysis of numerical democracy and corporate pluralism: 'votes count but resources decide'. Kvavik, who studied the role of Norwegian interest organizations in the 1960s, was 'surprised to discover the absence of "lobbyists"' in the Norwegian Parliament. He observed that 'legislation was shaped in the administration; once in parliament, the lines were fixed'. On the basis of interviews with leaders of interest organizations, Kvavik concluded that parliamentary institutions 'receive an exceedingly weak evaluation' (1976: 15, 120, 118).

Using the terminology in the previous section, one may say that in corporatist systems public power is concentrated in the hands of the executive. Corporatist researchers would subscribe to the 'decline of parliaments' thesis. This thesis accords well with widespread opinions on executive–legislative relations in Norway and many other countries. It is interesting to note, however, that the thesis about the segmented state does not ignore parliament. Members of parliamentary committees are included in the list of members of political segments, together with representatives of interest organizations and government ministries etc. (Christensen and Egeberg, 1979; Egeberg et al., 1978).

Recent studies clearly indicate that the Norwegian Parliament, the *Storting*, has strengthened its position. Norwegian governments confront nongovernmental majorities in the *Storting* more often than they used to. In 1979–81 the government lost less than one vote per month. In 1986–9 and 1990–5 governmental defeat occurred in more than seven votes per month (Rommetvedt, 1998: 67). A certain 'rise of parliament' has been noted in countries like Austria, Denmark and Sweden as well (Crepaz, 1994; Damgaard, 1994).

To summarize: the concentration of public power in the hands of the executive has been reduced in recent years. Parliaments have strengthened their position *vis-à-vis* governments. In other words, governments have been forced to share more of their power with the parliaments. As a consequence, one would expect organized interests to pay more attention to parliaments when they attempt to influence public policies. This expectation is more relevant, of course, in pluralist systems than in corporatist ones.

Corporatism and lobbyism

In this analysis, a distinction will be made between two different forms of political participation, or methods of exerting influence on the authorities: corporatist participation or corporatism on the one hand, and lobbyism on the other (cf. Christiansen and Rommetvedt, 1999; Rommetvedt and Opedal, 1995).

Needless to say, corporatist participation is related to corporatist government systems as described above. Lobbyism is more relevant in pluralist government systems. In simplified terms, *corporatism* can be defined as a highly institutionalized and formal method of political participation and influence, often with negotiations and agreements implying mutual obligations for the participants. *Lobbyism* is a form of political participation and influence that is less institutionalized, less formal and without negotiated obligations.[2] One of the conditions for corporatism is that the authorities establish institutional arrangements and bodies involving participation by affected organizations. Such bodies, on the other hand, are not necessary for lobbyism. Interest organizations and other lobbyists can lobby on their own initiative. Hence, lobbyism is a more flexible strategy than corporatism.

The concept of corporatism is related to the influence of organizations through the so-called corporative channel (Rokkan, 1966). An important element of the corporatist system is the formal representation and participation of organizations on governmental boards, committees and councils. The governmental boards and councils are focal partly because they are important parts of the corporative channel, and partly because existing studies by the councils facilitate the study of development over time (Nordby, 1994). Lobbyism is an informal means of political influence that is practiced through personal relationships, telephone conversations, informal meetings, correspondence, etc. However, informal relations are not necessarily equivalent to occasional and sporadic relations. The relations may be both frequent and stable, but are often more *ad hoc* than the formal and institutionalized corporatist relations.

The strategies of interest organizations may be directed towards administrative as well as parliamentary actors. Combining the two dimensions, institutionalization and direction, produces a fourfold typology as shown in Figure 5.2.

Strictly speaking parliamentary corporatism is based on functional representation in the legislature. This is not relevant in contemporary Norway. The composition of the *Storting* is based on territorial representation from the counties. In Norway the corporative channel has been dominated by representatives from organizations and civil servants. Accordingly, the

Institutionalization:

	Low	High
Parliament	**Parliamentary lobbyism**	**Parliamentary corporatism**
Administration	**Administrative lobbyism**	**Administrative corporatism**

Direction

FIGURE 5.2   *Types of relations between public authorities and organized interests*

Norwegian kind of corporatism can be characterized as *administrative corporatism.*

Originally, lobbyism was primarily connected with the lobby of the Parliament where outsiders could meet the elected representatives. In this chapter the key phrase *parliamentary lobbyism* is used as a label for informal relations between organizations and MPs. The informal relations towards civil servants and the attempts to influence them made by the organizations will be referred to as *administrative lobbyism.*

ORGANIZED INTERESTS, IDEOLOGY, STRATEGY AND ACTION

The next step of the analysis will focus on organized interests as political actors, and use Norwegian environmental policy-making as an illustrative case. It will concentrate on two dimensions of comparison at the national level, i.e., variations between different types of interest organizations, and changes over time.

Interest organizations have to operate within the wider context of power relations in society. Consequently, interest organizations are calculating actors, and the actions taken by organized interests in order to influence policy-making are based on strategic assessments. Strategic assessments are based on costs and benefits, on the ideologies of the organizations, and on the power relations of the political system. The actual influence on policy-making depends on the power relations in society and on the actions taken by the organizations. The relationships between these variables are specified in the scheme of analysis in Figure 5.3. In the empirical analysis below, hypotheses are specified according to this model.

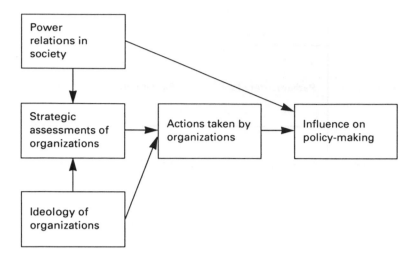

FIGURE 5.3 *Scheme of analysis*

Empirical data

The empirical illustrations will be based on information from various sources. The most comprehensive data originate from an *organizational survey* related to environmental policy-making (Klausen and Rommetvedt, 1997). The survey included two different questionnaires presented subsequently to administrative leaders and board members of the most important Norwegian organizations for environment, transport and agriculture.[3] A distinction will be made between two categories of organizations: *environmental organizations* include 12 organizations involved with environment protection and outdoor life; and *industrial organizations* include 19 industrial and business organizations, trade unions and other organizations within the areas of transport (11) and agriculture (8).

The primary units of analysis are the organizations. This represents no major problem with regard to the questionnaire presented to the administrative leaders who were requested to answer on behalf of their organizations. Somewhat more problematic is the questionnaire given to the board members, partly because they were requested to give their personal evaluations, and partly because the size of the boards and the number of respondents varied a lot from one organization to another. Thus, the number of respondents varies from one to 10 per organization. In the following presentation, the results are weighted in such a way that *each organization, not* each board member, counts as one unit.

Included in addition to the organizational survey is information from personal interviews with leading persons in 14 environmental and industrial organizations (Opedal and Rommetvedt, 1995a; 1995b; Rommetvedt and Opedal, 1995), and from a survey among Norwegian MPs.[4] Two databases at the Norwegian Social Science Data Services (NSD) will be utilized. They contain information on all nationwide nongovernmental organizations, and on governmental boards, committees and councils.[5]

In order to get a more concrete impression of the influence exerted by different organizations on environmental decision-making processes, also presented are some main findings from three qualitative case studies (Farsund, 1997; Opedal and Farsund, 1997a; 1997b). The case studies are based on interviews with civil servants and key informants in relevant organizations, as well as analyses of public documents and newspaper articles.

Ideology and strategic assessments

Integrated participation in the process of decision-making and close contact with political authorities may enhance the influence of interest organizations. However, integrated participation can imply responsibilities and losses of freedom and purity. The costs and benefits may, among other things, affect the organizations' spontaneity, their willingness to compromise, and their ideological identities (Olsen, 1983). Ideology can expand or restrict the organizations' room for action.

Environmental organizations are often regarded as anti-establishment with a grassroots image. This may sustain a wish among these organizations to keep a certain distance from the authorities. Environmentalists, like other activists and new social movements, are concerned with costs related to integrated participation (Gundelach, 1982; Jenkins, 1983; Melucci, 1985). In contrast, industrial organizations are more often regarded as parts of the establishment. Therefore it is less likely that they feel restrained in the same way towards the authorities as the environmental organizations do. As a result, one expects *environmental organizations, more than industrial organizations, to mobilize members, to be active in illegal actions, and to try to influence public opinion.*

Two questions in the organizational survey that were presented to the organizations' board members may be used to illuminate this hypothesis. The first question was related to the strategies and actions assessed to be most important in order to fulfill the goals of the organization. The second question concerned the decisions and attitudes that board members regarded as most important for the organization to influence. The answers are shown in Tables 5.1 and 5.2.

Table 5.1 reflects, to some degree at least, the social movement and grassroots profile of the environmental organizations. They are more concerned with recruitment of members, member mobilization, and mass media coverage than the industrial organizations. However, the differences are not at all overwhelming. The rank orders of strategies are almost identical for environmental and industrial organizations. The importance attached to demonstrations and civil disobedience is low, even among the environmentalists.

Table 5.2 shows that both the environmental and the industrial organizations view decisions in the Parliament as the most important ones

TABLE 5.1 *Most important strategies and actions to achieve the organizations' goals (weighted percent of board members)*

	Environmental organizations	Industrial organizations
Influence public policies through direct contact with central authorities	25	42
Seek mass media coverage on organizational initiatives	27	21
Mobilize members of the organization	20	16
Recruit as many members as possible	20	9
Stay in direct contact with companies and business organizations	7	11
Participate in demonstrations and actions	1	1
Participate in illegal actions and civil disobedience	0	0
Total	100	100

TABLE 5.2 *Most important targets of influence for the organizations (weighted percent of board members)*

	Environmental organizations	Industrial organizations
Decisions in Parliament	48	63
Attitudes in public opinion	27	13
Decisions in central administration	14	10
Decisions in municipal/county administration	9	3
Decisions in government	2	8
Decisions in international bodies	0	2
Decisions made by companies	0	1
Total	100	100

to influence. Surprisingly few regard decisions in the government as most important. The board members of the industrial organizations emphasize the decisions made in the Parliament and the government to a greater extent than the environmental organizations. Both the environmental and industrial organizations put people's attitudes and the decisions in the central administration in second and third places. However, a greater proportion of the environmental organizations than of the industrial organizations emphasize the importance of influencing attitudes in the overall population.

The last mentioned tendency is in accordance with what one would expect since so many of the environmental organizations are regarded as popular movements. However, the differences between the two types of organizations are less than one would expect. Altogether the answers give the impression that *the similarities between environmental and industrial organizations are greater than the differences*. Although the environmental organizations emphasize the importance of influencing public opinion more than the industrial organizations, it is obvious that *both the environmental and the industrial organizations attach greatest importance to influencing the political authorities and their decisions*. Among these authorities, *Parliament* is the most important.

Corporatist representation

The findings above are not consistent with what one would expect in a corporatist government system. Parliament is assumed to play a secondary role in corporatist systems. Corporatist representation is, first and foremost, a channel of contact between organized interests and civil servants. Governmental boards, committees and councils are important meeting places for representatives from interest organizations and the public administration. Previous research has shown that organizations within labor, industry and commerce, together with civil servants, have participated most frequently as members of governmental boards, committees and councils (Egeberg, 1981; Nordby, 1994). Therefore it seems reasonable to assume that *industrial organizations will participate more often in corporatist bodies than environmental organizations*.

However, during recent years the number of governmental boards, committees and councils has been greatly reduced in Norway, from 1155 in 1977 to fewer than 600 by the end of 1995. Denmark has experienced a similar trend (Christiansen and Rommetvedt, 1999). The decrease in the number of boards and committees *may suggest that there is no longer such a big difference* between industrial and environmental organizations.

Data from the Norwegian Social Science Data Services on governmental committees show that *a convergence has taken place between environmental and industrial organizations. Industrial organizations are still the most frequently represented in governmental committees, but the gap has been considerably reduced*. In 1983 fewer than one-fifth of the environmental organizations were represented in governmental boards and committees. Almost 50 percent of the industrial organizations were represented in such bodies. In 1993, one-third of the environmental organizations and 37 percent of the industrial organizations were represented in governmental committees.

There is still a great difference between environmental and industrial organizations as regards the number of representatives in governmental committees. However, this is because of the great number of representatives from the Norwegian Farmers Union and the Norwegian Farmers and Smallholders Union. In other words, *corporatism is still strong within the agricultural sector*.[6]

Thus, there has been a reduction in the overall access to authorities through governmental boards and committees for industrial organizations. On the other hand, environmental organizations seem to have obtained better access to the authorities through such committees. This may indicate a certain increase in the extent of corporatism for the environmental sector, although it is not particularly strong. The main conclusion to be drawn must be that *when the two farmers' unions are disregarded, administrative corporatism is rather moderate* for the organizations included in this study. The major distinction with regard to administrative corporatism is *not* to be drawn between environmental and industrial organizations. In this study's sample the major distinction is found between the farmers' organizations and other industrial organizations.[7]

Lobbyism

Since the degree of corporatism, with the exception of agriculture, seems to be rather moderate, *one expects lobbyism to be a more important method for interest organizations that seek to influence policy-making.* What kind of lobbyism, then, would we expect to be most important?

Over the last decades, the Norwegian Parliament has strengthened its position *vis-à-vis* the government. The level of activity and conflict in the *Storting* has increased substantially. Norwegian governments have been forced to tolerate defeat in parliamentary voting more often than before (Rommetvedt, 1998). As a consequence of this development, the outcomes of policy-making processes are more uncertain. This constitutes at the same time both a problem and an opportunity for interest organizations trying to make an impact on policy-making. Organizations that previously have been heard by the administration can no longer be certain that the Parliament will approve the proposals worked out in the corporative channel and/or in the administration, and then put forward by the government. Increasingly they will have to follow up the issues in the parliamentary channel to ensure that the final decisions correspond with the organizations' own interests. For organizations which have not succeeded in promoting their viewpoints through the corporative channel, the procedure in the *Storting* represents a new opportunity to influence the outcomes of the decisions. Hence, it can be assumed that *parliamentary lobbyism has become a more important element in both the environmental and the industrial organizations' attempts to influence policy-making.*

These hypotheses will be examined on the basis of questions regarding the interaction between organizations and public authorities in the organizational survey. These questions do not distinguish sharply between corporatist and lobbyist contacts, but formal corporative relations do not seem to be as extensive as lobbyism and informal relations between organizations and political authorities. Thus, it may be assumed that this part of the study is most relevant in relation to the *parliamentary* and *administrative lobbyism* conducted by environmental and industrial organizations.

The administrative leaders of the organizations were asked a question about the *frequencies of contacts* between their organization and various authorities and bodies during the last 12 months. The answers are shown in Table 5.3. These data show that a distinct majority of the organizations had been in touch with most of the mentioned authorities. The frequencies of contacts are particularly large as regards the central administration. More than 80 percent of the environmental organizations were monthly or weekly in touch with civil servants in ministries or agencies/directorates. Three-quarters of the industrial organizations had weekly or monthly contact with civil servants in ministries, while more than half had the same frequency in their relations with directorates. Most organizations are in contact with the various bodies within Parliament a few times a year.

TABLE 5.3 *Frequencies of organizational contacts with various authorities (percent of organization according to the administrative leaders)*

	Organizations	Weekly/monthly	Yearly
Parliament			
Single MPs	Environment	8	83
	Industrial	33	53
Parliamentary party groups	Environment	9	73
	Industrial	27	53
Parliamentary committees	Environment	8	83
	Industrial	6	82
County benches in Parliament	Environment	0	36
	Industrial	0	64
Central administration			
Minister/state secretary/ political adviser	Environment	18	73
	Industrial	31	46
Civil servants in ministries	Environment	83	17
	Industrial	77	18
Leaders/civil servants in agencies/directorates	Environment	82	18
	Industrial	56	38

In some instances one can find relatively distinct differences between the two types of organizations examined. A greater proportion of the industrial organizations than of the environmental organizations have weekly or monthly contacts with MPs or party groups in Parliament, and with cabinet members, state secretaries or political advisers in the ministries. The environmental organizations, on the other hand, are somewhat more often in contact with directorates.

The administrative leaders of the organizations were also asked about the *changes in the frequencies* of contact with the Norwegian Parliament and the political leadership of the ministries over the last 10–15 years. The answers clearly show that the *parliamentary lobbyism has increased the most.*

Sixty-seven percent of the environmental organizations and 40 percent of industrial organizations stated that their contacts with the *Storting* have increased. Further, 36 percent of the environmental organizations and 27 percent of the industrial organizations answered that their contacts with the political leadership of the ministries have increased. Only 7 to 9 percent of the organizations say that these kinds of relations have decreased.

The different frequencies of contact in the environmental and the industrial organizations fit well with the results of a survey carried out in the *Storting* during the spring of 1995 (Rommetvedt, 1997a; 1997b; 1998). Thirty-eight percent of the MPs indicated that they receive weekly enquiries from environmental organizations. Sixty-eight percent received weekly enquiries from business organizations, and 54 percent from trade unions. Forty-seven percent of the MPs said that their contacts with environmental organizations had increased during their service in Parliament. Sixty-four percent of the representatives stated that communication with industrial organizations had increased, while 52 percent told the same regarding trade unions.

In other words, the MPs' answers give an impression regarding the frequency of contact which is slightly different from the survey among the organizations. This may be connected with the existence of a far greater number of industrial organizations and trade unions than of environmental organizations. The MPs' assessments are based on industrial organizations and trade unions in general, while the survey among organizations only includes organizations dealing with agriculture and transport.

The main conclusion is that *both industrial and environmental organizations carry out an extensive lobbyism towards various political authorities. Although parliamentary lobbyism is considerable and increasing, administrative lobbyism is even more extensive.* This may result from the fact that there is a substantially higher number of issues and executive officers in the administration than in the *Storting*. A smaller number of decisions are made in the Parliament, but these decisions are considered to be of great importance to the organizations (cf. Table 5.2).

Changes in the importance of contacts with various authorities as regarded by the organizations can be illuminated by a combination of information from the Norwegian Social Science Data Services and from interviews with representatives of environmental and industrial organizations. Thus, one can map the changes in the organizations' assessments from 1982 up to 1992–5 for 21 organizations altogether. Of these 13 are industrial organizations and 8 environmental organizations. The results are shown in Table 5.4.

This table shows that the importance of contacts with MPs and party groups has increased the most, followed by the *Storting* and its committees, and by the government. The importance of contacts with the ministries and directorates has increased to a lesser extent. Moreover, several organizations report that the importance of contacts with the administration has been reduced. In other words, *the importance of parliamentary lobbyism has increased the most.*

TABLE 5.4 *Changes in the importance of contacts with different authorities, 1982 to 1992–5 (percent of organizations)*

| | Organization | Importance of contacts is: | |
		increased	reduced
Parliament/standing committees	Environment	38	0
	Industrial	31	15
MPs/party groups	Environment	50	0
	Industrial	46	15
Government	Environment	38	13
	Industrial	25	8
Ministries	Environment	13	0
	Industrial	8	8
Directorates/ agencies	Environment	13	13
	Industrial	15	0

THE POLITICAL INFLUENCE OF ORGANIZATIONS

The results from the previous section indicate that both environmental and industrial organizations make very active attempts at influencing political authorities. The next question to be analyzed pertains to the actual influence of the organizations. It is, of course, difficult to measure political influence and power. This study uses various indicators: first, some major findings in three case studies; and then the general assessments made by the organizations themselves and by Members of the Norwegian Parliament.

Illustrative cases

The three case studies were carried out in order to get a more concrete impression of the decision-making processes. All three cases are related to environmental policy-making: taxes on disposable packaging, climate change policy, and protection of conifer forest. The cases were chosen partly because they represent various kinds of environmental problems, and partly because they affect various parts of the society and of the political system.

The study of new *taxes on disposable packaging* covers the period from 1992 to 1995 (Opedal and Farsund, 1997a). There are two decisions in particular that call for attention. The first of these is the decision to introduce a basic lump-sum levy on packaging. Even though none of the pressure groups involved achieved their primary aims, it may be argued that the most influential groups were the environmental organizations and the brewery workers' organizations. The resolution of the *Storting* was in accordance with these groups' secondary preferences. Parliamentary lobbyism was the most important channel of influence for these organizations. The trade and industry organizations, who largely concentrated their efforts on lobbying the civil service, were not equally successful in getting their views across.

The other decision in this case was aimed at solving the waste problem by means of voluntary agreements with the business community, without the introduction of further taxes. In this case it appears in particular that the lobbying efforts of PLM Moss Glassverk (a major glass producer) towards the *Storting* contributed to a change in the Labour Party's stance on a lump-sum tax. The agreement seems to have been the result of parliamentary as well as administrative lobbyism on the part of these organizations.

The study of Norwegian *climate policy* covers the period from 1989 to 1996 (Farsund, 1997). In this case there are three major 'milestones' to consider. The first is the *Storting*'s 1989 decision to stabilize emissions of climate gases at the 1989 level in the year 2000. Here, it seems as if the Norwegian environmental organizations' efforts towards the Parliament contributed to ensure that the climate gas objective was established. In addition, international developments and the warnings put forward by respected research institutes were important for both the *Storting* and the government at this time. The industrial organizations were less active in this period and utilized their influence potential through lobbyism and corporatism to a lesser degree.

The other 'milestone' concerns the decision to introduce a charge on carbon dioxide (CO_2) emissions in the period 1990–3. Even though the environmental and the industrial organizations did not accomplish their primary objectives, they had success with some of their proposals. The introduction of the charge can to some extent be regarded as a victory for the environmental organizations, since instruments were implemented to ensure that the emissions target level would be reached. In 1992–3 we could observe that the 'wind' changed direction in climate policy in favor of business interests, who managed to exempt 40 percent of the emissions from charges. Both parliamentary and administrative lobbyism were significant methods in the organizations' work in this period.

The third 'milestone' relates to the work associated with a governmental report to the *Storting* on climate policy. When the government prepared the report, it was to a large extent influenced by business interests through administrative corporatism and lobbyism. Major victories for these organizations comprised the decision to withdraw from a heavily enforced implementation of climate policy, and that voluntary agreements on CO_2 abatement were introduced. This was somewhat leveled out in the proceedings in the Parliament's Standing Committee on Energy and the Environment. In the committee's recommendations there are statements that reflect suggestions from various interest groups. The environmental organizations were heard in their views on economizing on energy, bio-energy and the electrification of the oil and gas industry. On the other hand, industrial interests were served in that the main guidelines for climate policy would stay put until international developments made it feasible to change them. The most important channel of influence for both parties was parliamentary lobbyism.

The study of *conifer forest protection* covers the period from 1986 to 1996 (Opedal and Farsund, 1997b) and concentrates on a protection decision made by the Syse government in 1990, an escalation proposal put forward by the Brundtland government in 1995, and a decision to expand the conservation program made by the *Storting* in 1996. The result of the first protection decision was a protection level at less than a minimum proposal put forward by a governmental committee on conifer protection. The committee members were civil servants and representatives from the forestry and environmental organizations. However, the forestry organizations took the case off the committee's agenda. Instead, they focused on parliamentary and administrative lobbyism. The administrative lobbyism was particularly directed at the ministries' political leadership.

The Brundtland government's proposal to expand the protection program can be understood in light of the reactions to the previous stages of the decision process. The Syse government's decision led to a strong mobilization of environmental organizations and biologists. This pressure was to a great extent channeled through parliamentary and administrative lobbyism, especially at a political level of the ministries.

The *Storting*'s decision to escalate was largely in line with the government's recommendation. The influence efforts were characterized by the fact that the principles for protection were established earlier. For the industrial organizations, the paramount objective was to ensure improved economic frameworks for the forest owners affected by the policy. For the environmental groups, it was vital to get across that larger areas should be conserved. In this context, the decision to increase the conserved area by 120 km^2 can be regarded as a compromise between the two interest groups. The environmental organizations achieved a certain expansion of the protected area, whilst the forest owners and other business interests secured improved compensation schemes. In this part of the proceedings, administrative lobbyism and corporatism as well as parliamentary lobbyism played a part in determining the outcome of the case.

In sum, the three cases show that attempts at influencing the decision-making processes may be channeled through corporatist bodies as well as lobbyism. It is quite clear that organized interests have an impact on the outcomes. It is, however, also clear that no single interest group can dictate to decision-makers. Different interests compete with one another, and the influence achieved by various interest organizations varies over time. Concerning lobbyism versus corporatism, the overall impression is that parliamentary and administrative lobbyism are the most influential strategies.

General assessments made by organizations and MPs

It is always difficult to say how representative case studies are. Therefore, some general assessments can be made in addition to the illustrative cases presented above. These assessments were made by representatives of the organizations, and by the Members of the Norwegian Parliament.

In the *organizational survey*, board members were asked to make a statement about the impact of the organizations' views on the outcome of decisions made by various political authorities. Table 5.5 shows the weighted percentages of board members responding that the organization had exerted a 'considerable' or 'some' degree of influence on the decisions made by the various authorities. The answers show that most of the environmental organizations believe that they have an impact on the directorates/agencies. The industrial organizations most often experience an influence on the ministries and directorates. Both the environmental and the industrial organizations express difficulties in breaking through with their views in the government. Influence on the *Storting* comes in a position between the government and the public administration.

TABLE 5.5 *Impact of organizations' views on various authorities ('considerable' plus 'some' impact, weighted percent of board members)*

	Environmental organizations	Industrial organizations
Directorates/agencies	70	53
Ministries	51	53
Parliament	47	42
Government	22	17

In general, industrial organizations are regarded as powerful participants in the political arena. However, Table 5.5 shows that the board members of the environmental organizations to a greater extent feel that their opinions are taken into consideration. This is the case with respect to all instances of authority, with the exception of ministries where the difference between the environmental and the industrial organizations is insignificant. The most distinct difference between the two types of organizations lies in their relationship with directorates, where the environmental organizations feel that they play a more influencing role. A slightly larger proportion of the environmental than of the industrial organizations say that they have an impact on the Norwegian Parliament.[8]

Both the administrative leaders and the board members were asked to specify their influence towards the Norwegian Parliament. The figures in Table 5.6 are average frequencies for administrative leaders and board members (for details, see Rommetvedt et al., forthcoming).

The first impression from this table is that a considerable portion of the administrative leaders and board members believe that the enquiries from the organizations do have some influence on the work of the *Storting*. The enquiries are 'sometimes' or 'often' a contributing factor when the Parliament makes minor amendments to governmental proposals, and when MPs make dissenting remarks in the recommendations from parliamentary committees. To some extent these enquiries are also a contributing factor when MPs ask questions directed to ministers in Parliament. When more comprehensive amendments are made to governmental proposals or when private proposals

TABLE 5.6 *Impact of organizational enquiries in Parliament (percent, average of administrative leaders and board members of organizations)*

Organizational enquiries contribute 'sometimes' or 'often' when:	Environment	Industrial
Parliament makes minor amendments to governmental proposals	58	57
Parliament makes major amendments to governmental proposals	33	15
Dissenting remarks in recommendations from parliamentary committees	59	56
Questions and interpellations in Parliament	49	48
Private members' bills and proposals	13	24

are promoted in the *Storting*, this is less often because of organizational enquiries.

All in all, the effects of the contacts with political authorities seem to be more or less the same for the two kinds of organizations. It looks, however, as if enquiries from the environmental organizations contribute to adjustments of governmental proposals made by the *Storting* to a somewhat higher degree than enquiries from the industrial organizations. The latter, however, more often seem to prompt private proposals from MPs.

The previously mentioned *survey among* MPs also touched upon the influence of organized interests. Among the MPs, 25 percent and 27 percent, respectively, said that majority and minority statements in the recommendations of their standing committees 'very' or 'fairly often' are associated with enquiries from industrial organizations and trade unions. Fifteen percent of the representatives mentioned the same with respect to enquiries from environmental organizations. In addition, approximately half of the MPs mentioned that dissents and statements are 'sometimes' related to enquiries from industrial organizations (52 percent), trade unions (50 percent) and environmental organizations (50 percent).

Further, a question was asked regarding amendments to governmental proposals considered by the *Storting*. Again the question was related to each of the MPs' own standing committee and the area of jurisdiction belonging to this committee. Twenty-two percent of the representatives answered that amendments to governmental proposals are 'often' related to enquiries from industrial organizations. Twenty-two percent expressed the same regarding enquiries from trade unions, and 9 percent regarding environmental organizations. In addition, 43, 44 and 42 percent of the representatives, respectively, expressed that such amendments are 'sometimes' related to enquiries from industrial organizations, trade unions and environmental organizations.

After all this, the conclusion must be that *enquiries to the Norwegian Parliament, and to the administration, made from both environmental and industrial organizations may have a significant influence on the work and decisions of these authorities.* As far as the Norwegian Parliament is concerned this is a view shared by both the organizations and the MPs.[9]

CONCLUDING REMARKS

This chapter has analyzed relations between private and public power at the national level, using Norway as an illustrative case. It has shown how environmental organizations and industrial organizations operate within the general framework of power relations, in order to exert influence on Norwegian policy-making. An interesting element of the overall impressions from the empirical analysis is the apparent *coherence* between the various aspects of power relations in the theoretical part of the study.

Gradually, the character of the Norwegian government system seems to have changed, from a highly corporatist system in the 1950s and 1960s, via a segmented system in the 1970s, to a more pluralist system in the 1980s and 1990s. During the first decades after World War II, the power of organized interests as well as public authorities was highly concentrated. By the end of the 1990s, power seemed to be more dispersed. As a consequence, corporatist representation had lost some of its importance in Norway. One can still find many traces of corporatism, especially in the agricultural sector, but the less institutionalized lobbyism has become a more relevant way of exerting influence. The lobbying efforts of organized interests are directed towards civil servants as well as MPs. The growing importance of parliamentary lobbyism clearly indicates, however, that the Norwegian *Storting* has increased its power at the expense of the executive.

How representative, then, is the Norwegian case with regard to private and public power at the national level? Some references have been made to studies of other countries. These studies seem to indicate that the Norwegian development is part of a more general movement of formerly 'corporatist' countries in the direction of pluralism. In addition, of course, the former state-directed countries of East Central Europe have moved a long way towards pluralism as well.

An increasing degree of pluralism seems to be an important aspect of the globalizing world at the beginning of the twenty-first century. It is a paradox, however, that the pluralization that occurs at the national level is paralleled by homogenization at the global level.

NOTES

The author would like to thank the editors and Arild Farsund, Kjersti Melberg and Oluf Langhelle for their advice and assistance.

1 There is a lot to say about Schmitter's theory and other theories of corporatism (cf. Williamson, 1989). I will not, however, engage in that debate here. I use Schmitter as a point of departure for my discussion.

2 This definition does not preclude the regulations of lobbyism that many countries have implemented. Such regulations imply, of course, a certain degree of institutionalization of lobbyism.

3 The survey was carried out in 1995 and comprised a sample of 37 organizations with a total of 302 board members: 144 board members (48 percent) in 33 organizations responded to the questionnaire. The response rate for administrative leaders was nearly 84 percent. The responding administrative leaders represented 31 organizations, and here we concentrate on these organizations.

4 The investigation in the Norwegian Parliament was carried out in cooperation between research colleagues at the Institute of Social Sciences in Oslo and the Norwegian Research Centre in Organization and Management (LOS-senteret) in Bergen. Harald Espeli and Hilmar Rommetvedt were responsible for the part concerning lobbyism: 73 percent of the members of the Norwegian Parliament answered the questionnaire (Espeli, 1998; Rommetvedt, 1997a; 1997b; 1998).

5 See Hallenstvedt and Trollvik (1993) for further information about the organizations, and *Report to the Storting no. 7* about governmental councils. (The Report is presented once during each election period.) Endre Holmefjord (Norwegian Research Centre in Organization and Management) and John-Erik Ågotnes (NSD) have made the data available to us.

6 For more detailed information, see Rommetvedt et al. (forthcoming) and Klausen and Rommetvedt (1997).

7 Participation in governmental committees may be of greater importance to other industrial organizations. This is in particular the case for the Norwegian Federation of Trade Unions (LO) and the Confederation of Norwegian Business and Industry (NHO) which are not included in our research.

8 It is to be added that the feeling of being able to break through with one's opinions is not entirely 'objective'. It may be influenced by the expectation one had beforehand. It is possible that the industrial organizations had relatively higher expectations of their influence than the environmental organizations.

9 There exists a certain disagreement between MPs and organizations with regard to the question of whether it is the environmental or the industrial organizations that exert the greatest influence. Some of the differences may arise from the fact that the organizational survey only includes industrial organizations within agriculture and transport. The survey among MPs, on the other hand, contained questions about industrial and business organizations in general. This implies that an influential organization such as the Confederation of Norwegian Business and Industry (NHO) is included in the MPs' assessments, and not in our organizational survey.

6 Political Influence of NGOs on International Environmental Issues

Bas Arts

The concepts of *power* and *influence* are important issues in political science. For instance, one may want to know whether one or several elites determine political outcomes in different areas of urban decision-making (Dahl, 1961; Hunter, 1953; Mills, 1956), whether business organizations have an impact on local politics (Braam, 1973), or whether protest and pressure groups make a difference in the construction of highways (Huberts, 1989). This chapter deals with similar research questions. It examines the political influence of nongovernmental organizations (NGOs), such as Greenpeace International, Friends of the Earth International and the World Wide Fund for Nature, on global environmental policies.

However, the concepts of power and influence are also *essentially contested* concepts (Lukes, 1974). There is hardly any agreement on definition and it seems as if any student of power designs his or her own approach. Yet a limited number of traditions can be distinguished. This chapter builds on *agency-oriented*, *transitive* and *episodic* conceptualizations of power as well as on the *pluralist* tradition, and focuses on the *political* domain of society (Clegg, 1989; Dahl, 1957; 1961; Goehler, this book). With that, the concept of 'political influence' is preferred over 'political power'. In addition, this chapter brings the issue of 'power measurement' back in. While the measurement of power was a very popular subject in the 1950s and 1960s, this popularity ceased in the 1970s and 1980s (Waste, 1986b). Today, however, a comeback seems under way.

In this chapter, a specific methodology for the assessment of political influence of private actors in complex, global decision-making will be designed: the so-called EAR instrument. This instrument combines and renews elements of the reputation and decision-making methods (Dahl, 1961; Hunter, 1953). Furthermore, the focus of the chapter is on global environmental NGOs. These actors have become important players, since the process of globalization redefined the role not only of the nation-state, but of non-state actors as well (Waters, 1995; Gibbins and Reimer, 1999; Princen, 1994). This is also the case for global environmental NGOs. Some academics even believe that it is difficult to overestimate the importance of these NGOs for global environmental politics (Caldwell, 1990). To verify this proposition, this chapter assesses the NGOs' political influence on the Framework

Convention on Climate Change (FCCC) and the Convention on Biological Diversity (CBD) in the period 1990–5 (Arts, 1998). Both treaties were designed in the context of the UN system in the period 1990–2, signed by more than 150 countries at the Earth Summit in Rio de Janeiro in 1992, entered into force in 1993–4, and implemented since then. All these policy processes were heavily under pressure from global environmental NGOs.

The first section of this chapter briefly describes the role of NGOs in the age of globalization. It will be argued that these organizations can be considered *global players*. The second section focuses on the definition of political influence and addresses related concepts such as political power. The following three sections deal with the development and elaboration of the EAR instrument. In the sixth section this method is applied to one case: the issue of 'joint implementation' that is an element of the Climate Convention. The seventh section summarizes the findings of 18 cases from the Climate and Biodiversity Conventions. The final section discusses the conclusions of this chapter as well as the benefits and shortcomings of the EAR instrument.

ENVIRONMENTAL NGOs AS GLOBAL PLAYERS

The ecological dimension of the globalization process has been undervalued in the main literature so far (Yearley, 1996). Yet international environmental problems – such as global warming and the destruction of biodiversity on a worldwide scale – are themselves examples of globalization. This process has contributed to the further erosion of the nation-state, since policy-making within the nation-state model has proved to be insufficient to deal with global environmental problems (Caldwell, 1990; Gibbins and Reimer, 1999). Yet a system of global governance to manage these is still under way. Therefore NGOs try to overcome the 'governance gap'. They pressure governments and international organizations to recognize ecological problems (agenda setting) and to design policies that address these problems and transcend national interests of individual states (policy-making). In addition, they contribute to the realization of such policies at regional and local levels (policy implementation) (Hurrell and Kingsbury, 1992; McCormick, 1989).

An NGO is generally defined as any organization that is not established by a government or group of governments (Feld and Jordan, 1983). Others refer to NGOs as non-profit pressure groups (Thompson-Feraru, 1974). This latter definition matches the nature of global environmental NGOs quite well. However, the study of pressure groups has merely focused on the national level (van Noort et al., 1987). In international relations literature the emphasis on these groups is definitely less, since the mainstream view of *neorealism* focuses on nation-states in the international system of anarchy (Lieshout, 1993; Waltz, 1979). This state-biased perspective, though, has been challenged by many, given the process of globalization as described in the above. For example Morss writes: 'The era in which the nations ruled the world is over. With the information revolution and the demise of the United States as the dominant world power, three groups have joined nations as important global players: transnational corporations, international organizations, and special interest groups' (1991: 55). Morss's third type of global player – special interest groups – refers to NGOs. Arguments to defend the proposition that these have become global players are the following.

First, the number of NGOs has dramatically increased at the global level, from approximately 1000 in 1950 to more than 15,000 in the late 1990s (Hocking and Smith, 1990; van der Schot and van de Veen, 1997). Second, their constituencies have been tremendously broadened. For example, the environmental movement 'represents' millions of civilians worldwide today (McCormick, 1989). Third, the involvement of NGOs in the United Nations (UN) is formally recognized in Article 71 of the UN Charter. NGOs may have observer status at UN meetings, make oral statements, and disseminate written position papers. In addition, they may have access to working groups in which decisions are prepared; and countries may also add NGO representatives to their delegations at international meetings. Since 1945, this NGO regime has been enhanced and extended several times, so that even local groups can participate today. Apart from this formal access, NGOs can lobby in the corridors of UN meetings, and organize (protest) activities around the building where the negotiations take place. Fourth, NGOs seem to have become influential players. Willets (1982) refers, amongst others, to Amnesty International, trade unions and women's organizations (see also Arts and van Roozendaal, 1999).

Claims with regard to the power and influence of NGOs are also made in the literature on global environmental policies:

- Global environmental NGOs were key players in the final acceptance of the ivory trade ban under CITES, the Convention on International Trade in Endangered Species (although this ban has recently been amended). They were the only ones in this arena who were able to truly link the local level (knowledge on the hunting of elephants and the trade in ivory) to the global (knowledge on the diplomacy within the context of CITES) (Princen, 1994).
- NGOs were involved in the ozone layer issue since the beginning of the 1970s. They successfully campaigned against aerosols with chlorofluoro-carbons (CFCs) and against McDonald's fast-food packaging, and lobbied for an immediate ban on the production of CFCs. In 1990 the countries that are parties to the Montreal Protocol adopted a phase-out of CFCs before the year 2000 (Rowlands, 1995).
- NGOs, particularly Friends of the Earth International and Greenpeace International, have lobbied for a total ban on whaling since the 1970s. A great deal of this lobbying was directed at the International Whaling Commission. Today a commercial moratorium is in place under the banner of this commission (Burke, 1982; Rowlands and Greene, 1992).

POLITICAL POWER AND POLITICAL INFLUENCE

To repeat, power is an essentially contested concept and many interpretations do exist. Authors therefore make categorizations of power, however differently. Common distinctions are, amongst others: (1) agent versus structural power, (2) transitive versus intransitive power, (3) episodic versus dispositional power, and (4) power versus influence. Below, these categorizations are used to position this chapter in the power debate as well as to formulate appropriate definitions.

The first distinction – *agency* versus *structure* – has determined most of the power debate in social and political sciences in the last few decades (Guzzini, 1993). It has dealt with the question of whether power has one or two faces, three dimensions, and the like (Bachrach and Baratz, 1962; Clegg, 1989; Giddens, 1984; Lukes, 1974). Agency-oriented approaches have focused on the observable power of social or political actors ('first face'), while structural approaches have dealt with processes of non-decision-making ('second face'), latent power mechanisms ('third dimension'), and structures of hegemony and domination. Given the focus of this chapter on global environmental NGOs, its nature is definitely agency-oriented. With that, it stands in the so-called *pluralist* tradition of the political sciences (Self, 1985). Although this tradition is (rightly) criticized by structuralists, since agents are constrained by given rules and divisions of resources in any social system, this chapter nonetheless focuses on agent power and *not* on structural power.

Goehler extensively elaborates on the second distinction in this book (Chapter 1). According to him, transitive power relates to agency, conflict and zero-sum games ('one overruling the other'), whereas *intransitive* power relates to social integration, consensus and collective action ('to act in concert'). His main argument is that the former builds on the latter. There is no transitive power without intransitive power. This is also the case for global environmental NGOs. As a collectivity, they draw heavily upon intransitive power: the ability to act in concert on the basis of shared values, identities, norms and symbols. In day-to-day politics, however, they have to engage in political struggles to achieve their goals in decision-making; and that is related to transitive power. Given its orientation, this chapter definitely focuses on the latter, on how NGOs achieve (or fail to achieve) their goals in global politics. Although the importance of intransitive power as a prerequisite for political influence is acknowledged, it will not be further analyzed below.

The third distinction is elaborated on by Clegg (1989; Chapter 3 in this book). *Episodic* power refers to *exercising* power, whereas *dispositional* power refers to *having* power. The famous definition of Dahl is an example of the former: 'A has power over B to the extent that he can get B to do something B would not otherwise do' (1957: 202). This definition definitely refers to A *exercising* power over B. Cox and Jacobson, however, relate their definition to *having* power: 'Power means capability; it is the aggregate of political resources that are available to an actor' (1973: 3). What Dahl names *power*, they would probably refer to as *influence*, and this is the fourth distinction that was presented in the above. Cox and Jacobson write: 'influence means the modification of one actor's behaviour by that of another' (1973: 3). And they add: 'Influence is to be distinguished from power . . . Power may be converted into influence, but it is not necessarily so converted at all or to its full extent.' In their opinion the US is powerful because it *possesses* nuclear weapons, not because it *uses* them. Others, though, hold that it is impossible to assess the power of players on the basis of their capabilities. Good examples in this respect are the military adventures of the US in Vietnam and the USSR in Afghanistan: both failed (Ray, 1987). Therefore, there is hardly a one-to-one relationship between resources and outcomes (Keohane and Nye, 1989).

This position is, of course, contestable as well. Resources may, according to Huberts and Kleinnijenhuis (1994), indeed give an indication of someone's power, at least if these resources proved to be effective in the past or elsewhere in the world under comparable circumstances. Following Kuypers (1973), they make the distinction between *power as the (more or less) permanent ability to influence, and influence as the realization of a single effect*. This distinction is also adopted in this chapter, because it has the advantage of putting the position of global NGOs *vis-à-vis* nation-states, for example the US, in the right perspective. The latter has a permanent ability to influence global politics and may be rightly considered a powerful player. But this cannot be said about the NGOs; they are probably influential, or a bit powerful, at best. Hence, the concept of 'political influence' is preferred over 'political power' to refer to the effects of global environmental NGOs (cf. Banfield, 1961). Note that the adjective 'political' is added to the concepts of power and influence here, which is no surprise given the fact that the focus of this chapter is on the (global) polity.

However, with political influence it is not intended to refer to *any* modification in decision-making. The impact of an actor A by definition regards something that is of value to A. This may be an ethical rule or an ideal, the achievement of a material or immaterial goal, a service or the solution of a problem. In this chapter this is referred to as *goal achievement*. Goal achievement may be either positive or negative. In case of *positive* goal achievement an actor A, whose influence we want to assess, *accomplishes* something. By *negative* goal achievement we mean the *prevention* of something.

In general, definitions of influence are formulated in terms of a dyad, just as is the case in the definitions above. However, in this chapter the final aim of A is not so much to influence a decision-maker, being a subject, but to modify a *decision*, being an object (cf. Riker, 1964; Stokman, 1994). Besides, influence is not necessarily exercised through bilateral contacts between two actors A and B, as an actor C may transmit A's preferences to decision-maker B (Potter, 1996). Also, some definitions of influence include unintended effects, as the possible impact of the *presence* or *thoughts* of players are part of the concept (Huberts, 1988; 1989; 1994). It therefore includes the possibility that A changes B because of the simple fact that A exists. This phenomenon is referred to as *anticipation* in the literature (Bell et al., 1969; Clegg, 1989). Although it is recognized that this phenomenon exists, it is excluded from this chapter for pragmatic reasons. It is simply too difficult to assess such unintended impacts (van Schendelen, 1981; Bos and Geurts, 1994).

Given the above considerations, political influence is defined as *the achievement of (a part of) an actor's goal with regard to a political outcome – e.g., an intergovernmental decision – which is (at least partly) caused by one's own and intended intervention in the political process concerned*. It is also possible to rewrite this definition in terms of the so-called counterfactual (Biersteker, 1993; Lukes, 1974). Then political influence implies that the outcome concerned is more in line with the goal of the player involved than would have been the case had the latter not intervened.

THE ASSESSMENT OF POLITICAL INFLUENCE

Particularly in the 1950s and 1960s the measurement of power was a very popular subject (Banfield, 1961; Bell et al., 1969; Cox and Jacobson, 1973; Dahl, 1957; 1961; Hunter, 1953; Mills, 1956; Riker, 1964). This popularity, however, ceased because criticism was directed at both elitist and pluralist approaches as well as at positivist methodology in the 1970s. The focus of the debate shifted from power measurement at the individual or group level to theory building on power at the structural level of society (Bachrach and Baratz, 1962; Clegg, 1989; Lukes, 1974). Recently, though, the actor-oriented and empirical focus of the old community power debate has been revalued, probably as a result of the current popularity of post-structural, post-Marxist, rational choice and social-constructivist approaches in the social sciences (Dowding and Dunleavy, 1995; Giddens, 1984; Huberts, 1989; Waste, 1986b; Westerheijden, 1987). As a consequence, the measurement of power seems to have become a relevant issue in political science again. In this chapter, though, the notion of *assessment* instead of *measurement* will be used, as the latter notion gives the impression that the extent of power can be known in objective, exact terms. At best, such figures are *well-educated guesses* (Everts, 1985; van Noort et al., 1987). This 'post-positivist' proposition is also shared in this chapter.

With regard to techniques to assess power, authors generally classify three classical approaches: the positional, reputational and decision-making methods (Dahl, 1961; Huberts and Kleinnijenhuis, 1994; Hunter, 1953; Mills, 1956; van Schendelen, 1981). Given the fact that this chapter focuses on how NGOs affect global environmental policies, the decision-making method seems to be the most appropriate to employ (Banfield, 1961; Dahl,

1961). A contemporary example of this approach is Huberts's *intensive process analysis* (Huberts, 1988; 1989; 1994). In short, he assumes that the chance that pressure group A indeed caused the change of decision-maker B increases if: A really intended to change B ('intention'), A had access to B ('access'), the time between A's attempt and B's change is short ('time lag'), B's policy change is in A's interest ('goal achievement') and B remained the same individual during the decision-making process ('personnel'). Besides these indicators, *resources* – according to Huberts – are important. If several players with similar objectives undertake similar (or collective) attempts to influence a political player and they succeed, then one might discriminate among them on the basis of resources. The player who possesses or invested most resources is assumed to be the most influential.

Although Huberts's intensive process analysis is quite elegant in nature (Aarts, 1991), its application is questionable in *complex* decision-making at the *global* scale (Arts, 1998). First of all, decisions on highways are of an unequivocal and zero-sum nature. That is, decision-makers have to choose between two or three different options for the stretches of a highway. Hence, the policy positions of the different participants are rather easy to identify and the decision is either X or Y or a compromise between the two. However, many decision-making processes are much more complex. For example, the Climate Convention contains some 8500 words over which political players may have struggled one-by-one. Hence, the adoption of such a convention theoretically leads to thousands of 'subdecisions'. Moreover, the end result is not a zero sum, either X or Y, as the outcome of a treaty is not fixed at the moment a negotiation process starts. Given the complex nature of the former decision, one may wonder whether the premise of the intensive process analysis, i.e., that a decision-making process should be *entirely* reconstructed, is realistic.

Second, the cases Huberts analyzed take place at one level of policy-making, that is the national level of political decision-making in the Netherlands. However, many decision-making processes are multilayered. Consider again the formation of treaties at the global level. International politics can be characterized as a two-level game: played domestically and globally (Putnam, 1988). This implies that the number of players involved is often immense. In case of the FCCC more than 150 countries, hundreds of NGOs, and at least 10 intergovernmental bodies are involved. Obviously the reconstruction of the intentions, the goals and the activities of *all* those players at *all* levels of decision-making involved is beyond the control of a researcher. Therefore Huberts's method needs some adaptation in the case of global decision-making. The first adaptation to be presented here is the selection of key topics, key actors and a key level of decision-making, as will be shown in the next section. A second adaptation is the adoption of some additional assessment tools, which are derived from the reputational method.

Huberts would probably reject this latter choice, as he shares the classical critique of the reputational method, since perceptions do – according to the critics – not say much about *actual* influence (Polsby, 1960). However, this critique should be put into perspective given the recent rehabilitation of the reputational method, both in rational choice and social-constructivist studies (Dowding and Dunleavy, 1995; Wendt, 1992; Westerheijden, 1987). In addition, the perceptions that participants in the decision-making process have of the political influence of the different players may yield additional information. This application of more than one methodology to assess the same phenomenon is in line with the concept of *triangulation*, and may improve the validity of the assessment (Verschuren and Doorewaard, 1995).

THE EAR INSTRUMENT

The proposed EAR instrument consists of three dimensions: ego perception (E), alter perception (A) and researcher's analysis (R) (see also Arts, 1998; Arts and Verschuren, 1999).[1] 'Ego perception' refers to the perception of key player A, whose political influence is being assessed, of his *own* influence, or lack of influence. 'Alter perception' indicates the perception that the other key players B to Z have of A's influence or the lack thereof. 'Researcher's analysis' finally regards a check by the researcher of the validity of these perceptions (see Table 6.1). This check is based on a reconstruction of the players' goal achievement, which should be the result of their own interventions (see the definition of political influence in the second section).

TABLE 6.1 *The EAR instrument*

Dimension	Meaning
Ego perception (E)	Views of key players with regard to their own (lack of) influence on key topics in complex decision-making
Alter perception (A)	Views of the other key players with regard to the (lack of) influence of 'ego' on key topics in complex decision-making
Researcher's analysis (R)	Validity check of ego and alter perceptions by the researcher on the basis of the indicators 'goal achievement' and 'own intervention'

The selection of key players is based on two criteria. A player to be selected (a) has been involved in the entire decision-making process and (b) holds an important position in this process, as either stakeholder, policy-maker or decision-maker. This selection of key persons can be based on a pilot study of the political arena or on a study of relevant documents. The selection of key topics, next, is based on the ego and alter perceptions. The selection of the key level of decision-making, finally, depends on the nature of the research questions under investigation.

The ego and alter perceptions of the key players are to be reconstructed by open, in-depth interviews. These interviews should produce, among others, specific examples of the (perceived) influence of A – the player to be studied – and specific examples of lack of influence. Crucial is the *openness* of the interviews, as the expert respondents should come up with their *own* examples of influence (or the lack thereof). The key topics that result from these ego and alter perceptions are to be subjected to the 'researcher's analysis'. This analysis builds on Huberts's approach and consists of the following elements. First of all, the researcher needs to check to what extent A achieved his or her goal regarding the key topic under consideration. This check is based on a comparison of A's initial policy goal, as deduced from documents and interviews, on the one hand, and the actual political outcome on the other. In cases in which A has not achieved its goal, it is assumed that he or she had not been influential at all. In cases in which A has entirely or partly achieved his or her goal, it was checked whether this goal achievement could be ascribed to A's own interventions and not those of governments, international organizations, science or business. This check consisted of an analysis of: (1) the goal achievement by other relevant players; (2) the access of A to the political arena and decision-making; (3) interventions that A and other players made; (4) the number and intensity of those interventions; (5) the adoption of A's views/proposals by the decision-makers; (6) the possible effects of external events and autonomous developments.

The identification of three perceptions, i.e., ego, alter and researcher perceptions, raises the question of how to construct a final judgment on the NGOs' political influence. It is obvious there is no problem of interpretation if the three dimensions support one another. If they do not support one another, then the researcher's analysis is considered dominant *vis-à-vis* ego and alter perception in principle. The reason is that the former is mainly based on 'fixed' policy documents, whereas the ego and alter perceptions are the result of a stimulus–response technique. As all players have strong and sometimes opposite interests, this may lead to biased answers.

EXTENT OF POLITICAL INFLUENCE

The EAR instrument also raises questions as to the *extent* of political influence. Given its definition, the extent of political influence coincides with the extent to which goal achievement may be ascribed to one's own intervention. However, it is quite obvious that 'goal achievement' and 'ascription' may vary independently. For example, A may achieve all his policy goals, but this may result only a little from the intervention of A, and in large part from the interventions of others. In that case A is said to have moderate influence. On the other hand, A may achieve only part of his goals, but this goal achievement is in large part attributed to A, with the same conclusion. We may put this in a formula as follows: $PI = GA \times AS$, in which PI is the extent of political influence of actor A, GA is the extent of goal achievement of A, and AS is the extent to which goal achievement can be ascribed to A. This formula, which is heuristic in nature, makes clear that neither goal achievement GA nor ascription AS is assumed to be a sufficient condition for political influence PI separately, but their *combination* is. For that reason we use a multiplication instead of an addition in the formula. As soon as either GA or AS is zero, PI is nil as well. Therefore both GA and AS need to produce at least some minimal score before we may conclude that there is political influence. Note that PI will be positive too if both GA and AS are *negative*. However, this possibility is excluded here, as negative scores for these variables are meaningless.

A limitation of this formula is that it does not take into account that the political relevance of decisions may differ. As van Schendelen (1981) noted, such relevance should definitely be taken into account in assessing political influence. A bit of influence by player A on a very relevant topic might be as important as, or even more important than, much influence by A on a less relevant one. Therefore we add *political relevance (PR)* to the formula. There are three indicators of this variable: (a) the degree to which a decision is a political key issue; (b) the extent to which a decision is binding to the stakeholders; and (c) the extent to which a decision is controversial to the stakeholders. Each of them indicates that real interests of players are at stake. If all three may be considered 'highly significant', the political relevance is considered 'strong'. On the other hand, if a rather trivial topic, a non-binding outcome or a symbolic decision is influenced by a stakeholder, then the relevance of such influence will be 'weak'. And, of course, some cases may be in between ('moderate' relevance). Now the formula becomes $PI = GA \times AS \times PR$, in which PR – the abbreviation that was added – refers to the political relevance of the political outcome. As all three components – goal achievement, ascription and political relevance – can be measured ordinally at best, it is proposed to use four categories for each component: 0 = none, 1 = weak, 2 = moderate and 3 = strong. Hence, the resulting outcome of this formula ranges from 0 to 27, with several scores that are not possible. In order to avoid a false suggestion of exactness, it is preferred to translate these scores into verbal equivalents as follows: 0 = no influence; 1–4 = weak influence; 6–12 = moderate influence; and 18–27 = strong influence.[2]

AN EXAMPLE: 'JOINT IMPLEMENTATION'

The three dimensions of the EAR instrument and the application of the formulas may be illustrated by assessing one case in depth. Of the 18 cases that were originally studied (Arts, 1998), the topic 'joint implementation' (JI), which is an element of the Climate Convention, was chosen for elaboration below.[3] Before doing so, a few general characteristics of the study should be highlighted. First, the analysis focuses on the *global* level, so only NGOs that are active at that level are taken into consideration. Examples of the most important ones are Greenpeace International, Friends of the Earth International, World Wide Fund for Nature, Third World Network, Natural

Resources Defense Council, World Resources Institute, Climate Action Network and World Conservation Union. Second, the study is limited to the period 1990–5. The year 1990 marks the beginning of the formal negotiations of the Convention, whereas 1995 is the year in which its formal implementation started. Finally, the following key players were identified. Next to NGO representatives, country delegates and UN officials were selected as expert respondents. Some observations and inquiries at international negotiation sessions sufficed to select about 25 NGO representatives and 25 policy-makers and decision-makers.

The UN Framework Convention on Climate Change (FCCC) is the first global and legally binding instrument to address the risks of climate change (Bodansky, 1993; Mintzer and Leonard, 1994). Article 4.2 deals with specific commitments. It states that industrialized countries should stabilize their CO_2 emissions at 1990 levels by the year 2000. With the 1997 Kyoto Protocol to the FCCC, new targets for the industrialized countries were adopted which should lead to an average reduction of greenhouse gases of 5 per cent in the period 2008–12, compared to 1990 levels. Article 4.2 also states that the industrialized countries may implement this stabilization target *jointly* (subparagraph (a)). The background to this concept of 'joint implementation' (JI) is the following (Woerdman, 1997):

- Given the global nature of the problem, it makes little difference to the greenhouse effect *where* emissions are reduced or removed, either at home or abroad.
- It is more effective to invest in environmental technologies and measures in less developed and, hence, less efficient economies than in highly developed countries. As the marginal costs of environmental gains rise proportionally with efficiency standards, it is less expensive to make such gains in the East or in the Third World than in the West.

The concept can be put into practice as follows. A rich country starts a project on energy efficiency (to cut emissions) or reforestation (to absorb CO_2) in an Eastern European country or developing country and the resulting gains in terms of less greenhouse gas (GHG) emission or more GHG removals should be shared and booked as *credits* under the FCCC. All parties warmly welcomed this idea in the first instance. Developing countries would be able to implement the Climate Convention on the basis of additional foreign assistance, while rich countries would be able to implement their commitments abroad at lower costs.

Most NGOs, however, immediately criticized the mechanism (Climate Action Network, 1992; Eco, 1993). They feared that the industrialized countries would buy off their domestic commitments, and so prevent painful interventions at home by unloading the burden on the poor. Although developing countries were initially in favor of the concept, most of them slowly turned against joint implementation as a general mechanism to put the Convention into operation (G77 and China, 1995). The reason for this shift was threefold. First, Third World countries feared that JI would be mixed up with other commitments of industrialized countries under the FCCC, such as the obligation to provide financial resources and technology to assist developing countries to implement the Convention. Second, the South started to share the NGOs' concern that through JI industrialized countries would 'soften' their domestic commitments. Third, the G77 and China used JI as a bargaining chip *vis-à-vis* the North. They knew that the industrialized countries were very much in favor of it, but were at the same time dependent on them for its realization.

Joint implementation was an important issue at the first Conference of the Parties (COP) to the FCCC (Berlin, April 1995). It was decided to establish a pilot phase. Projects should be among industrialized states only, but developing countries might participate as well, on a voluntary basis (FCCC, 1995). Moreover, crediting was excluded, which means that the reduction of GHG emissions realized abroad could not be added to that realized at home. However, since 1995 new developments have taken place (Woerdman, 1997). During the third Conference of Parties in Kyoto in 1997, more priority to the mechanism was given. It is now accepted that industrialized countries will achieve about 50 per cent of their commitments abroad, amongst others through JI. Moreover, joint implementation projects in the East and the South were conceptually separated, the former being still referred to as JI, the latter being termed CDM (clean development mechanism).

Ego perception

A relatively large group of NGO respondents from the climate arena claim at least some influence on this topic (six out of 13). They refer to their critical assessment of the concept, which was to some extent taken over by the Third World. Some NGO representatives also claim success with regard to pressure on Northern countries to soften their position on JI.

Alter perception

Three out of the 10 key government respondents from the climate arena are convinced that NGOs played an important role in the whole debate on JI, in particular with regard to clarification of the concept and its potential drawbacks for developing countries. Some believe that this was a positive contribution to the debate. Others, though, have a more negative view, as NGOs according to them were among those players who blocked an immediate and unrestricted adoption of the concept by the COP. Also, the NGOs' views on JI were, according to some government respondents, influential, but not relevant in Berlin.

Researcher's analysis

It is difficult to distinguish 'the' NGO goals, as some were partly in favor of the JI mechanism, while others were dead set against (Eco, 1993). Still, the

NGO umbrella Climate Action Network (CAN) managed to operate with reasonable unity on this topic. Its position was that JI could be an option only for the future and only for those industrialized countries that would already have achieved substantial GHG reductions at home (Climate Action Network, 1994). Furthermore, only a fraction of the commitments should be realized through JI and this should not include the export of nuclear technology. But *if* a pilot phase was established in Berlin, according to CAN, it should be among industrialized countries and without crediting. This 'if' word makes clear that most NGOs were not very enthusiastic about a pilot phase. The fact that it nevertheless was established implies that they did not achieve their main policy goal. So NGOs may have delayed the unrestricted introduction of JI, but the fact that it *has* been introduced cannot be overlooked. On the other hand, they achieved some of their second-order objectives, given the substance of the pilot phase (no crediting; JI only for industrialized countries), which was decided on in Berlin.

It is obvious that the policy outcome – the Berlin decision on the pilot phase – is a compromise between advocates and opponents of JI. As their positions were more or less known in advance of Berlin, it does not seem that NGOs could have played a significant role there, as the compromise and decisions were made behind closed doors. Nonetheless, the role of NGOs *before* COP1 is difficult to deny. They were the first to formulate criticism on joint implementation (VROM, 1991) and their views were to some extent adopted by others at a later stage. Examples are several key developing countries, such as India (G77 and China, 1995). This impact of NGOs is confirmed not only by the alter perceptions in the above, but also by several government policy documents (e.g., VROM, 1991; 1994), as well as by a second check among key negotiators at the time (amongst others: Vellinga, the Netherlands; Ripert, France; Luiz Meiro Filho, Brazil). Therefore the conclusion that NGOs indirectly affected the negotiation and decision-making process on joint implementation in accordance with their policy goals is considered plausible.

Extent of political influence

Given the above conclusion, the counterfactual is considered different. But as JI is still legitimized and institutionalized by the Berlin decision and as most NGOs had not wanted to go that far, their policy goals were only weakly attained ($GA = 1$). This can, however, be substantially ascribed to their own interventions, as NGOs were the original critics of the whole concept and persuaded the G77 to partly adopt that criticism ($AS = 2$). The political relevance of this topic is definitely high ($PR = 3$). JI was really a key topic at the negotiation sessions and industrialized states perceived it as one of their main interests. All in all, the political influence of global environmental NGOs on JI in the period 1990–5 should be considered *moderate* ($PI = GA \times AS \times PR = 6$).

THE CLIMATE AND BIODIVERSITY CONVENTIONS

Eight and 10 cases respectively from the Framework Convention on Climate Change (FCCC) and the Convention on Biological Diversity (CBD) have been assessed in accordance with the EAR procedure as applied in the previous section. The notion of 'case' as used here refers to a specific policy topic within the climate arena or the biodiversity arena. Such a topic has been covered either by one or more articles of the Convention concerned or by one or more decisions of the Conferences of the Parties to the two Conventions. NGOs claimed to have influenced all 18 cases (ego perception). However, only half of these claims could be confirmed on the basis of alter perception and researcher's analysis (Table 6.2). Therefore, one has to conclude that NGOs *did* influence the policy outcomes of the FCCC and CBD, but only to a limited extent, all the more so since no specific case was strongly influenced.

TABLE 6.2 *FCCC and CBD cases and the extent of political influence of global environmental NGOs*

	Strong political influence	Moderate political influence	Weak political influence	No political influence
FCCC cases	–	• AOSIS Protocol • Joint implementation	• Target • Berlin Mandate	• Objective • Principles • Implementation • First review
CBD cases	–	• Preamble • Financial mechanism	• *In situ* conservation • Indigenous people 2 (decision COP) • Marine biodiversity	• Indigenous people 1 (treaty text) • Genetic resources • Biosafety 1 (treaty text) • Forests • Biosafety 2 (decision COP)

CONCLUSION

In the first section it was assumed that NGOs have become global players, because of their impressive numbers, their increasing constituencies worldwide, their formal position in the UN system, and their political influence on a global scale. This latter claim was verified in this chapter. It follows that NGOs indeed make a difference in global climate change and biodiversity policies, although the effects should not be exaggerated. In any case, global environmental NGOs do *not* have a *permanent* ability to influence these – and probably other – policies. Hence, global environmental NGOs are *influential* global players at best, not *powerful* ones so far.

This main conclusion is based on the EAR instrument. Its aim is to produce plausible and transparent assessments of political influence, while addressing the complexity of political processes on a global scale. The latter is achieved by interviewing expert respondents, which yields a quick introduction to the object of study, and a selection of relevant topics for further analysis. Transparency is achieved by analyzing selected cases of possible influence in accordance with one format (the dimensions of 'ego', 'alter' and 'researcher's analysis', and a formula). Finally, plausibility is achieved by confronting the perceptions of the expert respondents with available data from documents and additional interviews (triangulation). Given these characteristics of the EAR instrument, it is believed that it is especially well equipped for the study of the influence of players in complex decision-making by one researcher.

Of course, the proposed method has some drawbacks as well. First of all, since the EAR instrument is rooted in both the reputational and decision-making methods, some general drawbacks of both approaches are involved. The researcher should be sensitive to possible biases in ego and alter perceptions. Respondents may have reason to respond strategically or reify general beliefs. The researcher's analysis, next, has – just as the decision-making method – a bias in favor of pluralist theory. After all, there is hardly any decision-making process in which players do not have some influence. Therefore the conclusion that both stakeholders and decision-makers are to some extent influential in complex negotiations is not really a surprise. More important then is the political relevance of such influence, and that aspect should be given due attention.

Second, the presented methodology is based on the selection of key respondents, key topics and key levels of decision-making. Obviously *any* selection procedure implies methodological problems, as one may select the 'wrong' persons and items and leave the 'good' ones out. Hence, some in-depth knowledge of the decision-making process, and several checks with experts, are prerequisites for any researcher in order to make a valid selection.

NOTES

1 Note that in the original study (Arts, 1998) the abbreviation EAC is used. In that book the third dimension is called 'causal analysis'. Here the terminology 'researcher's analysis' is preferred for two reasons. First, the notion of 'causal' may have a traditional-positivist connotation and give readers the (wrong) impression that the 'causal truth' will be unraveled. Second, EAR as an acronym sounds better, as it indicates that *listening* to expert respondents is an important aspect of the instrument.

2 Note that in the original study (Arts, 1998) other, more complex formulas are used to assess the extent of political influence. For reason of parsimony, the formulas presented here are preferred (see for example Waltz, 1979 for a debate on 'parsimony'). Although the outcomes have changed somewhat as a consequence, the general conclusions on the NGOs' political influence remain similar. Also, the scores and verbal qualifications in the above differ compared to

those in Arts and Verschuren (1999) (a score of 4 indicates *weak* influence here, and not *moderate*). The reason is that the boundaries between the verbal qualifications are arbitrary and depend on a decision by the researcher at face value.
3 See, for a more extensive analysis of this case, Arts (1998: 138–43).

III GLOBALIZATIONS

Previous chapters have focused on debates about the timeless characteristics of political power and the various elements that make it up. This final part, in contrast, considers whether some fundamental characteristics of power were already changing significantly by the end of the twentieth century – in particular, with regard to the highly complex and contested phenomena associated with globalization. Indeed, these four chapters focus on four quite different interpretations of globalization – the four 'globalizations' implied in the title of Part III. Nevertheless, these contrasting interpretations intersect and overlap (even where they disagree) in a range of key ways: first, in their understanding of liberalism and neoliberalism as both 'truth' and discourse; second, in their evaluations of the crucial role of the United States and of American political and economic power; third, in their assertion that, whatever form globalization takes at the macro-level, it makes power relations *at all levels* (i.e., Clegg's three circuits of power) more complex, even where the primary focus of analysis has thus far been on the third or systemic level; and finally, in their agreement that new – but not always predictable – configurations and dynamics of power may emerge and crystallize as we get deeper into the new millennium.

With regard to globalization, it is usually thought to be not so much the endogenous nature of political power *within* essentially national societies that may be changing (although that is happening too), but more the wider transnational and international context within which power operates. For the way power as we have known it has evolved over the past several hundred years at the macro-level has depended in several deep structural ways upon the emergence, consolidation and structural primacy of one organizational feature of the political landscape – the modern nation-state and the political order it represents. Even from most Marxist perspectives, the economic power of capitalism has been crucially mediated and exercised through the nation-state and the interstate system.

Most observers see the most important feature of the nation-state to be its internal coherence and stability. For Goehler (Chapter 1 in this volume) it forms a 'common space of action'; for Crozier and Friedberg (1977) a 'structured field of action'; and for Spruyt (1994) an 'arena of collective action'. The existence of such an arena, differentiated in space from other arenas, has always been seen as a crucial precondition for politics, whether in Plato's *Republic*, Aristotle's *politeia*, Hobbes's *Leviathan* or Marx's *The Eighteenth Brumaire of Louis Bonaparte*. Only when there is such a coherent internal space available can political (and economic) power transcend the limits of mere force, i.e., coercion and compulsion (Goehler's 'transitive power'), and become the basis for a collective social structure – hopefully pursuing some sort of ideologically legitimated 'general good', but also capable of actualizing Bentham's (and Foucault's) *Panopticon* – keeping people in disciplined order for the pursuit of wider social values and objectives – or Marx's 'state monopoly capitalism'. Thus the state internally is essentially *hierarchical* in its organizational structure – a 'hierarchical structure of imperative coordination', possibly (from the perspective of many political and social philosophers throughout history) the highest or most overarching form of hierarchical imperative coordination available.

At the same time, however, at another level of analysis, the nation-state has been the fundamental building block of an *international* or interstate order (sometimes called 'inter-national' with a hyphen). Since the Peace of Westphalia (1648) ended the post-medieval Wars of Religion, the most crucial political norm of that order has been the mutual recognition by the rulers of states of each other's internal sovereignty and territorial integrity. But there has been no international *government* as such, no organizational feature above and beyond the state to enforce that or any other norm – in other words, the structure of the international system has been seen as *anarchical* rather than hierarchical in form. Only the self-interest of states in avoiding their own destruction in the pursuit of their various goals has kept them in line through self-restraint, backed up by the existence of (a) a particular international *balance of power* amongst states (usually major states and their allies) which can explode into war if upset, and (b) *growing practices* of interstate interaction such as diplomacy, international trade, etc. 'Relative gains' are more important than 'absolute gains' in such a context. Such self-restraint is a fragile reed at times, as can be seen in the expansion of warfare in the modern world through industrial warfare, total war (the two world wars), guerrilla warfare and terrorism, and potential nuclear war (the Cold War or, today, the threat of proliferation).

Modern manifestations of political power, therefore, have been to a great extent shaped by the development of nation-states and the international system. Without the Janus-faced state as the dominant form of political organization – in contrast to other major types of society throughout history, including village societies, nomadic patterns, tribal societies, feudal systems, traditional empires, transnational economic elites and so on – neither the 'common space of action' within states nor the balance of power amongst them could hold. The threat of a return to a Hobbesian 'war of all against all' always lurks beneath the surface. The significance of globalization is that several aspects of that phenomenon have been seen by both academic and non-academic commentators as having the potential to undermine or transform the modern world order and to provoke or engender fundamentally dissimilar kinds of power relationships which the world would need to adjust to in novel ways.

Globalization is a very complex phenomenon which can be analyzed from several different perspectives and on several different levels. The four authors in this section have identified a number of interlinked but contrasting dimensions of globalization which both reflect the traditional characteristics of the nation-state and the international system and yet chart fundamental changes.

In Chapter 7, Erkki Berndtson argues that while little has changed at one level, much has changed at another. The international system, however anarchic in terms of its basic organizational form, has always been marked by the fact that different states have possessed different types and amounts of power resources; balances of power have not been between equal states, but between coalitions of states, often in flux – which is why balances of power have come and gone, with changes usually coming about through re-equilibrating wars. The most powerful states in both military and economic terms have had a disproportionate impact on the distribution of power and the enforcement of power relations in the international system; they have been called big powers or great powers, or, in the Cold War, superpowers. But globalization has worked on two levels to alter this situation.

In the first place, since the end of the Cold War, there has been only one superpower, the United States of America. Thus the balance of power today, Berndtson argues, is less a balance between shifting coalitions than the growing *unbalanced* hegemony of the USA. In this sense, the nature of power in the international system is becoming less anarchical and *more* hierarchical, although the restructured circuits of power generated by such a change are also becoming more complex at several levels. Thus if there is a common 'global' space of action emerging, that action is lopsidedly organized. This lopsidedness can therefore also have a destabilizing aspect, as it can engender resistance at a variety of levels; American power may be broad, but in some ways it seems shallow, lacking the legitimacy of true intransitive power. Furthermore, and more importantly, American power is more than just 'American' power, or the power of the American *state*; it is also the objectification of *economic* globalization, i.e., the spread of American-style capitalism with its neoliberal discourse and practices to the rest of the world. In this sense, Americanization may be making the world look more like the inside of traditional nation-states in some ways, with for example an emphasis on common goals like unrestrained trade, economic growth, human rights, etc. – but without the legitimacy and sense of common identity characteristic of political power within 'modern' nation-states, and therefore without the glue that makes political power genuinely intransitive.

In Chapter 8, Philip Cerny, although agreeing that American agency has been crucial in pushing towards globalization, goes farther than Berndtson in claiming that the very structure of political power is being fundamentally transformed in a global context. For Cerny, globalization leads to a *disarticulation* or breakup of the contextual preconditions for the coherent, organizationally centripetal exercise or practice of political power as we have known it in the modern era. This disarticulation essentially involves the unpacking of the different tasks, roles and activities of the nation-state. The state has traditionally been a *multifunctional* or 'multitasking' organizational structure organized around, if not an *a priori* coherent domestic society, at least the political project of creating a coherent domestic social order (especially through nationalism, as with Bismarck's *Kulturkampf* – i.e., the 'cultural struggle' to *build* a German nation in the late nineteenth century out of the various diffuse local and regional social, political and economic orders that had previously prevailed – and with postcolonial nationalism in the Third World).

In this sense, the nation-state is a relative newcomer to the world as a form of political organization, as can be seen by the list of alternative structural forms given earlier (village societies and the rest). It may be that the emergence, consolidation and development of the nation-state and the states system are time-bound phenomena, not eternal or even particularly durable, and especially vulnerable to the impact of globalization. In this sense, both the capacity of the state to 'perform' in domestic terms, especially to 'deliver' certain so-called public or collective goods, and the ability of states collectively to stabilize the international system through balances of power and intergovernmental practices of various kinds, are compromised by globalization. Power is being redistributed among a range of claimants, new and old, with the state – although still very much to be reckoned with in many ways – finding itself increasingly faced, Cerny argues, both with a 'governance gap' with regard to some of its most important modern functions, especially in terms of its capacity to redistribute economic resources, and with the crystallization of a range of complex, multilayered webs of governance linking the local, the regional and the transnational as well as the national and international. In this sense, globalization is transforming political power into the kind of complex, messy webs of power which we usually associate with the Middle Ages rather than retaining the neat categories associated with the 'modern' state and states system.

In contrast, Howard Lentner in Chapter 9 argues that states and the kind of political power associated with them are alive and well, and are indeed being strengthened by globalization. At one level, the essential change is not from the state to something else, but from the coexistence and competition of different state forms – especially between politically and economically liberal states and more authoritarian and interventionist states – to a greater convergence around a liberal norm. Lentner also agrees to some extent with Berndtson that this process and associated trends are to a great extent the result of the power and hegemony of the USA and the kind of world order American leaders in both public and private sectors have sought to export to the rest of the world.

More important for Lentner, however, are not the discontinuities but the continuities. Despite its 'neoliberal' label, he says, the liberal state has a long pedigree going back at least to the Enlightenment, and its philosophical proponents have always linked effective political power with certain limitations on the scale and scope of that power. Individuals have political rights, and a division of functions keeps the bounds of the political fairly narrow while leaving production and employment mainly to business and the market; liberal politics and the liberal marketplace are two sides of the same coin. Indeed, globalization not only is the product of the liberal state (especially in its American manifestation) but also expands and reinforces that liberal state as the dominant nation-state model both at home and in making the quasi-anarchic international system work by building in liberal norms through states and through expanding international institutions. Even economic matters have to be underpinned by political power; 'investor confidence' requires essentially political foundations. And no other structural phenomena – neither individuals, nor families, nor firms, nor criminal gangs, nor nongovernmental organizations (NGOs) – are in a position to provide the most important political goals and values. Those goals and values – security, identity, welfare and macroeconomic stabilization – can only be provided by the continuing strength of states, of the international system and, increasingly, of the intergovernmental institutions established and guaranteed by states to undertake particular tasks in a more integrated global context.

Finally, in Chapter 10, Elina Penttinen develops a full-blown Foucauldian model of globalization, both overlapping and in stark contrast with the others. In this analysis, it is not merely American capitalism, nor the restructuring of the nation-state and the interstate system, nor the political desirability of liberal values that is in question. It is the way contemporary capitalism (American-style, but inherently global as well) transforms not the third or systemic circuit of power (the main focus of the previous three authors) but the second and, most importantly, the first too. It is the commodification of the individual that characterizes globalization first and foremost. 'Individuals' are not born as such, but *become* so, through liberal and now (in a more inexorable form) neoliberal *discourse*. Neoliberal discourse reconstructs the individual as a pure consumer, for whom the act of consumption subsumes other physical and psychological needs and necessities in its all-pervading sensuality. When the going gets tough, the tough go shopping. This extends to the commodification of human body parts and genetic material.

Thus we have come full circle. At one level, the discourse and practices of power are fragmented downwards to the individual, undermining the collective discourses or grand narratives of modernity. But of and by the same token, globalization and global capitalism create a new common space of action – but one which is not of collective political action but of individualized consumption, the arena of which is, and can only be, the world as a whole. Nevertheless, such a transformation can never be complete or exhaustive, which will open up spaces for new discourses and practices to evolve which might well include not merely those of dominance and subjectification but also those of resistance and emancipation.

For all of these chapters, therefore, the key issue of globalization is how the macro-level, systemic circuit of increasingly globalized power is articulated (efficiently or inefficiently, evenly or unevenly) with the new discourses and practices of neoliberal fragmentation. Will the liberal state remain at the core, holding the ring between the global and the local, as Lentner believes?

Or will American hegemony play this role, as Berndtson argues? Or, in contrast, will the world become politically and socially fragmented, undermining state structures and creating a governance gap, as Cerny argues? Or, finally, as Penttinen suggests, will the many internal contradictions and microcircuits of postmodern global power relations alter the whole way we perceive power itself, making traditional political macro-institutions into vestigial relics of modernity in a world of hyper-capitalism from below? Thus from the perspective of contemporary debates on power, we are talking about not merely one 'globalization' but many (or at least four!) 'globalizations'.

7 Globalization as Americanization

Erkki Berndtson

POWER AND GLOBALIZATION

Power is usually analyzed in the context of the state. Individuals, groups and institutions use power within the state. Or states use power in relations with one another. On the other hand, it is increasingly argued today that the state is losing its sovereignty. Globalization has become a symbol of our time. If that is true, who uses power in today's world – and how?

In the discourse on the nature of power one can stress the role of agencies of power or systemic properties of power (Haugaard, 1997b). Stressing only one or the other aspect of power, however, the analysis is bound to overlook important elements in today's situation. Power should always be looked at as a process in which many elements interact with one another. It is as important to ask 'who has power?' as it is to ask 'how does power work?' Conceptualizing only one aspect of this process as power *per se* easily leads to misinterpretations. Power consists of numerous forces, counterforces and relations which dominate people and make them act the way they do, placing people in different social positions with different resources. That is why it is necessary to focus at least on resources of power, institutional bases of power, techniques of power, networks of power and conditions of power.

This can be illustrated by looking at the agencies of power and systematic properties of power. As for the agencies of power, power does not exist as such: 'it is not a resource, but the mobilization of resources by an actor' (Wrong, 1988: ix). Because power becomes apparent through the mobilization of different resources, it is important first to identify these resources, whether they are linked to force, economic sanctions or charisma. Different social positions already have different resources, but resources also create positions.

From the perspective of political process, one of the most important elements in the use of power is the institutional structure of the political system. Institutional factors are too easily forgotten today, when there exist so many other interesting possibilities for analyzing power. Their importance should not, however, be forgotten. The institutional system of making decisions in society offers positions to use power at different social levels. The political structure also determines how values and wants are allocated for a society. It partly determines also the importance that force, money or charisma have in politics in a given political system.

Another aspect of power that is often neglected involves techniques of power. How to use different power resources in different situations requires skill and knowledge. What is useful in some situations may not be so in others. Techniques of power are very much linked to specific situations.

Actors create different networks of power. Societies are structured in such a way that behind one process of power there is always another one (Malecki, 1990). Structures of power vary from language to social practices that are sedimented in time, and, by socializing people, they form conditions of power. These refer to ways in which actors understand their situations and react to power. If people fight against the people in power all the time and are even ready to die rather than to consent, the use of power is different from that in societies in which people accept the authority of decision-makers (Merriam, 1964: 21). An efficient use of power actually needs authority, because lack of authority often leads to violence and chaos. In that sense conditions of power link together agencies and networks of power as systemic properties of power.

Power in a globalized world should be understood as a process of these interacting elements. A problem with much of the globalization literature, however, is that it treats globalization as a natural process, a process without actors seeking and using power. A debate on globalization seems to rely more on the systemic approach than on actors using power. Some globalization theorists have even claimed 'that there are forces operating beyond human control that are transforming the world' (Waters, 1995: 3). This perspective, however, presents a wrong image of globalization. It is just as important to understand processes of globalization from the perspective of the systemic properties of power, but it is as important to understand who are the key actors in the system.

CONCEPTS OF GLOBALIZATION

Is the contemporary world system qualitatively different from the past? The problem is that globalization itself is a contested concept. There are at least three different approaches to it. The first one is economic. It takes a rather narrow historical perspective as the term refers mainly to processes beginning in the 1970s, gaining strength in the 1980s, changing the rules of the game in the 1990s and expected to become dominant in the twenty-first century. In this sense globalization has been linked to recent changes in the role of the state and to the growing influence of market forces. Governments have reduced public expenditures by eliminating social services and privatizing state enterprises. Liberalization of trade and capital movements as well as an overall deregulation of society have become dominant political ideologies.

All over the Western world politicians and business leaders have argued that there are no alternatives to these policies. The economic growth period from 1945 to 1973 is over and old industrial states have to face new global challenges. Hans-Peter Martin and Harold Schumann (1997: 6) have pointed out how this ideology is continuously strengthened by opinion-makers, who argue that the welfare state 'has become a threat to our future' and that 'greater social inequality is unavoidable'. Although the result has been a cutting of real wages and a rising unemployment in the West, also many on the left have accepted these problems as an unavoidable calamity resulting from the demands of globalization.

Globalization mixes economics with politics. Advanced industrialized countries are compelled to change their economic and political systems because of the growing economic challenge from the former developing countries. Western economic powers have helped their new adversaries to grow, but now the world has changed into a new globalized system with its own laws. An the end, the need for transformation in the industrialized West seems to arise from outside. The message is that 'Western society with its high level of demands, is colliding with the self-denial typical of Asiatic society' (Martin and Schumann, 1997: 5–6).

Not everybody accepts this interpretation of globalization, however. It has been pointed out that economic globalization has much longer historical roots. Usually one refers to the 1870s (e.g., Lentner, 2000) as a period of the beginning of modern industrialization and international trade. From this perspective the present economic globalization is nothing new and contemporary protagonists of globalization have a poor sense of history. The international economic system before the 1970s was not as closed as it is often claimed to have been. In fact, the period from the 1870s to the First World War marked more a open international economy than was the case later (Hirst, 1997b).

According to some critics, globalization theorists also misinterpret basic facts. Paul Hirst claims that true transnational corporations are still relatively rare and, on the other hand, foreign direct investment happens mainly in the Triad of Europe, North America and Japan: 'Capital is not fleeing the developed world to low-wage countries. Foreign direct investment is flowing to a select minority of developing countries – Singapore, Malaysia, Mexico, and the coastal provinces of China taking the lion's share' (1997b: 213). That is why Hirst sees globalization as a myth and argues that the nature of the world society is more international than global at the moment. It is still based on nation-states (cf. Lentner, 1999). What is called globalization is still essentially a Western phenomenon (cf. van Elteren, 1996: 59).

The second approach to globalization is cultural. Malcolm Waters (1995) looks at globalization as a history of modernization beginning in the late fifteenth century. The cultural approach to globalization also comprises politics and economics, but looks at them from a perspective of broad historical tendencies shaping values and behavior patterns of individuals and nations. Globalization refers to the spreading of European culture to other parts of the world. As Waters writes, 'Globalization is the direct consequence of the expansion of European culture across the planet via settlement, colonization and cultural mimesis' (1995: 4). Western colonialism, beginning in the sixteenth century, systematically reached around the globe, until at the beginning of the twentieth century the 'European world' comprised 74 per cent of the globe (Braudel et al., 1992: 141–2). This world was very heterogeneous, but it slowly became a true global international system, paradoxically through the spread of modern nationalism by the Western colonial powers and the subsequent creation of new independent states through the process of decolonization.

But although the Western domination still exists, some optimistic cultural theorists believe that globalization is also changing things. Globalization is best understood as a process in which socialization of citizens happens increasingly in the context of global knowledge, global awareness and global imagery (Spybey, 1996: 151). This process has been hastened by technological advances that have brought us satellite and cable television, cellular phones, faxes and the internet. And although these are Western products, they seem to offer possibilities for the spreading of alternative information around the globe. Globalization is nothing to be afraid of, but something to take advantage of. Optimistic cultural theorists believe that Western domination is turning into a global culture.

The third approach to globalization is politico-ideological. It has been claimed that globalization 'is the international system that has replaced the cold-war system' (Friedman, 1999: 42) and that the concept is the functional equivalent of the concept of 'Free World' during the 1950s and 1960s (Bacevich, 1999: 8). This argument makes globalization a general metaphor, which describes a qualitatively new international system which came into being after the collapse of the socialist world system. One consequence of the end of the Cold War was that it has been easier for Western corporations and political leaders to push policies which are nowadays identified as economic globalization.

Because of these different interpretations it is often difficult to evaluate the globalization debate. Scientific analyses mix with political and economic hopes, fears and ideologies. Different interpretations of globalization deal with the same elements, but the problem is the periodization of history and the meaning that is given to economics, politics and culture.

GLOBALIZATION AND THE UNITED STATES

Because I am mainly interested in power in the contemporary world, I use the concept of globalization loosely throughout the text, as a metaphor describing new economic, political and social conditions at the beginning of the twenty-first century. This perspective does not deny globalization as a long process of Westernization. From the perspective of this chapter, it is not important whether a contemporary world is characterized by globalization or internationalization, or whether globalization began in the sixteenth century or in the 1970s. What is interesting is that the concept of globalization came into wide use only in the 1990s (Waters, 1995: 2). Different concepts imply that today there are not only different approaches to globalization, but different (and often contradictory) 'social demands' for the use of the term.

In this sense it is interesting to note that the term has been most widely used in political debates in the United States. All American presidents, from Jimmy Carter to Bill Clinton, have pushed vigorously for economic transformations and eliminated controls on currencies and capital (Kennedy, 1999: 56), but it has above all been Clinton who has given a name to these policies: globalization. Social processes identified as globalization are clearly not natural processes, but conscious ones with specific interests. Even the concept of globalization has become a rhetorical instrument of persuasion, a form of power itself. One must submit to its laws, whatever they are, claim its advocates.

It is no wonder that many argue that features identified as globalization are a process set in motion by American politicians and corporations: 'globalization . . . is for most nations a brute fact from which they cannot escape. For America, it is a process that its own economic and political elites deliberately launched and keep in motion' (Martin and Schumann, 1997: 216), and 'there is no way the United States can retreat from the worldwide wave it has set in motion' (Whitman, 1999: 81).

Indeed, the United States has been a key actor in opening up the world to trade (GATT and WTO), to foreign direct investments and to liberalization of money markets, while other industrialized countries have been compelled to follow its example (1999: 67). As Secretary of State Madeleine Albright has said, 'What we've done is kind of open the whole system up' (quoted in Bacevich, 1999: 9). International agreements have become a reality only when the government of the United States has been willing to sign them and it is still the case that 'although America may not be everything, nothing adds up to anything without America' (Martin and Schumann, 1997: 216).

The United States is a major player in the economic field: 'at least on the money markets, globalization so far means little more than the Americanization of the world', and 'the great majority of global players in the money market are American institutions . . . Besides, the hardiest speculators do not cross swords with the world's largest bank of issue, because its dollar reserves are unlimited' (Martin and Schumann, 1997: 73).

The same argument is made by George Ritzer (1998) from the perspective of culture. Ritzer has been one to criticize studies on globalization, because many of them seem to reject an impact of any single nation, the Western nations in general and the United States in particular, on globalization (1998: 81). As a student of consumer society Ritzer is interested in the role of the United States in the birth of mass society, and he argues convincingly about America's continuing impact on the world: globalization means

Americanization. American cultural products are an important part of keeping the American Dream alive. It is not only that American movies and popular music can be seen and heard everywhere, but 'it's a real thing' and 'just do it' may be still more effective mechanisms of socialization. As Ritzer argues, American business innovations such as credit cards, fast food restaurants and shopping malls have already changed the way of life around the world. McDonaldization of society has meant the spreading of efficiency, predictability, calculability and control of social processes. It has also meant dehumanization and homogenization of world culture.

If the United States has played a major role in economic cultural and politico-ideological globalization of the world, why is this fact often 'forgotten'? There are many possible answers for this. First, although globalization has been presented as a social necessity, it has not been possible to convince some because, while this 'necessity' is beneficial for some countries, others may nonetheless suffer from this process. Second, there is a natural resistance around the world to acceptance of the idea of the domination of the United States. And because 'Americanization' is never total, but rather partial and selective, it has been easy to underplay the American influence. America's cultural products do not necessarily replace extant cultures, but often coexist with them and are becoming in a sense 'everyone's second culture' (1998: 74). As French television commentator Christine Ockrent has pointed out in regard to Europe, 'the only truly pan-European culture is the American culture' (quoted in van Elteren, 1996: 77).

There are, however, two additional reasons for underestimating the role of the United States. First, it was not so long ago that many scholars, politicians and business leaders thought that the United States was in economic decline and losing its economic hegemony in the world. In particular, the rise of the economic power of Japan in the 1970s seemed to pose a serious threat to the American economy. And in the 1980s the whole Pacific region was often presented as a new center of the world economy.

Second, if globalization has been understood as a general Westernization process, the United States has been treated as an offspring of European culture. The United States was born from European heritage and it is not American culture which is spreading around the globe, but a culture that is 'Western', 'modern' and 'capitalist'. Both of these latter arguments need a more detailed analysis.

THE UNITED STATES AND ECONOMIC HEGEMONY

Although the image of American economic decline still lingers in the minds of some scholars, it is clear that recent economic developments have changed the situation prevalent in the 1970s and in the 1980s. Since the 1997 Asian economic crisis Americans have increasingly argued that the crisis showed the vulnerability of the 'Asian economic model' and the strength of the

American economy (Emmerson, 1998: 48). The crisis seems to have proven what Manuel Castells argued even before the crisis, i.e., that a 'Pacific region' is culturally extremely diverse and most countries of the area are characterized by strong cultural nationalism which divides them. That is why the internal dynamics of the region still make it fundamentally dependent on the performance of non-Asian markets, especially the United States (Castells, 1998: 206–15).

A good example of the change of attitude is the testimony which Federal Reserve Board Chairman Alan Greenspan gave before the Senate Subcommittee on Foreign Operations after the Asian Financial Crisis. He stated among other things:

> Although East Asian economies have exhibited considerable adherence to many aspects of free-market capitalism, there has, nonetheless, been a pronounced tendency toward government-directed investment, using the banking system to finance that investment. Given a record of real growth rates of close to 10 percent per annum over an extended period of time, it is not surprising that it has been difficult to convince anyone that the economic system practiced in East Asia could not continue to produce positive results indefinitely. Following the breakdown, an increasing awareness, bordering in some cases on shock, that their economic model was incomplete, or worse, has arguably emerged in the region. As a consequence, many of the leaders of these countries and their economic advisors are endeavoring to move their economies much more rapidly toward the type of economic system that we have in the United States. The IMF . . . is trying to play a critical role in this process, providing advice and incentives that promote sound money and long-term stability. The IMF's current approach in Asia is fully supportive of the view of those in the West who understand the importance of greater reliance on market forces, reduced government controls and the scaling back of government-directed investment. (Greenspan, 1998)

A new rise in the economic role of the United States did indeed happen in the 1990s. Also, Europe's economic condition still seems problematical to many Americans. Europe is seen to be plagued with 'Eurosclerosis', high unemployment and slow economic growth. For American free-market ideologists, European labor markets are too rigid and its social safety nets too large (Wallace and Zielonka, 1998: 65). It is no wonder that Americans have been eager to point out that the economy of the United States is flourishing at the same time as Europe and Asia face severe economic problems.

Many trust that the United States will keep its position as a leading economic power for a long time to come. Although the United States had severe economic difficulties during the 1970s and the 1980s with its huge fiscal deficits and loss of competitiveness in the global economy, it is believed that downsizing and restructuring in the 1990s led the United States to a new start and 'what people thought was American decline in the 1980s was actually America adjusting to the new system before anyone else' (Friedman, 1999: 42; cf. also Zuckerman, 1998: 18–20).

The 'new' economic power of the United States is based on many factors. One factor is that it controls many industries of the future, 'such as advanced semiconductors, computer network servers, personal computers, software and service, entertainment, finance, and telecommunications . . . the world of internet. Some 90 percent of web sites are American' (Zuckerman 1998: 20).

Second, the world's scholarly, scientific and technological skills are concentrated in the United States. As Paul Kennedy has argued, the country 'possesses incredible intellectual assets in its great research universities, with which the higher education systems of other countries simply cannot compete' (1999: 56).

An additional factor is the set of requirements of financial markets, which centralize the financial world. At the moment only New York and London have the resources and skills to carry out complex financial operations worldwide fully. Frankfurt, Hong Kong and Tokyo are still secondary cities compared with these two, while other financial centers operate more locally, with relations to these centers and subcenters (Sassen, 1999: 75–6).

Furthermore, the economic power of the United States is more than ever strengthened by non-economic factors. The importance of cultural products was noted above. Moreover, the presence of American military power globally gives the United States a leading role in world affairs. Having been the backbone of the whole Western world since the Second World War, it continues to act in that role even after the collapse of the Soviet Union. In doing so it also advances its own interests vigorously among its allies. As the US Deputy Secretary of State Strobe Talbott said when he talked about globalization and its challenge to America:

> we are pushing Japan to deregulate and open its economy in ways that will reduce our persistent bilateral trade deficit. We are urging the South Koreans, with whom we currently have a trade surplus, to open doors to U.S. products in key areas such as automobiles and telecommunications. (Talbott, 1997)

The globalized economy needs regulation and someone at the same time to guarantee its 'openness' (Bacevich, 1999: 8–9; Hirst, 1997b: 212). The discipline and cohesion of the system must be maintained, and the United States is, in fact, the only country at the moment able to guarantee the existence of the present global economy. As President Clinton has asserted, the United States is 'helping to write the international rules of the road for the twenty-first century, protecting those who've joined the family of nations and isolating those who do not' (quoted in Bacevich, 1999: 10).

EUROPE AND THE UNITED STATES

Those who understand globalization as a long Western modernization process do not wholly accept the claim of globalization as Americanization.

They argue that the United States is part of the general Western culture, an heir to European cultural heritage. But is the contemporary United States an offspring of European culture anymore? Western Europe and the United States share many values and ideas, but there are also basic differences in their cultural, political and economic systems. Although from a non-Western perspective the difference between the United States and Western Europe may not be big, for citizens of these two cultural entities, differences are evident (Ellwood et al., 1994: 34; Miller, 1990).

Besides, as William Wallace and Jan Zielonka (1998) have argued, there has always existed an uneasy relationship between the United States and Europe. The former was built by immigrants who often were disappointed with the Old World and were searching for a new beginning in life (1998: 65; Walt, 1998–9: 7). The birth of the United States was based on 'the central idea of putting New World opportunity in the place of European privilege' (Spybey, 1996: x). The same attitude can still often be seen in American criticism of European practices.

On the other hand, at least since Alexis de Tocqueville many European social theorists have looked suspiciously at American consumer society and mass participation in politics. The nature of American democracy has been evaluated with hope, skepticism or mixed feelings. For some the United States has been the 'land of the future' and a model to be learned from, but for many it has also been a model to be avoided. Like de Tocqueville, many European commentators have believed that Europe will follow in some respects the example of the United States. At the same time they have not been sure if that will be good for Europe.

It is no wonder that after the United States had made its first incursion into the affairs of Europe in the First World War, the criticism of 'Americanization' began to spread as fast as American movies and popular music began to capture European audiences. This same ambivalence prevails in Europe today, although the criticism towards the United States varies in different European countries. In some countries the criticism is more open and specific (e.g., in France), while in others the attitude is more pragmatic (e.g., in Germany and in Italy). And of course Britain has always had a special relationship with the United States. But even taking these differences into account, it is true that among European economic and political elites some feel deeply uneasy about tendencies pointing towards an Americanization of the Continent (Martin and Schumann, 1997: 237).

There are a number of reasons why Americans and Europeans look at each other in the late 1990s with a growing skepticism. The partnership between the United States and Western Europe after the Second World War was based on three unifying forces (Walt, 1998–9). The basic factor was a Soviet threat. Even America's economic interests in Europe were partly molded by it. Western Europe had to be economically strong to oppose the Soviet Union and socialism, although the American–European economic partnership in itself was also beneficial for the development of the American economy itself. This special relationship between the United States and

Western Europe was then maintained by the existence of a generation of American and European elites with a commitment to the idea of an Atlantic community.

But now these unifying forces are gone or eroding. The end of the Cold War changed the situation. Besides, economic relations between the United States and Europe had already begun to change earlier. Asia had surpassed Europe as the main market for US trade as early as 1983 (1998–9: 4). And Europe's own integration process has worried many Americans for a long time 'for fear it could produce a true global rival' (Wallace and Zielonka, 1998: 66).

Neither is the commitment to the idea of an Atlantic community so certain. Europeans have especially been worried that 'Americans suffer from dwindling information and expertise on Europe as the American media retreats into domestic coverage and exotic human interest stories and the generation of exiled Europeans teaching in American universities passes on. In the end, American elites are increasingly left with a crude picture of European politics, society and economic development' (1998: 66).

Although there is no reason to overplay differences between the United States and Western Europe, because they still have many common interests and their relationship is fundamentally sound, the United States and the European Union have nevertheless been involved in persistent trade disputes since the 1960s (Dinan, 1999: 531–54). The collapse of socialism has also clearly sharpened the economic competition between the two Atlantic powers.

With the foundation of the WTO in 1995, many disputes have also become more open and formalized. Two striking examples are the quarrels over bananas and hormones in beef. The European Union has for a long time set quotas on the import of bananas, favoring banana growers from the former European colonies. The United States, on the other hand, has tried to advance the interests of American banana companies in Central America, accusing the EU of breaking the WTO rules on free trade. The United States has also retaliated by applying heavy duties to certain European imports to the US. Another persistent row has been the one over hormones in beef. The EU has banned the use of hormones in the production of beef and all importation of such meat. The United States has taken the case to the WTO and although the WTO has ruled against the EU (as in the case of banana war), the EU has not yet given in, but has demanded more scientific information on the effects of hormones (1999: 545–6, 549–51).

Although no one expects the relationship between the United States and the European Union to evolve into a breakdown of relations, there are real differences of political and economic outlook of Americans and West Europeans. The banana and hormone wars are trade disputes, in which each side is defending its interests, but there are also more fundamental differences in the political and social outlook between Americans and Europeans, 'ranging from the role of foreign policy in economics to the role of governments in ensuring public safety and managing scientific risk'

(1999: 553). American capitalism is too individualistic and hard for many Europeans.

That is why Europeans often feel alienated from American society. In the aftermath of the Second World War Europeans looked at the United States for help and accepted its leadership, but new European generations no longer do that (Walt, 1998–9: 8). There does not exist the same admiration for American things as before. Many Europeans cannot understand the Clinton–Lewinsky affair or the removal of references to Darwinian evolution in state examinations in Kansas schools. The postwar Europeans were eager to see 'America', but contemporary Europeans are more interested in Gaudian Barcelona than in Los Angeles freeways (Pells, 1997: B5).

But while West Europeans may sneer at the crassness, greed and uncaring nature of America's capitalism, millions of people from other countries – in Eastern Europe, the Caribbean, East Asia – are all eager to get to the United States (Kennedy, 1999: 56). And this is, in fact, a key factor why the United States is not a European culture anymore. Basic differences concerning economics, politics and culture between the United States and Western Europe are strengthened by a new social and cultural composition of Americans. With a new African-American and Hispanic consciousness, with more and more people with Asian and Pacific backgrounds, Americans who have their roots in South America, in Africa or in the Pacific do not find Europe to be a natural target of identification. The United States has clearly become a multicultural global society, a new American model, which is qualitatively different than the old European model. The United States is already a global society in a sense that no other country is.

THE MEANING OF AMERICANIZATION

Differences between Europe and the United States do not deny the existence of American influence in Europe. Many Europeans have accepted the 'necessities' of economic globalization, because of American politics and policies. Without the United States, European countries would not necessarily have taken steps that they have now taken. The 'American model' of rugged individualism and eschewing of the role of the state is still contrary to European culture.

The 'Americanization' process is in many ways paradoxical. Americans try to influence the decision-makers of other countries in a number of ways and, with the strong international position of the United States, no country is able to overlook its views. Besides, American influence often results from social theories and ideologies which are used in science, consulting and international administration. These direct means of influencing social practices and policies around the world comprise one form of globalization as Americanization.

But the hegemonic position of the United States often creates strong anti-American sentiments around the world (Kennedy, 1999: 56–7) which lead to conscious opposition to American power. That is why it is possible to argue at the same time that the world is being Americanized and that it is not. A good example is East Asia after the 1997 financial crisis. Asian countries have seemingly adopted some of the demands of the United States and the IMF, but at the same time they have maintained many of their old economic practices (Emmerson, 1998: 56).

That is why Americanization is often more efficient through other means. Many technological advances have come to reality because of research and development work in American universities and corporations. The mass production of cars, electromagnetic broadcasting, innovations based on the DNA sequencer, etc., have profoundly shaped life in the world. More importantly, it has been 'the changes in social technology – the institutions and practices that evolved along with the material culture and established its context' which have had the most profound impact in other countries (Moglen, 1998: 11). The McDonaldization process has transformed the world in the direction of American life models more thoroughly than the conscious efforts of Americans to influence policies around the world have been able to do (Ellwood et al., 1994: 39; van Elteren, 1996: 81).

Globalization as Americanization does not mean total influence by Americans. The reception of American culture in other countries has always been selective. Different countries have adapted it in ways and degrees that have suited their own needs and cultures (Ellwood et al., 1994: 41). Besides, in many cases American influences have reached one country through another, which has already reformulated the original American impact. Globalization as Americanization means only that because of the position and resources of the United States, it will be the major originator of the globalization process.

The nature of the globalization process is inherently American also in another important way. As the world is becoming more and more hybrid, it begins to resemble the United States in some respects. As in the United States 'polyglot, multicultural constituencies selectively assimilated, challenged and recombined the dominant culture with their own cultures in a complex process that can best be called "creolization"' (van Elteren, 1996: 53), so in the future global society the same kind of creolization process will in all probability develop identities that combine 'global' and 'local' dimensions in countless different ways (1996: 54).

Americans learned a long time ago that in order to sell, cultural products have to transcend regional and ethnic differences in multicultural societies. That is why there is no 'national' culture in the United States: instead, its culture is a 'global' culture, more a form of entertainment than a builder of national consciousness (1996: 49–50, 56; also Kimmelman, 1999). Compared to many other countries, the United States is an 'illusory' state in the sense that although it is kept together by forces of order both internally (law and order) and externally (military), it is above all an idea, the 'American

Dream', that forms the basis of social life, while in other countries it is still the 'nation' that constructs the state as the state.

A problem of national consciousness shows, however, how long the world still is from a true globalization. Globalization as Americanization is above all a metaphor describing some important and profound tendencies affecting the world society. In this process the United States has a unique position. Although it is possible to talk about 'Toyotization', no one would argue that the world is becoming 'Japanized'. Although the European integration process is advancing in giant leaps, it is yet too soon to argue that there is a 'Europeanization' process going on globally. Americanization goes beyond America, because the United States is the only country in the world today offering a model of a global society.

AMERICANIZATION, GLOBALIZATION AND POWER

Globalization does not mean that the future world will look like the United States today. The future will depend on relations of power both in the United States and in other countries. The striving for globalization was, however, born in the United States because of its economic, political and social system. Institutional factors as well as changing power resources between different political and economic actors have made it easier for recent American governments to push for deregulation, privatization and liberalization of international economy than has been possible for governments in other industrialized countries.

A part of the 'American exceptionalism' is that there has never been any strong socialist party in the United States. The development of American political parties has followed more pragmatic than ideological considerations. In contrast, European party systems were formed in relation to socialism, and the left–right dimension has always been the major political cleavage in Europe. European politics has been organized by ideological parties based on class cleavages of industrial society (with additional religious and language cleavages). And although a strong socialist component in European culture and politics with its state traditions and practices has begun to erode, it is hard to see that the European societies would suddenly move to an American direction in politics (cf. Birnbaum, 1977: 215). Moreover, although socialist parties have declined in popularity, the rise of green parties in Europe will still guarantee the difference between European and American politics in the near future.

The classical question of why there are no important socialist parties in the United States can have many possible answers, from the early political formation of parties to political repression (Berndtson, 1985), but an important element has also been American federalism, a design by James Madison and others to balance different interests (Lowi, 1984: 376). The existence of many states has helped to disorganize the working class and it has always been possible for corporations to play states against one another.

This can be seen in the development of American trade unions. During the 1980s the balance of power between labor and capital changed markedly in favor of capital. Manufacturing centers began to move to the South where labor unions were weak. With liberalization of capital movements multi-national corporations also began to move their production outside the United States, to countries where labor costs were low. At the same time the supply of labor grew enormously when the global workforce increased from 1.3 billion in 1965 to 2.5 billion in 1995 as a result of population growth in developing countries and women entering the labor market in advanced industrialized countries. The threat of unemployment and plant relocation began to weaken the power of labor in the United States. Additionally, the structure of work began to change. The traditional industrial sector was diminishing and the majority of new jobs were created in the service sector, where, at least in the United States, trade unions were traditionally weak (Newland, 1999). In fact, temporary employment and contracted business services are the fastest growing employment sectors today (Whitman, 1999: 62).

Power in the United States has also become more fragmented and difficult to understand. This has undermined the ability of politicians to control social processes. The United States has always been a pluralist society. But from the stratified pluralism described by Robert A. Dahl at the beginning of the 1960s, power relations have developed into forms of hyper-pluralism and privatized pluralism (cf. Waste, 1986a). Dahl has even argued recently that a new political order has been created in the United States over the last 30 years (Dahl, 1993). There are more conflicting and independent interest groups than before, while governmental institutions have become weaker. President and the Congress are not leading the country but adapting to outside pressures. At the same time the plebiscitary nature of American politics has increased. People vote for short-term benefits and do not always understand the consequences of their own actions.

The same has happened in regard to capital. Marina v. N. Whitman has noted how a tradition of separating ownership and control began to reverse itself in the United States in the mid 1970s. The share of publicly held stock (for the 1000 largest firms in terms of their market value) owned by pension funds, mutual funds and other large institutional investors rose from 16 per cent in 1965 to 57 per cent in 1994 (Whitman, 1999: 69). It is these new institutional investors who have played a major role in the globalization process. They have also increased the volatility of the whole economic system, while ordinary citizens have become its prisoners, as 'each of us is both a producer and a consumer, putting us at war with ourselves; in Pogo's words, "we have met the enemy and he is us"' (1999: 81).

These changes coincide with a rise of a new era in American politics. Kevin Phillips (1990) has described the period from 1932 to 1968 as the 'Democratic New Deal Era' which represented America's searching for common ground for its citizens. The new global strategy of the United States began to emerge only when the Democratic New Deal Era had broken down. Economic globalization has been a product of the 'Civil-Disturbance Republican Era' from 1968 onwards, allowing American rugged individualism to reign. Economic elites have successfully been able to turn American populism to their own advantage. The present nature of globalization has deep roots in American relations of power. The future of globalization, however, is still open.

8 Globalization and the Disarticulation of Political Power: Towards a New Middle Ages?

Philip G. Cerny

POLITICAL POWER FROM THE CENTRIPETAL STATE TO DURABLE DISORDER

The very foundations of the way power works are being dramatically transformed today by wider changes in the nature of economy and society. In the modern era – broadly speaking, over the past 300 years – world politics has been characterized by the structural dominance of one level of political organization, the nation-state. Other levels of political organization, whether endogenous (i.e., domestic political systems) or exogenous (i.e., the international system or states system), have crystallized around or through the Janus-faced state. The very notion of political power itself has issued from and depended upon there being states and a states system to give it coherence and substance – what Goehler in this volume calls a 'common space of action' and Crozier and Friedberg (1977) a 'structured field of action'. In analytical terms, this assumption affected social science as a whole, and not merely political science; it was built into mainstream sociology through the works of Weber and Durkheim, in particular, and economists have long assumed for theoretical purposes that the world economy is made up of national economies ever since theories of comparative advantage were developed by Smith and Ricardo. Of course, Marxism was an internationalist perspective, but nation-state-based revisionism came to dominate both social democratic and Leninist forms in practice.

Domestic political scientists have seen politics as involving the resolution of social conflicts through the development of common institutions and patterns of behavior which would obviate the direct use or even threat of force, aims which could only be realized if there were a single, centripetal playing field with common and enforceable rules of the game and a certain infrastructure of common values. International relations specialists, in contrast (with the long-standing exception of the most dedicated of idealists), have resisted attempts to translate the kind of relations and structures of power, interest group politics, democratic (or authoritarian) principles, notions of social justice and the like, which are characteristic of the domestic sphere, into the international. Instead, they have overwhelmingly believed that the self-interest and self-help imperatives of a world of states would cause those states to defect from more binding institutional settlements at key times, causing the whole structure to revert to a state of nature if not a state of outright war. Indeed, states are virtually compelled to act as power-maximizing unit actors in the international system, despite domestic divisions or cross-border interdependencies, because the system itself forces them to (Waltz, 1979). And without an international balance of power among such unit actors, the capacity of societies to maintain stable domestic political systems would be fatally undermined too by a Hobbesian state of endemic warfare.

The central question today is whether this dual mechanism retains both its internal logic and its wider stabilizing capacity in a rapidly changing world. In a structural environment more and more characterized by so-called globalization – essentially the dynamic intersection (or even synergy) among several uneven processes of internationalization and transnationalization – how do such changes affect the nation-state itself and, in turn, the structural coherence of the states system? Are there *other* ordering mechanisms in the process of evolving? This chapter argues that there is such a process of reconfiguring of political power going on – indeed, of its effective disarticulation or *disordering* in a more complex world – integrally rooted in and arising from globalization, making traditional state-based notions of political power increasingly problematic and in some ways redundant.

Two major aspects of the impact of globalization on political power again reflect the orthodox distinction between national and international levels of analysis in political science. On the one hand, the *domestic* nation-state today is more permeable and vulnerable to transnational and international developments – not only more 'interdependent' but more 'interpenetrated'. The choices open to politicians and bureaucrats, and therefore to political publics, are narrower today in significant ways than they have been since before the First World War. At that time, states and state actors were in the early stages of a process of discovering how to imagine and construct an *industrial state* around the new, large-scale industries of the Second Industrial Revolution (what Chandler, 1992 called the 'modern industrial enterprise', built on expanding economies of scale and scope), involving trade unions and mass political movements, new middle classes, managerial elites and the 'corporate state'. Alongside the industrial state came the *welfare state*, which involved governments in increasingly complex tasks of distributing and redistributing resources. The structural ascendancy of this 'modern' nation-state led to what Polanyi (1944) called the 'Great Transformation' – a new way to reconcile the competing imperatives of capitalist development and social justice. Globalization, however, erodes the capacity of the state to pursue such a broad-based project in a coherent or strategic way (Cerny, 1995; 1999a), leading state actors themselves to undermine their own power by promoting globalization through the 'competition state' (Cerny, 1997) and thereby also narrowing the scope for democratic decision-making (Cerny, 1999b).

On the other hand, globalization undermines and transforms *international* relations, i.e., relations among discrete, unit-actor-like nation-states. Complex multilayered webs of governance are proliferating and expanding, often rooted in private sector relationships and private–public networks (such as those found in international financial markets: Cerny, 2000a) rather than traditional intergovernmental regimes alone. Individuals, groups (including both old and new social categories), firms, voluntary associations, industrial sectors, 'special interests' and the like often do not see their values and interests as being simply – or appropriately – channeled through and achieved by the nation-state alone (or at all, in some cases). Rather, they are tempted to 'defect', to find new ways of pursuing their ends outside, above, through, and also below state processes and institutions. In this 'new security dilemma' (Cerny, 2000b), the international system is ordered no longer by balances of power among states (and by threat of states *per se* defecting from the fragile cooperative arrangements which result from such balances) but rather by a quasi-pluralist or 'plurilateral' (Cerny, 1993) process of the diffusion and diversification of power among a wider range of actors and across a more complex range of structures. The result looks more like some aspects of the Middle Ages than the era of the modern nation-state.

THE CHANGING INTERNATIONAL CONTEXT: GLOBALIZATION AND INSECURITY

The bottom line of any structure of political power is its capacity to provide the basic, underlying public good of *security* to its constituency. Since 1648, both external security *and* domestic political and social security have primarily been organized through the state and the states system. The Peace of Westphalia, although at the time concerned with the clash between emperors and kings on the one hand and the Roman Catholic Church on the other hand as to which religion should be established in the various territories of the Holy Roman Empire (thereby ending the long wars of religion), established the twin principles that rulers (at that time monarchs and dynasties, rather than impersonal, institutionalized nation-states) recognized each others' *internal* sovereignty and *external* territorial integrity. In other words, sovereigns (later states) agreed not to interfere in the internal affairs of other sovereigns (states). The modern international order, despite the rise of trade, economic and political imperialism and the Industrial Revolution, has since continued to be 'governed' without an international 'government' through the workings of these principles, despite ever larger wars up to 1945 resulting mainly from the attempts of revolutionary *states* to alter that situation. (The appropriation of Marxism – originally an internationalist ideology of working-class revolution – by the Soviet Union and other Marxist states merely proved the rule and indeed reinforced it during the Cold War.) Internal upheavals also seemed to reinforce the need for, and capacity of, states to guarantee basic security.

Even globalization has not undermined the principles themselves or replaced the states system *per se*. Rather it has *eroded the capacity of states to perform certain key functions* attendant on their traditional role and also has generated more diffuse and complex transnational webs of governance which increasingly perform some state-like functions – sometimes in conflict and sometimes in collaboration with various state actors and agencies. In this context, security itself is becoming more diffuse and uncertain. Indeed, what is called the 'new security dilemma' starts from the growing perception by actors themselves as well as by academic observers that *the states system itself has become the key source of insecurity* in the contemporary world, rather than the basic source of stability – and that, in turn, the search for security increasingly involves the resort to different forms of *exit* from that system. In seeking to exit the constraints of the states system, actors (whether state actors or non-state actors, and whether seeking prosperity, power or justice) further undermine or erode the capacity of the states in the system, individually or collectively, to provide either external or internal security. Thus actors are *rationally* induced to resort to non-state decision-making mechanisms in order to provide security (and other goals and values which security is thought to make possible).

On the one hand, this process can lead to the emergence and development of a range of newly embedded, but originally *ad hoc*, private or quasi-private regimes and circuits of power, both formal and informal, surrounding and criss-crossing the state in a new web of complex relationships. In this sense, the new security dilemma is inextricably intertwined with the processes of internationalization and transnationalization which comprise our wider notion of globalization and would reflect any synergies or interaction effects stemming from their intersection. On the other hand, however, the same process can lead to the breakdown of existing bulwarks of order without replacing them with new institutionalized mechanisms, leading to a self-feeding expansion of endemic, low-level conflict and spreading violence, no longer monopolized in Weberian fashion by the state. In this sense, the reconfiguring of power in a globalizing world may lead not to a new world order but to a *new world disorder*, a vicious circle which cannot be counteracted by states at home or abroad. The most crucial question for the future of political power is whether a new kind of *post-state* ordering mechanism can develop to replace the old balance of power with a more complex balance of intersecting groups and overlapping institutions in the future.

In the meantime, however, it is crucial not to attribute this transformation to more immediate causes. This is a real danger. In particular, there is today a widespread tendency to see the 'end of the Cold War' as producing such a fundamental realignment of the international system. But this is to confuse cause and effect. The end of the Cold War *per se* resulted not so much from the breakdown of a particular balance of power – the bipolar balance between the United States and the Soviet Union – as from the *increasing ineffectiveness of interstate balances of power generally* to regulate the international system. For example, the failure of large powers to determine outcomes in the Third World through traditional security means – the most salient examples being Vietnam for the United States and the Sino–Soviet split (and later Angola and Afghanistan) for the Soviet Union – was merely the first major shock to the balance of power system. Many more were to follow.

The demise of the Soviet empire (and the Union of Soviet Socialist Republics itself) in turn did not result just from some change in its relative overall power position *vis-à-vis* the United States of America. The USSR collapsed because of an evolving configuration and interaction of several fundamental structural trends – domestic and transnational pressures stemming from technological backwardness, international economic interdependence, awareness of social and cultural alternatives by individuals and groups made possible by international contacts and communications, the growth of consumerism and other pressures for 'modernization', etc. – with which the USSR was less and less able to cope. Likewise, growing complex interdependence in the West as well as in the East undermined the hierarchical alliance structures set up in the postwar period by the superpowers (the North Atlantic Treaty Organization and the Warsaw Pact), at first through the development of the new nationalism of the 1960s and 1970s such as Gaullism in France and the Sino-Soviet split, and later through the growing ineffectiveness of those alliances in controlling new forms of conflict, especially the breakdown of the Iron Curtain in Europe, endemic tensions in the Middle East, the spread of civil wars and state collapse in the new Fourth World (especially Africa), etc. (Indeed, the crisis in the Balkans more recently brought together elements of all three.) But the most important systemic consequence of all this is that towards the end of the Cold War *both* superpowers became *weaker* in systemic terms because traditional forms of power could not cope with the challenges of the late twentieth century international order.

This erosion of exogenous state capacity to control conflict, along with the rapid development of new transnational interdependencies like the integration of international capital markets, has thus reduced the power of *all* states, not merely the superpowers, to play their traditional systemic roles. In terms of the means of violence in particular, both nuclear weapons (increasingly seen as unthinkable and unusable, except perhaps by the governments of India, Pakistan and North Korea) and also limited 'low-intensity warfare' (more and more costly and counterproductive, as demonstrated not only in Vietnam and Afghanistan but in Bosnia and Algeria), have lost their utility, leading to a common-sense realization that neither national nor collective security can any longer be reliably based on interstate balances of power *per se*. Furthermore, this change has entailed not merely the replacement of interstate competition for military security by new forms of interstate competition, e.g. for 'economic security', but rather a realization that security based on the simple interaction of unitary nation-states itself is becoming *a cause of even greater insecurity*. A new sense of generalized insecurity has emerged, symbolized not only from above by a general threat of uncontrollable nuclear annihilation, but also from below by the rise of civil wars, tribal and religious conflicts, terrorism, civil violence in developed countries, the international drugs trade, etc. This sense of insecurity has led to a growing realization that the provision of security itself as a public good – the very *raison d'être* of the states system – can no longer be guaranteed by that system.

This *insecurity from below* is bound up with the dual character of globalization as a global–local dialectic, whipsawing the state between the international and transnational on the one hand, and an increasingly complex set of micro- and meso-level phenomena on the other – what Rosenau (1997) has called 'fragmegration' (i.e., both fragmentation and integration at the same time). Post-feudal state formation and consolidation, from Westphalia to the twentieth century, revolved around the capacity of the Janus-faced state to provide security simultaneously at two levels: Weber's 'monopoly of legitimate violence' in the domestic sphere; and the capacity for Clausewitz's war as the 'pursuit of politics by other means' in the international sphere. Institutionalizing a more rigid inside/outside distinction – providing a stable internal arena for collective action, alongside the capacity of states to make 'credible commitments' externally – made politics into an increasingly coherent two-level game articulated around and through structurally differentiated states (Spruyt, 1994). States today, however, are increasingly challenged at both levels. Changing payoff matrices crystallizing at the start of the twenty-first century are creating a range of incentives for players to defect from the states system itself – unless restrained from doing so by the as yet embryonic constraints of complex, especially economic, interdependence.

The decline of interstate wars at the end of the twentieth century and the increasing prevalence of local, civil and cross-border wars today therefore mirror deep structural changes in the international order itself. Whether a layer of institutionalized power will crystallize and converge to provide effective collective security at a global level is highly problematic. Of course, new constraints are also being created by expanding intergovernmental and multilateral cooperation. However, these essentially involve a process of 'catch-up', lagging the development of micro- and meso-level processes. They are also vulnerable to micro- and meso-level defection, while attempts to provide international and domestic security through the state and the states system actually become increasingly dysfunctional. On the one hand, the pre-existing monopolization of political power by sovereign states can actually *obstruct* and *stunt* the development of new forms of institutionalized international governance (Lake, 1999). On the other hand, such attempts can create severe *backlashes* at both local and transnational levels, backlashes which in turn weaken the state and undermine wider security. These backlashes do not develop in a vacuum. They interact with economic and social processes of complex globalization to create overlapping and competing cross-border networks of power, shifting loyalties and identities, and new sources of endemic low-level conflict – a 'durable disorder' analogous to some of the key characteristics of the medieval world (Bull, 1977: 254–5; Cerny, 1998; Minc, 1993). This chapter, then, seeks to examine the complex interaction of globalization, on the one hand, and the fragmenting of security, on the other. Its underlying theme is that this interaction challenges a wide range of familiar understandings of social structure and change.

GLOBALIZATION AND THE GROWING GOVERNANCE GAP

Critics of globalization discourse present the very idea and image of globalization as representing an oversimplified linear approach. 'Globalizers' argue, these critics say, that the world is increasingly being pushed by market forces (or, in the Marxist version, by the requirements of global capital accumulation) into becoming a homogenized, undifferentiated economy – and, ultimately, society and polity (Hirst and Thompson, 1996). I argue, on the contrary, that globalization is constituted not by unambiguous homogeneity, but by the *interaction of differences* (see especially Cerny, 1995; 1999a). These are not just national differences, of course – indeed, they are not primarily national differences at all – but differences which persist or arise on a number of levels and along a variety of dimensions in a complex process of divergence and convergence. Existing conjunctural conditions, previously embedded structural constraints and underlying tensions, interact to shape and channel change. At the same time, the very complexity of that change gives particular strategically placed actors some influence on outcomes (Cerny, 1999c).

Even the structural predominance of nation-states and the international states system *per se* represents the crystallization of a particular set of successive, path-dependent equilibria in global politics. Broader social, economic and political structures beginning with the transition from feudalism to capitalism became absorbed and locked into this increasingly embedded order; indeed, states and the states system became the core around which other complex structures in turn emerged and developed (Cerny, 1990). Of course, the fully fledged 'modern' state did not thoroughly develop until the Second Industrial Revolution and Polanyi's 'Great Transformation'. Globalization, however, impacts that system in a range of complex ways which challenge both of the main characteristics which gave the nation-state the edge in the last round of 'institutional selection' (Spruyt, 1994) – i.e., the *multitasking* or multifunctional character of the nation-state as an institutional structure, on the one hand, and the ability of state actors and their allies to make the *side-payments* necessary to effectively maintain the provision of collective goods and the credibility of international commitments, on the other (Cerny, 2000b). Both are under threat. With regard to the first, the different tasks, roles and activities of nation-states and state actors are being increasingly 'unbundled' or 'unpacked' by cross-cutting linkages among different economic sectors and social bonds. With regard to the second, the capacity of the state to make effective economic policy, especially redistributive policy, along with challenges to state ideological and cultural supremacy in the ongoing quest for loyalty and identity, have significantly transformed – and, some would say, undermined – the ability of the state to marshal both material and ideational resources in its interaction with other social and economic (and political) structures. Thus, the state itself is in the process of 'disarticulation' (Lake, 1999). Complex globalization thus creates a *governance gap* which is likely to persist and deepen.

If the state is in the process of disarticulation, then what kinds of rearticulation might conceivably occur in the next phase of institutional selection? For example, to expect the sort of fragmented, disarticulated international and transnational governance structures which are emerging from the processes of globalization to maintain, expand or even defend the institutional gains of existing liberal democratic nation-states is simply not credible. Even as nation-building and democratization processes are ostensibly being extended in the Second and Third Worlds, state policy capacity is being both hollowed out and put at the service of enforcing the outcomes of globalization themselves (Cerny, 1999b).

On the one hand, states today are increasingly bad at certain key tasks which have been important for their social, economic and political development and effectiveness in the modern era. These underperformed tasks include redistribution, structural regulation (the broad 'design capacity' to structure the way social and economic activities are carried out) and the direct delivery of public services. Conservative neoliberals applaud such changes. Even social neoliberals, for example the 'reinventing government' school, try to make a virtue out of this: 'Governments should steer but not row', say Osborne and Gaebler (1992). The 'New Labour' government in Britain today is pursuing such a course (Cerny and Evans, 1999). Of course, state capacity is being eroded at different rates in different sectors, and these different sectors are evolving distinct public, private and mixed governance structures – on multilayered domestic, global and transnational levels.

On the other hand, states are left with a range of important but nonetheless normatively residual tasks, and some of those tasks may paradoxically be expanded and reinforced in a complex globalizing world. In the first place, states will still be left with ensuring the provision – increasingly indirectly, however – of some distributive public services, i.e., those which are not sufficiently profitable or altruistically motivating for transfer into the private or voluntary sector. Minimal welfare states will have to be maintained; the absence of any public safety net would lead to social unrest and destabilization. This function, however, is primarily in evidence in the advanced capitalist world; in areas of the world where the welfare state has remained underdeveloped or essentially absent, there will be little effective structural pressure to create or develop one. Second, some states are still relatively good at prudential regulation and the *ex post facto* enforcement of contracts, as well as the promotion of certain forms of competitive advantage in a more open world through limited industrial and trade policy measures (Cerny, 1997). Furthermore, older, more entrenched states still have a comparative advantage in providing a sort of ersatz *Gemeinschaft*, but such ties are less compelling in newer states or latent and manifest non-states. However, the *Gemeinschaft* function too – the ability of states to provide a deep psychological sense of social identity and belonging – is being unevenly eroded by the postmodern fragmentation of national identities.

In fact, however, what the state is *best* at is enforcing the norms generated and decisions made at the international and transnational levels, whether by public (state) actors or, increasingly, by private markets or institutions and private–public networks. As market outcomes, the transformation of production processes, technological innovation, socio-cultural globalization and the marketization of the competition state combine to transform nation-state structures and processes – in the absence of effective direct international 'police powers' and judicial/legal systems – state capacity in terms of enforcement will continue to grow and certain kinds of state intervention to expand. Indeed, the *weight* of state intervention overall – and its penetration into social and economic substructures – is actually increasing, not declining, as the result of globalization. What is different, then, is the *substance* of the tasks, roles and activities that fall within the state's remit, with a particular emphasis on enforcement – and with a growing deficit with regard to redistributing resources among different socio-economic groups or to designing the structural contexts within which social and economic processes take place.

Therefore the range of goals that political actors, both elite policy-makers and mass publics, can aspire to is becoming increasingly circumscribed. The process of enforcement, furthermore, increasingly involves enforcing norms, rules and decisions which have not in the first place been arrived at through autonomous, endogenous (including democratic) *political* processes, but which instead reflect market decisions and the preferences of transnationally imbricated, private oligarchic/oligopolistic structures. Challenges to the legitimacy of enforcing such decisions and preferences may therefore in some circumstances rapidly evolve into challenges to the state's primordial claim to represent the public interest or common good and therefore to its supposed monopoly of legitimate violence. A policy deficit is leading to a legitimacy deficit. This is already having far-reaching effects, especially in weaker states.

With nation-state-based institutions and processes having been transformed into transmission belts and enforcement mechanisms for decisions arrived at on different levels of the wider global system, but with that system as a whole becoming increasingly incapable of generating effective, authoritative, multifunctional coordination and control mechanisms or governance structures, the international system is likely to be characterized once again by a number of attributes usually associated with the medieval era: (1) competing institutions with overlapping jurisdictions (states, regimes, transgovernmental networks, private interest governments, etc.); (2) more fluid territorial boundaries (both within and across states); (3) a growing alienation between global innovation, communication and resource nodes (global cities) on the one hand and disfavored, fragmented hinterlands on the other; (4) increased inequalities and isolation of permanent subcastes (the underclass); (5) multiple and/or fragmented loyalties and identities (ethnic conflict and multiculturalism); (6) contested property rights and legal boundaries (e.g., disregard for rules and dispute resolution procedures, attempts to extend extraterritorial jurisdiction, etc.); and (7) the spread of what Alain Minc has called *zones grises* (gray zones), or geographical areas and social contexts where the rule of law does not run (both localized ghettos and international criminal activities) (for a more extensive consideration of these categories, see Cerny, 1998).

Today we live in an era of increasing speed, global scale and the extremely rapid diffusion of information and technological innovation, characteristics too which seem to be outgrowing the political capacities of the existing institutional order (Douglas, 1999). An extended phase of low-level disorder, punctuated by episodic structural mutations and the uneven maintenance of pockets of pluralism and elements of sectoral hegemony, seems the most likely scenario. But in the longer term, this is nothing new. In contrast to our modern notions of statehood or governance, as local societies in the past have become interlinked and interpenetrated with one another, they have generally *not* done so – prior to the consolidation of the modern nation-state – in terms of establishing consolidated, integrated, multitasking administrative hierarchies with a general grant of social authority analogous to the authority of village chiefs or big men, Roman *potestas*, or modern sovereignty (Hinsley, 1966). Rather, their structures have been *multilayered* and *asymmetric*. Different, asymmetrically structured hierarchies have usually held various kinds of authority, competing and overlapping with each other within the same broad territorial expanse. The shift of society to a wider base of inter-actions and linkages has usually been accompanied by locking in *suboptimal* equilibria (with the partial exception of the modern nation-state era) as layers of new and old social, economic and political relationships have essentially been imposed and juxtaposed around and on top of each other in patchwork fashion.

The development of human politics and society has not on the whole been a teleological process, of evolution towards a particular goal, but one of *bricolage*. Indeed, the development of the modern state is the exception that proves the rule. Village and tribal/clan societies, unless highly isolated, have usually been drawn into wider systems of competing landlord/warlord relationships, in which layers of hierarchy are permeable and territorial frontiers fluid – sometimes merely around border areas, sometimes in terms of core territories and cities too. Such overlapping and cross-cutting landlord/warlord societies have also usually become imbricated in wider quasi-monarchical and imperial systems, ranging from tributary and suzerain systems within which the concept of 'unity' has little social or economic depth or penetration, to complex, quasi-confederal, quasi-patrimonial empires.

Religious hierarchies have frequently cross-cut such systems in complex ways; trade routes and fairs have sustained a limited market economy, usually on the margins but with growing structural impact; and cities have provided havens for groups which find themselves either on the periphery of, or able relatively easily to navigate across, the complex inner boundaries (and often external frontiers too) of such multilayered, asymmetric social formations. Communications and transport systems have obviously constituted a key set of technological constraints and opportunities within which such societies could evolve.

Today, the global system ought in principle to be able to transcend such limitations of pre-state societies. Indeed, nation-states have been the incubus of the transnational as well as the international; the capacity for globalization processes to occur in the first place is due to the pre-existence of the nation-state/states system and its capacity to overcome many of the bounds of such parochialism. For example, national economies themselves evolved in the context of an increasing global division of labor and the spread of international markets for commodities and finance. National societies provided the breeding ground for both the Enlightenment and the spread of modern universalistic religions (in contrast to the 'civil religions' of ancient Greece or the insulated, centripetal belief systems of village societies) where previous social formations, even traditional empires, were more particularistic in their belief systems; and the emergence of the modern state – in both its European or Western form and later attempts at 'nation building' – gave rise to different yet analogous political systems based on an 'international of nationalisms', bureaucratic rationality, economic modernization and the like. The fact that modern states have had crucial structural similarities indicates that the states system is not the antithesis of globalization, but its precursor.

THE FUTURE OF THE NATION-STATE

The main problem, of course, is that the very success of the state is also its prison – i.e., that its success limits *both* the capacity of the state to operate transnationally in a global context *and* the capacity of latent or potential global-level equilibria to consolidate into analogous multifunctional transnational and international governance structures with the capacity to make the necessary side-payments for survival and effectiveness. The nation-state both creates and underpins globalization processes, on the one hand, and prevents those processes from effectively rearticulating governance at a 'higher' level, on the other (Lake, 1999). The result may well be the crystallization of increasingly suboptimal forms of international governance too and the threat of growing institutional entropy in world politics generally. The 'hollowing out' of the state is not matched by any equivalent 'filling in' of multilateral, transnational, regional, or whatever, governance structures – thereby creating not only a 'democratic deficit' but also a wider and deeper governance gap as we begin the twenty-first century. One of the main consequences, of course, is the increasing breakdown of the state's monopoly of legitimate violence, and thus the growing incidence and structural significance of civil wars.

However, disputes over the decline of the nation-state need not imply that nation-states will simply be replaced by some sort of integrated global order; they may merely be transforming themselves into structures which will be better able to *survive* in a multilayered global context, i.e. into 'competition states'. Monitoring and regulating economic activities are likely to differ from sector to sector, depending upon the scope and scale of the microeconomic and mesoeconomic characteristics of that sector – especially its degree of transnationalization – with the effective purview of states limited to those sectors whose organization structurally corresponds to the requirements of effective monitoring and control at a national/territorial level (Cerny, 1995).

Nation-states will probably look more like American states within the US federal system – with circumscribed remits, but retaining important residual policy instruments and the ability to exploit niches in the wider system through limited taxation and regulation. They will resemble those residual aristocracies left over from the Middle Ages that remained powerful within nation-states (Mayer, 1981) in an increasingly globally integrated capitalist environment, focusing on what is good for their own estates and seeking not to lose too much power and prestige to the *nouveaux riches* or transnational elites of the global economy. At the same time, it follows that the more transnationalized a sector, the more it will tend towards developing trans-national self-regulatory institutions – whether with the implicit or explicit authoritative delegation of nation-states, as in traditional international regimes, or in increasingly unaccountable private regimes. When added to transnational interest group formation and the development of transgovern-mental coalitions bringing regulators and policy-makers in overlapping spheres into regular networks cutting across 'splintered states', the rapid but asymmetric multilayering of political and economic institutions will lead, at best, to an emergence of quasi-public, quasi-private dispute settlement regimes seeking to arbitrate competing claims for rights and privileges in this patchwork system (Aman, 1999; Cutler, 1995).

The main causal factor missing from this process today that was present in the transition from feudalism to capitalism is the spur of exogenous systemic competition. It was the institutionalization of competition and conflict between increasingly powerful dynastic families in the late medieval period which led to the consolidation of state bureaucracies and their growing penetration into more and more exclusively territorialized social and economic bases. With the exception of unexpected intergalactic warfare, there will be no external consolidating pressure on the contemporary system analogous to the interdynastic struggles of the Hundred Years' War, the Thirty Years' War and the subsequent three centuries of interstate competition both within Europe and across the world as Europe expanded. Just as the Chinese empire, in Kennedy's analysis, stagnated because it experienced no fundamental external threat for many centuries, so the neomedieval international order will face no direct exogenous political or military pressures for institutional consolidation at a transnational level (Kennedy, 1987: 16–30).

Thus an increasingly dense, multilayered and asymmetric set of suboptimal competing institutions with overlapping jurisdictions – including, not breaking up, a residual nation-state – will muddle along, untroubled by exogenous pressures to consolidate. In this context, nation-states will find – weaker states first, stronger states later on – that their territorial and authoritative boundaries will effectively become more fluid. Even if legal sovereignty is not formally threatened, state borders will still appear as real lines on the map, and guarantees of diplomatic recognition and membership of certain international institutions will remain. Collapsing states like the Lebanon and Somalia; 'transnational territories' such as those unevenly controlled by the National Patriotic Front of Liberia; so-called 'archipelago' states like the Democratic Republic of the Congo; and substate ethnic and separatist movements, will threaten state cohesion at the same time that existing borders are clung on to for dear life in the name of elite legitimacy.

However, it is unlikely that the actual breakup of nation-states *per se* will be as significant a development as the exogenous and endogenous differentiation and disarticulation of their authority – especially for the older and wealthier nation-states of the North. Nevertheless, centrifugal pressures on 'empire-states' like Russia and China are likely to grow in importance as the penetration of cross-cutting sectoral and market pressures expands within those territories. Some authors have always believed that even if China does not break up (with, for example, its long externally interdependent southern coastal region and hinterlands breaking away, among other oft-canvassed potential developments), its premodern structure of regional quasi-warlords loosely held together by a weak imperial bureaucracy will return in a form adapted to the structures of a complex global economy.

At another level, the emergence of international or transnational *regions* is playing an increasing role in territorial organization. However, what is most interesting about these regions is not their institutional coherence or suprastate-like structural form; indeed, the European Union is the only region with that sort of quasi-state coherence. What is most interesting is that they are themselves multilevel, asymmetric entities, with criss-crossing internal fault lines – subregions, cross-border regions, local regions, not merely 'nested' but often conflicting, with national, transnational and subnational rivalries poorly integrated – based mainly on the density of transactions which also reflect the complexity and circularity of wider globalization processes (Higgott, 1997). Will regions in the future reflect the macrostructures of the European–North American–Asian 'Triad'? Or are they fundamentally much smaller but overlapping nodal areas in which the density of particular (especially sectoral) socio-economic transactions and infrastructure is forming *de facto* cross-border regional clusters, such as around the Sea of Japan, the emerging German–Central European industrial economy, the *maquiladora* export zones in northern Mexico, or the much poorer cross-border social economies of Kurdistan or eastern Liberia? Regionalization is thus itself a multilayered phenomenon, reflecting the interaction of processes of convergence and divergence in international politics – a world in which the whole is increasingly less than the sum of its complex parts.

NEW COMPLEXITIES OF SPATIAL ORGANIZATION

The main structural fault lines – political, social and economic – in this complex world reflect not clear territorial boundaries enclosing hierarchical authority structures, but new distinctions between different levels of economic cleavage and urban/rural splits. The academic sociological and geographical literature on global cities reflects the concept that a range of 'virtual spaces' in the global political economy will increasingly overlap with and possibly even replace the 'real' space of traditional geographical/ topological territories. These new spaces are embodied – and increasingly embedded – in transaction flows, infrastructural nodes of communications and information technology, corporate headquarters, 'edge city' living complexes for 'symbolic analysts', increasingly 'dematerialized' financial markets, and cultural and media centers of activity (and identity). Control of new ideas and innovations will come to be increasingly concentrated in such areas, protected and secured by a growing panoply of international and transnational intellectual property rights (May, 1997).

On the one hand, therefore, the specific spaces which people perceive and identify with are likely to become increasingly localized and/or micro-level in structure, while on the other hand, people may even lose their very perception of space being partitioned vertically and learn over time to 'navigate' between different overlapping, asymmetric layers of spatial perception and organization. The poorer residents of such areas will find themselves increasingly excluded from decision-making processes. And in those areas where navigation among complex structural layers is more difficult – for example, where such nodes, infrastructure, activities, etc., do not exist within easy reach and perception, such as across large geographical spaces – many people will simply be 'out of the loop', country bumpkins or even roaming, deprived bands, like Hobsbawm's (1972) primitive rebels (consider the Hutu ex-Interahamwe in the African Great Lakes region) forced once again to become predators or supplicants on the cities, as in the Middle Ages.

Changes in institutions, the fluidity of territorial boundaries and the increasing hegemony of global cities will interact with new forms of 'flexible' labor processes and economic organization to increase inequalities and turn downwardly mobile workers (especially the less skilled, the ghetto dwellers, etc.) into a new lumpenproletariat, underclass or subcaste – a process well under way in the First World and already dominant in large parts of the Third World. In this context, it will not be merely ethnic loyalties and tribal enmities that undermine the ersatz *Gemeinschaft* of the nation-state, although they have so far been the leading edge of cultural fragmentation. It will be the development of complex new inequalities of both real class and virtual geography. Such inequalities will be far more difficult to counterbalance and neutralize without effective or legitimate state institutions, and, especially when they are allied to other cleavages, they are likely to comprise an increasing source of civil and cross-border violence. Such a situation will be not merely one of fragmentation, but one of *multiple loyalties and identities* – of social and political schizophrenia – with shifting patchwork boundaries and postmodern cultural images. Any truly global cultural identity structure will have to be not so much homogeneous or unifying as intrinsically multilayered and flexible, able to adapt chameleon-like to a wide range of differentiated contexts.

Finally, in a reconfigured world there will not only be 'niches' for the maintenance of pluralist autonomy for individuals and groups; there will also be increased escape routes – and organizational opportunities – for those operating more or less 'outside the law'. *Exit* from political society is likely to become a more viable option for a wider range of actors and activities. At one level, such phenomena involve more than just international (and domestic) criminal activities such as the drugs trade or the (semi-transnational) Russian mafia; they also involve the areas where excluded people live – especially urban ghettos at one geographical extreme, and enclaves in inaccessible areas (jungle, mountains, etc.) at another (Kaplan, 1997; Minc, 1993). Indeed, the toughest problem in this area is where different dimensions of extra-legal activities intersect with legal or quasi-legal ones, for example where the resources and networks of the drugs trade not only create alternative power structures and social identities for members of the underclass physically located in ghettos but also extend into state bureaucracies and 'legitimate' private firms, as mafias have always done. Excluded rural hinterlands may also become such 'gray zones'.

At another level, however, it is likely that many traditionally mainstream social and economic activities will expand as much through gray zones as through legitimate means, much as the informal market economy has done in many areas during the modern era. A transnationalized black economy constitutes a major challenge to the enforcement function of even the residual state, and the inclusion or integration of such areas and activities into the complex governance structures of a globalizing world is likely to be extremely uneven (Friman and Andreas, 1999). At a third level, too, Singer and Wildavsky (1993), in distinguishing between 'zones of peace' and 'zones of turmoil' in the wider world order, were inadvertently pointing to another dimension of this phenomenon which cuts across borders and regions too – shifting the focus and locus of conflict and violence even farther away from the interstate pattern and towards the intractable complexities of the micro- and meso-levels. The impact of insecurity from below will create conditions in which increasingly intractable and complex civil and cross-border wars will become the norm, while social, economic and political actors will increasingly be limited to searching for *ad hoc* partial solutions.

CONCLUSIONS: THE DISARTICULATION OF POWER AND THE SEARCH FOR NEW FORMS OF GOVERNANCE

In today's globalizing world, as in the medieval world, there is no external threat to the system as a whole which could galvanize a sufficiently hierarchical response to engender the emergence of genuinely 'global governance', and no prospect of a sufficiently autonomous and powerful collective vision – religious, social, economic or political – to transform such a world into a new transnational *res publica*. There is still no international equivalent of Goehler's 'common space of action' in the global context. Consequently, if political power in the international order is eventually to be rearticulated into a more hierarchical and authoritative global system, capable of effectively pursuing genuinely collective values on a wider, global level, then the sources of that transformation must come from *within* the newer, essentially transnational structures of such a world. They are unlikely to come from nation-states as such, however much states engage in multilateral cooperation as a pragmatic response to transnational challenges. Nation-states are (a) too limited in the scope and scale of what they can do and (b) too beholden to narrow domestic interests to be able to lead such a transformation process. They can, of course, play a facilitating role, especially as domestic enforcers of global norms and practices, and – paradoxically – as 'competition states', in pushing forward a process of economic globalization in order to maximize domestic returns, a kind of barrier-lowering tit-for-tat. However, such developments will merely widen the governance gap, not fill it in.

In reality, further consolidation of genuine global governance will have to come from a *political* process involving both the increasing international and transnational entrenchment of property rights, on the one hand, and consequent claims for countervailing rights and privileges from specific transnational economic actors and sectors, on the other – restructured through an ongoing process of interaction with and among transnational interest groups and policy networks. The 'governmental process' (Bentley, 1908; Truman, 1951) – i.e., the predominance of pluralist functional representation over territorial representation – would have to be refocused on genuinely global structures, however uneven. But such actors and groups are most likely to interact *outside* the formal-legal bounds of both state sovereignty and/or multilateral political processes. Indeed, the most powerful and effective actors and groups in the globalization process are likely to be the most monopolistic or structurally homogeneous ones, such as multinational firms, transnational strategic alliances and global financial markets.

In any case, the range of potential equilibria will be increasingly diverse, and complex situations are likely to produce complex outcomes. It can only be hoped that in the much longer run, the global order will prove to be structurally adaptable enough, as was its medieval predecessor, to leave open the possibility of its eventual evolution into something more structurally cohesive and normatively acceptable.

9 Politics, Power and States in Globalization

Howard H. Lentner

In today's world, the attempt to banish politics from public life emanates from many corners. Neoliberal ideology not only dominates discourse about the international political economy; it is pervasive in framing public questions and insinuates itself into most intellectual analyses of public choice. Neo-liberals have reached such a dominant position in public discussion that even non-ideological journalists write about contested views as if they were settled truths. For example, when governments opt for market principles, they are said to have made 'economic' decisions, whereas more interventionist policies are labeled 'political'. Yet, neither choice is less political than the other. For three decades in American politics anti-government rhetoric has sounded a powerful theme of disparaging public servants. Advocates declaim on behalf of privatization. In practical applications, corporations have come to run prisons and to provide such public services as street cleaning and welfare services. Some intellectuals even disparage those who study politics, claiming that they cling to a past that, if it no longer exists, is at least on its way out.

Before acquiescing in the treatment of politics as a disposable product, one needs to get behind the cant, to examine exactly what the empirical rela-tionship between globalization and politics is, and to grasp what is going on in this debate. Clearly, the world is undergoing changes related to reduced costs of transportation and communication as a result of modern technology. One cannot presume, however, that technology determines specific decisions. Neither can one know implicitly who does or does not control the technology without investigation, for the issue remains an empirical one. Globalization tends in general to be regarded by observers to encompass primarily economic and cultural activities. Among the more overblown claims, new worldwide phenomena are eroding the state to a point of helplessness. In more sophis-ticated analyses that admit power as a primary consideration, a consensus has developed that markets continue to gain power at the expense of states as economic producers and that the regulatory powers of states have diminished.

To engage these issues, this chapter does three things. First, it provides a brief definition and analysis of globalization. Second, it shows that politics and governance are clearly related to global trends in several ways: through power relations among states and international institutions; through insti-tutional reforms that are required by the leading states at the national level as well as societal political reforms; through the advance of the liberal state against other forms of state; and through institutional developments at the international level. Third, the chapter more explicitly examines how power works in globalization processes. A brief conclusion brings the chapter to an end.

GLOBALIZATION DEFINED AND ANALYZED

The buzzword 'globalization' refers to the rationalization of production on a worldwide basis, the spread of best production and administrative practices, the diffusion of cultures beyond their areas of origin, extensive migration, and varied effects of computer technology, including communications as well as data and financial transfers. These phenomena comprise current expressions of movements that have been occurring throughout the world since roughly 1870, the approximate beginning of modern industrialization and of a distinctive modern phase of the spread of the Enlightenment (Everdell, 1997).

Like that of Randall White, the position outlined in this chapter holds that 'the national state . . . remains the most important political framework for coping with many of the new problems . . . [generated by] globalizing trends' (1995: 12). This formulation may be contrasted with others. Some writers (Robertson, 1992; Waters, 1995) associate globalization with modernity. Others (Albrow, 1996) claim that the present period is a postmodern one in which the world has moved beyond the Enlightenment and is entering a new historical period in which consciousness is being transformed. Axford avers that 'globalization processes are creating a single world' (1995: 26), even as he recognizes the potential for fragmentation (1995: 206). To confirm or disprove any of these hypotheses must await the future, for all embody a good deal of guesswork and speculation. The argument of this chapter, however, suggests that there is a dominant system of power in the contemporary world that might be thought of as analogous to a Foucauldian dominant discourse and that also resembles Clegg's third (system integration) circuit of power (Haugaard, 1992: 53–4).

As a continuation of what has gone before, the present international system rests upon the domination of the United States and its allies who have put into effect a liberal international political economy. In trade, the coalition developed a regime that operated for nearly half a century under the principles and rules of the General Agreement on Tariffs and Trade. That regime was broadened and given greater institutional expression in the World Trade Organization in 1993. International management of economic development, trade, and related balance of payments matters is also conducted through the international financial institutions, the World Bank and the International Monetary Fund. International financial transactions, which have drawn considerable attention following the increased complexity of new instruments such as derivatives and hedge funds, rely for their regulation and management upon the administration by each state of financial institutions within its own territory, though international negotiations have succeeded in fashioning a limited set of agreed standards (Kapstein, 1994). Consequently, to refer to the international political economy as if it could be treated as a global unit remains a fallacy. One hastens to add that no one really knows what may be required for, or how to go about, the construction of adequate mechanisms for regulating international financial flows (Stiglitz, 1998).

With respect to the other major dimension of globalization, the intermingling of cultures afforded by reduced costs of travel and by modern communications technology enriches many lives in many different societies. However, the claim that a homogeneous world culture has gained ascendancy overlooks the remaining cultural diversity that one finds in every place. Even with the spread of English as a world language, thought patterns, food and social habits, religion and other ethical foundations, personal and societal tastes, and artistic expressions continue to exhibit great ranges of distinctiveness.

If the term 'globalization' refers to real phenomena in the world but not a homogeneous and overarching conceptual and empirical unity, a different conceptualization is required. Succinctly, globalization means that there exists a set of pressures emanating largely from the more powerful countries, that these are able to be projected rapidly and over great distances, and that all but particularly less powerful countries are placed in a position of coping with those constraints. In the contemporary world, pressures are composed of economic threats and opportunities, cultural challenges, and the unsought flow of people, pollution, disease, crime and drugs. In other times, weaker countries faced invasion, imperialism and colonialism, pollution, disease, crime and drugs. More powerful countries are not immune to the forces at work in the world, just as they were not in the past.

Thus, globalization turns out to be a faddish word for modernization as manifested in the late twentieth and early twenty-first centuries, combined with the continued presence of quite ancient interactions. Certainly, the present world offers different forms of pressure and opportunity; and new and marvelous technologies have been made available. Nevertheless, we live in an international system that shares more with the past than it differs from it. Continuity rather than discontinuity more nearly characterizes the age in which we live. Certainly, the world has not been transformed.

Still, change fills the air, and, in order to cope with change on a societal basis, politics remains necessary for formulating responses and effecting them. So, let us turn to considering how politics pertains to the changes that are going on.

POLITICS AND GOVERNANCE RELATED TO GLOBAL TRENDS

Politics and governance accompany global trends in two fundamental ways. First, a Gramscian hegemony underlies the spread of a liberal international economy and the transfer of culture. The power sector of the hegemony is constituted by a broad coalition led by the United States and its allies, which forms a military and economically productive base from which multinational firms can rationalize production on a global basis, financial institutions and individuals can pursue their transactions, and citizens and commerce can communicate and travel freely. Liberal market tenets provide the ideological sector of the hegemony. In as much as no competing ideological and power base offers an alternative, the world witnesses only pale criticisms of the prevailing hegemony and the absence of an alternative hegemonic shelter for the disenchanted and the marginalized. Moreover, the hegemony gains adherents and commands consent because of its instrumental advantages of providing economic growth, accumulation of wealth, and rising standards of living.

The second fundamental way in which politics and governance accompany global trends lies in the absolute necessity for effective states to furnish the security and stability, legal frameworks and administration of justice, management and regulatory regimes, policies to sustain social peace, and foreign policies for dealing with other states in order for complex markets to operate. In recent years, governments have reduced their roles as direct producers and employers; but that reduction should not be allowed to obscure their increasing institutionalization and effectiveness in carrying out other functions.

Those functions relate to both economic and non-economic aspects of societal life. In addition to exercising central bank activities, putting into place and directing macroeconomic fundamentals, providing currencies, enforcing contracts, managing foreign exchange, issuing licenses, and monitoring and regulating various aspects of business, governments perform many other important roles. Fundamentally, as Nye (1993: 184) has written, states provide security, identity and welfare.

In the liberal state, the operation of the market and a dominating neo-liberal ideology tend to overwhelm other aspects of society through a process that Marxists refer to as commodification. Religion, the arts, philosophy and other realms of life tend to be weakened rather than supported; but the loss of space and significance in modern life of these desirable and valuable dimensions of social life occurs with the connivance of the state which supports economic forces. States are not losing to markets; instead, states and markets gain as other societal power centers lose. On the other hand, the state remains the locus for appeal by those social groups that are disadvantaged by the forward march of impersonal market forces. In reality, a reference to impersonality actually obscures the fact that participants in markets do have faces. And some of the individuals and groups to which they belong find their wealth and position increasing while others stand still or fall back economically.

Beyond these general dimensions of politics in the operation of the 'globalizing' world, politics and governance form part of several discrete aspects of the dynamic arrangements being put into place in the contemporary world. The first of these involves international institutions designed to facilitate and channel economic transactions. Moreover, those economic transactions flow freely only because of generalized international peace and stability, a condition stemming not just from state power but also from international cooperative arrangements to assure the continuation of stability and to control actual and potential disruptions.

POWER, STATES AND INTERNATIONAL INSTITUTIONS

In wishful thinking, international institutions act autonomously outside the control of states. Taking the European Union as a paradigm for the future, some observers project the fairly complex interactions of states, regions, supranational authorities, firms and organizations to the broader international system, assuming that the world is moving in the direction exemplified by Europe (Ruggie, 1993). Despite its being far from clear what permanent and stable arrangements will in the end be put into place in Europe, the evidence for substantial integration there seems clear. The situation in the world as a whole, however, proves quite different. International institutions have not just been created by states, particularly the major powers, but also provide instruments that they manage and use for their own purposes.

Taking just the post-Cold-War period as the time frame, the powers – particularly the United States – demonstrated the continuing efficacy of military power in the 1991 Gulf War, in 1995 and subsequently in Bosnia, and in the coercive diplomacy in early 1998 that insured compliance of Iraq with the United Nations Security Council inspection regime (UNSCOM) to monitor Iraq's production facilities for weapons of mass destruction. With less effect since UNSCOM ceased inspections in late 1998, an American bombing campaign has continued against Iraq. In addition, the 1999 bombing war against Yugoslavia/Serbia in support of Kosovo's autonomy proved effective in gaining compliance from the resistant Milosevic regime. In his 1998 diplomatic intervention, Secretary-General Kofi Annan called attention to the armada in the Persian Gulf and the ground-based forces in Kuwait that stood ready to rain devastation upon Iraq should the Saddam Hussein regime not comply with the resolutions of the Security Council. Moreover, those resolutions were largely devised by the United States and deferred to and endorsed by other members. The Clinton administration made clear that it was prepared to act alone in taking military action against Iraq if, in Washington's judgment, full compliance by the Iraqi regime should not be forthcoming; and the United States has carried out that pledge.

The essentiality of the powers to the operation of other institutions, such as the International Monetary Fund, continued to be revealed in 1998 in the face of the East Asian financial crisis. Whatever the errors of judgment in policy that may have been made by the IMF (Feldstein, 1998), it remains an essential tool for managing the problems associated with trade deficits and the problems of the economies standing behind international trade. Additionally, the ragged, constitutionally provided process in the United States of allocating sufficient funds to allow the IMF to persist as an effective institution reveals the ongoing dependency of this international economic institution on the United States, as well as on other wealthy countries. Beyond that, the evolving international political economy relies for leadership on state finance ministers, in 1998 during the East Asian crisis led by Robert Rubin, then US Secretary of the Treasury.

Obviously, changes in patterns of trade and investment continue to occur. Moreover, the financial sector, having been freed of a rigid international regime, has proved itself a creative innovator of novel financial instruments. Computer technology has assisted the development of this sector and the speed and volume of financial transactions, posing new challenges to regulators, who have to deal with the broader ramifications of the new instruments, and to economists, who face the tasks of gaining insights into the rapidly evolving financial world and of building theories that can grasp the new developments.

The volume and speed of financial transactions and the appearance of new instruments does not inevitably carry the implication that the state has been diminished or is in the process of eroding. Although it may be the case that such implications will follow, the evidence thus far suggests that financial markets, like others, continue to rely upon state interventions to operate properly and to come to the rescue in cases of untoward consequences resulting from market activity. Thus, in the 1997–8 Asian crisis, the response called for construction or reform of central banking systems and more effective financial sector regulatory regimes and for interventions by IFIs and the United States. Clearly, banks have not come to the rescue: governments and their international institutions have.

In part, these responses have proven to be *ad hoc*. Permanent solutions to national problems rely upon governments which need to construct more effective arrangements to insure the prosperity and continued development of their respective economies. At the same time, it has also become clear that, as the international system evolves, new arrangements need to be made to deal effectively with the international political economy, specifically with the financial sector. Who will devise and put such arrangements into effect? It seems that no one suggests that it be done by banks, brokerage firms, insurance companies and related institutions. The tasks involved need to be performed by governments.

Responsible governments are not in a position to deal with problems of the international financial sector by themselves discretely. Movements internationally require cooperative arrangements among all of the states involved, if societies are to take advantage of the benefits of the free flow of capital through the varied financial instruments available. However, it is not now clear what sorts of arrangements will be put into place. Thus far, the international financial regime consists of internationally negotiated standards which are implemented by states. Such a regime may be perpetuated and enhanced, but other arrangements may be devised to supplement and/or replace it. Given the limited knowledge base available, it would be foolish to make any forecasts. What one can say with confidence is that governments will continue to be the agents to which firms as well as general populations turn in their search for means of governance over these quite complex matters.

GOVERNMENTAL AND SOCIAL REFORM WITHIN: STATE BUILDING

Three developments contribute to the plausibility of the thesis that states are eroding and/or are losing power to firms or to market forces. First, the developing countries – especially in Latin America – since the 1970s have moved away from an import substitution industrialization development strategy that had been prominently advocated by the United Nations Economic Commission for Latin America (ECLA) and that entailed a major governmental role in production. Second, the failure of the Soviet Union eliminated the world's most prominent centrally directed economy, and its many imitators turned away from the government-owned production arrangements that the Soviet system modeled. During the existence of the Soviet Union, a command economy in which a central state bureaucracy directed all production provided an alternative to the liberal pattern of two distinct realms of government and business, in which the latter holds primary responsibility for production (Heilbroner, 1990). A less prominent practice that had grown, especially during periods of economic stress, entailed using the government as a last-resort employer, which had led to bloated public payrolls which are regarded as misallocating resources and are thus unsustainable in a competitive production system.

Under the pressures of imitation and socialization from the international political system, governments have dismantled command aspects of their economies and engage in one or another form of privatization, transferring assets from direct government control to some form of private enterprise. Moreover, long before their withdrawal from public ownership of the means of production, the exhaustion of the import substitution industrialization model led many states to shift the emphasis in their economies to production for export. This move to increasing emphasis on the export sector stemmed as much from the intrinsic rationality of enhancing economic growth as from international systemic pressures. On the other hand, reduction of government payrolls more often resulted from insistence by international financial institutions and donors as well as investor states on the need to reduce public expenditures on unproductive labor.

These three moves have reduced the space that the state occupies as a producer and employer and have expanded the scope for private production activities. Inferring from this transfer of economic activities from state to private sector, some observers conclude that states have lost power to private actors and that states as autonomous entities are eroding (Strange, 1996). In addition, the rapid expansion since the end of the Cold War in 1989 of international trade, foreign direct investment, and international financial transactions has led some observers to regard the changes as a transformation to a global system in which states have lost the ability to control economic activities within their borders.

Despite the obvious shifts that have occurred in the international political economy and in the international political system following the disintegration of the Soviet Union, states persist and, in some ways, increase in importance. Undoubtedly, many states are being restructured, but they retain important functions with respect to the economy, and state and political activities encompass many non-economic responsibilities. Indeed, states remain essential to the effective operation of the liberal economic systems that are being put into place in so many of them.

Commerce that is free flowing relies upon effective states to provide a variety of underpinnings, of which some are directly related to economic activity while others remain largely unrelated but nevertheless essential to the conduct of business.

In the business-oriented economic community perhaps the most frequent invocation mentions the need to establish and retain investor confidence in order for a national economy to prosper. Although the refrain emanates from the business side of human affairs, the actions called for lie almost entirely in the political realm and need to be effected by governments. Personal and property security and political stability form the base, and a transparent legal system provides the next layer for retaining investor confidence. Beyond those essential matters, governments manage their currencies and macroeconomic policies, their trade flows, and other so-called economic fundamentals. Then, regulatory regimes must be put into place to create rules for business operations and to insure adherence to legal norms. Behind financial and industrial institutions stand central banks as lenders of last resort and legislatures as protectors of failed industries whose collapse threatens the larger economy. Finally, states negotiate and in other ways deal with other states with respect to economic interactions and to the construction and maintenance of regimes for regulating international commerce.

One cannot imagine that a modern, complex economy could operate without the performance by states of these essential tasks. But many observers limit their vision of the state to the role of supporting the economy. Unfortunately, such a view overlooks the immensely important things that states do that are, at most, only incidentally related to economic activities. More frequently than not, social groups comprising states possess distinctive identities and hold different aspirations. States provide the mechanisms both for forging overarching identities and for deliberating over common futures. Public authorities in well-ordered states work to overcome societal divisions like race, ethnicity and class. States provide protection to their citizens not just from one another but also from predatory neighbors, illegal immigration, and such plagues as epidemic diseases, drugs and other contraband. In cases of war, states mobilize for the defense of territory and population; and, even in defeat and occupation, they provide the symbols for resistance and/or restoration when the occupation ends. To avoid war and/or to prepare against its eventuality, states enter into military alliances with other states for mutual defense. States also provide the organs for deliberation to settle conflicts among social groups and to forge policies that map out and pursue the directions that societies want.

Faced with extraordinary pressures combined with immense opportunities, states find it both advantageous and often necessary to adapt to international constraints. A developing country aspiring to economic growth may alter its laws and incentive structures to attract foreign direct investment. Having opened its economy to international trade and investment, a country may then find itself under pressure from currency speculators as well as international financial institutions, requiring it further to adapt its institutions and legal arrangements in order to continue to take advantage of immersion in the international political economy. The adjustments and changes to be made in such circumstances have to be done by governments; they cannot be performed by the private sector. When strong governments are not in a position to make the necessary adaptations and changes, those modifications do not occur. Ineffective governments find it impossible to take the actions necessary to achieve public goals in their economies; and private actors are not in a position to fill in. For those private firms to take advantage of the international marketplace, it is absolutely essential that states remain effective to bring about changes in institutions, infrastructure and policies to enable the functioning of the growth economy.

TRIUMPH OF THE LIBERAL STATE

Both in theory and in practice, many different kinds of states have formed across the world. These have ranged from despotic entities like Mao Zedong's China and theocratic states like Iran under Ayatollah Khomeini to constitutional democracies like Britain and India, and from militarized states like Argentina under the generals before the Malvinas/Falklands War to unarmed and peaceful democratic states like Costa Rica. During the Cold War, the United States and the Soviet Union offered two models of large, powerful states organized along very different sets of principles, one with an authoritarian polity and a command economy, the other with a liberal regime embodying political democracy and a capitalist economy. With the disintegration of the former, more and more polities have moved toward the adoption of liberal principles.

At a casual glance, this phenomenon looks like a triumph of the liberal state over other forms of political and economic organization. In the rhetoric of those trumpeting the advance of the market, no distinctions are made among the variety of forms that have been adopted by different countries, the incompleteness of the liberal triumph, and the limited application of the liberal model to fewer than half of the world's countries. Moreover, such rhetoric overlooks such exemplars of different arrangements as Afghanistan, Iran and others that have not moved at all in the direction of the liberal model. Thus, it is important to determine how extensive the triumph really is, where liberal principles have been planted and where not. Additionally, distinctions need to be made between market principles and political democracy, particularly drawing attention to a tension that characteristically exists between them. Another worthwhile inquiry concerns variations among democratic states, particularly involving alternative models such as the government–business partnership of the Japanese model, the *laissez-faire* American variant, and the social democratic, welfare systems of Western Europe. Finally, in those places where liberalism has taken hold, one wants to examine the conformity of practice to the ideal types offered by the various models.

The liberal state forms out of two distinct traditions, political democracy and industrial capitalism. Tracing its roots back to classical Greece, modern political democracy gained its first footholds in the American and French Revolutions at the end of the eighteenth century. Huntington (1991) has formulated the spread of democracy in the modern period as having occurred in three waves. The first lasted from the 1820s to 1926 and produced 29 democracies. A fascist reaction reduced this number to 12 by 1942. With the victory of the Grand Alliance in World War II, a second wave 'reached its zenith in 1962 with 36 countries governed democratically' (Huntington, 1993: 3), with that number reduced by 1975 to 30. From 1974 to 1990, in Huntington's calculation, 'at least 30 countries made transitions to democracy' (1993: 3). Since that time, this third wave has been sustained, although Sudan's and Nigeria's fall[1] from Huntington's third wave list, and Colombia's and Mexico's drug-related corruption that undermines popular rule, remind us of the fragility and absence of consolidation of democratic rule. Beyond the well-documented reverses that have occurred, one should note that very problematical cases tend to be counted in formulating such lists. For example, an expensive and large international operation conducted a democratic election in Cambodia in 1993 only to be followed by a military *coup d'état* in 1997. Another election was held in 1998, though inclusion of the country on democracy's roster rests on a slender reed of legitimacy, illustrating that the criteria for such inclusion seem pretty flexible and based on a good deal of optimism.

Industrial capitalism sometimes accompanies political democracy, but the two do not necessarily go together. Germany and Japan formed two of the three new industrial giants – the third was the United States – that rose to prominence at the end of the nineteenth century. Although those two enjoyed periods of political democracy in the early twentieth century, it was not until after their defeat in World War II that democratic consolidation was imposed on them. In the case of Germany, of course, only in 1990 was democracy extended to the whole of the country. Chile, too, combined industrial capitalism and democracy in an interrupted pattern. Following a century of stable liberalism, first an attempt at socialism was tried in 1970 and then capitalism without democracy triumphed in 1973. Only lately has liberalism been restored to Chile. China remains an authoritarian polity, run by the Communist Party, even while it builds an industrial capitalist economic system. Thus, a variety of combinations of elements of liberalism has been produced. Undoubtedly, the contemporary liberal state does offer an appealing model of citizenship and production. So long as wealth and individual person enhancement continue to be produced by liberal states, the model seems likely to continue to hold its appeal.

Aside from competition against it by states and elites holding assorted other values, the liberal state itself embodies inconsistencies resulting from the very different traditions from which it is derived. Liberal democratic politics embodies a vision of equality, in which each person possesses rights and duties in a balanced measure. On the other hand, liberal capitalist or market economics embodies an image of equal opportunity, which has the result in practice of unequal accumulation of wealth and, derived therefrom, of power within the polity. Unless the tensions are held in balance through policy actions, the economics side of the liberal equation can undermine the political dimension. Similarly, as such examples as Nazi Germany and Abacha's Nigeria attest, the political aspect can trump the economic side.

Apart from the problems that beset the liberal state and the ascendancy that it enjoys in the 1990s, the current situation does not represent a universal triumph. Many states remain outside the liberal circle. Some of these, like China or Indonesia, have adopted enough of the economic accoutrements of liberalism to appear related. In contrast, other states – such as Sudan, Algeria, Iraq and Afghanistan – present exemplars that not only cannot be confused with liberal states but also embody such directly anti-liberal attributes as arbitrary arrests, extra-legal killing and general repression by the governments.

With all of these exceptions and reservations, nevertheless, the spread of the liberal state over the course of the last two centuries proves impressive. Even its particular success in the 'third wave' leaves much of the world outside its ambit, but in those areas where the liberal state has been planted, it provides one of the necessary pillars that support the processes of globalization.

INSTITUTIONALIZATION AT THE INTERNATIONAL LEVEL

Institutions facilitate cooperation among states and those entities that they wish to encourage, such as multinational firms and humanitarian non-governmental organizations. Moreover, institutional cooperation among states advances their attempts at controlling or suppressing undesired activities, such as drug trafficking and piracy.

Building on earlier antecedents, the victors of World War II created both security and economic institutions in order to promote international cooperation. For the most part, those institutions remain in place, though some significant modifications have occurred. Additionally, the powers have created other institutions to handle the increasingly complex matters newly inscribed on the international agenda. Discussions go forward about additional arrangements needed to manage international problems.

Central to the dominant vision in 1945, the United Nations Security Council formed the main security institution; but the emergence of the Cold War led to its overshadowing by the North Atlantic Treaty Organization (NATO) and a less formal Soviet-led alliance, which in 1955 became the Warsaw Treaty Organization. With the removal of any threat to NATO and the demise of the latter, NATO launched an expansionist plan that has added three new members in Eastern Europe. From March to June 1999, NATO conducted an aggressive war against Yugoslavia; and, in its aftermath, the alliance operated an occupation regime in Kosovo province that holds out the possibility of creating a new state there. Meanwhile, the Security Council has passed through various phases that include its eclipse through most of the 1950s and 1960s, and then its restoration to an important instrument of the powers during the 1990–1 Persian Gulf crisis and war against Iraq. In this stage, other countries have largely deferred to the wishes of the United States. Thus, the Security Council has become less a mechanism for managing the differing interests of the leading powers and more an instrument for the United States to build support, and thus legitimacy, for those of its interests that it chooses to pursue through the Council.

In the economic sphere, the primary institutions came out of the Bretton Woods Conference in 1944. Two of the institutions remain pillars of international cooperation over 50 years later. The International Bank for Reconstruction and Development (IBRD or World Bank) has added new facilities, in particular its soft lending and private investment encouragement arms, and continues as a vibrant agency for promoting economic development and, lately more directly, poverty relief. Meanwhile, the International Monetary Fund has remained an important institution for stabilizing the monetary arrangements underlying international trade; and it has enhanced its capacity to assist countries in adjusting their economies as a means of getting at the basic structural problems underlying exchange difficulties. In part, those difficulties stem from the collapse of another pillar of the Bretton Woods arrangements: fixed exchange rates. In 1971, the United States unilaterally decided to end the exchange rate system that it had provided since the end of the Second World War. With the creation of a market for foreign exchange, the burden of adjustment was transferred from the provider of a fixed rate to other countries which were forced to cope with foreign exchange uncertainties.

Negotiators at Bretton Woods also agreed to an international trade regime, though their plans came to naught as the United States decided not to support the arrangements. Instead, the General Agreement on Tariffs and Trade provided a weaker, though still very effective, set of arrangements that led to the impressive expansion of international trade that has occurred over the course of the last 50 years. With the successful conclusion of the Uruguay Round and the creation of the World Trade Organization, the trade regime has been broadened to include the less developed countries, agriculture, intellectual property rights and non-tariff barriers.

Foreign direct investment increased over the years, and its volume has grown substantially in the post-Cold-War period. For the most part, states bargain with firms for access to their respective territories. On the other hand, partly in response to IMF pressures for liberalizing their economies, many less developed countries have adopted policies welcoming to foreign direct investors as well as to financial speculators. These developments represent political bargains, however; they do not evidence increasing autonomy of international institutions over states. Furthermore, control over access to territory for investment as well as other purposes remains with states.

The greatest increase in international transactions has occurred in the finance sector, with flows through banking, stock markets and other mechanisms soaring over recent years. If any sector of economics were to symbolize globalizing trends, finance would be the prime candidate. With the volume and velocity of transactions growing since the early 1970s, alarming events over the years have focused the attention of concerned bankers, insurers and other dealers in financial instruments and their governmental supervisors. From the failure of the Bankhaus Herstatt in 1974 to the 1997–8 Asian financial crisis, these participants have sought to develop tools, first for managing financial crises, and second for putting into place institutions and principles for managing risk that do not also stifle the efficient functioning of private entities.[2] In general, the direction of financial supervision has rested with home countries (Kapstein, 1994), although the management of major crises threatening the international financial system has lain with *ad hoc* international management, led primarily by the United States but also involving other countries and importantly employing the IMF. Nevertheless, some advances in institutionalization on a more permanent basis have been made. The Basle Committee on Banking Supervision at the Bank for International Settlements was created in the 1970s; the International Organization of Securities Commissions was set up 1984; and most recently, in 1995, the International Association of Insurance Supervisors began to function. The Mexican crisis at the end of 1994 and the Baring banking crisis at the beginning of 1995 prompted the Windsor Declaration by representatives of 16 countries, which 'called upon supervisors to cooperate in responding to market disruptions, and to share information regarding large exposures in individual markets' (Group of Thirty, 1997: Appendix A, p. 32). At the G7 summit meetings, state leaders have continued to attend to the need for development of international institutions to deal with the new financial instruments and massive increases in transactions in such a way as to head off any systemic threats to international banking and finance. In the wake of the 1997–8 Asian crisis, both government and private sector participants continue to strive for appropriate institutional arrangements. Given the complexity of the subject as well as the rapidity of changes that have occurred, it must be expected that the solutions do not present themselves as obvious. Because responsible private sector parties recognize their own exposure and vulnerability to risks, they accept the continuing need for appropriate supervision by governmental authorities. What remains unclear is the final shape that supervision will take. It is possible that the system of national state supervision will persist, but the potential of creating international organizations continues. In the final analysis, though, no uncertainty remains concerning the fact that whatever supervisory institutions may be put into place, they must be created and be enforced by state authorities.

POLITICS AND POWER IN GLOBALIZATION

The analysis in this section examines the ways in which power shapes globalization. It leaves aside some of the more interesting questions that political analysis more broadly gives rise to through treating power and justice together.

Every relationship contains an element of power, though political science tends to focus on matters involving large numbers of people, mostly acting through governments and thus involving authority as well as public purposes. In as much as globalization pertains to a wide range of human activities involving a great many people, analysis of power requires attention to many manifestations. Because the phenomena associated with globalization operate across international borders, it can be expected that power in one country may be affected by cross-border operations and that international power relations may also be partly shaped by shifting power relations within countries.

First, power relations underlie globalization. The United States' military and economic power provides the stability that allows a liberal international political economy to bloom in cooperation with other liberal states that have joined the United States. Such formidable power grew over the course of the last century and a quarter, to some extent stimulated by the contests waged against non-liberal adversaries. That is to say, the United States gained a recognition of its worldwide security interests at the end of 1941 with the Japanese attack on its territory and the German declaration of war against it (Gaddis, 1997). Similarly, it was Soviet hostility and competition that prompted the building of the immense military capabilities now possessed by the United States (Rhodes, 1995).

Within the United States, the growth of the neoliberal ideology that dominates discussions concerning the international political economy resulted from a shift of the political coalition governing American politics from that based on the ideas of Keynes to one founded on the notions of Hayek. The effects of those ideas rested upon the power lost by a coalition of New Dealers, social democrats and labor unions and won by another grouping of bankers and business people (Helleiner, 1994). An ongoing struggle persists in the United States over elements of the international political economy that can be expected to continue to affect the progress of globalization. Issues involved in that struggle include financing for the International Monetary Fund to assist other states in the liberal coalition with balance of payments and other problems; extending the authority of the President to negotiate a western hemisphere free-trade agreement; and other matters affecting continued United States' participation in the fomenting and maintenance of the liberal international system. Although the evidence for a turn inward by the United States remains scant, the rise of isolationist sentiment in the American polity would provide a serious threat to the processes of globalization.

Similarly, power arrangements within other countries have effects upon the channels and methods by which globalization processes proceed. For example, within Malaysia the governing coalition has remained committed for over two decades to opening the economy and to industrialization. Since the mid 1980s, its privatization program has persisted as an opaque endeavor favoring rentiers within the reigning political party coalition as well as family members of leading politicians (Gomez and Jomo, 1997). Moreover, one of the causes of the country's vulnerability to currency speculation in late 1997 was its semi-fixed exchange rate; and behind that policy lay the power distribution in which bankers dominated the decision-making process against the interests of exporters (Jomo, 1998).

Furthermore, the Malaysian case offers evidence about a proposition put forward by some of those who exaggerate the effects of globalization processes, namely, that countries have lost control of their borders. As it industrialized and grew economically, Malaysia has relied heavily on immigrant labor. Estimates at the beginning of 1998 indicated that approximately 2 million immigrants resided in the country. As the Asian financial crisis unfolded in 1997 and 1998, increasing numbers of illegal immigrants entered Malaysia in search of relatively better conditions than in their own lands, especially Indonesia. Such a great influx alarmed Malaysian authorities who employed the police, backed by the armed forces and vigilante citizen groups, to stop the flow by arresting and repatriating the illegal entrants (Cohen and Sigli, 1998). Given the will to protect their own economy, the Malaysians wielded effective state power to deal with the problem.

Global pressures also worked some effects on the power-holders in Malaysia. In response to the 1997–8 economic crisis, Prime Minister Mahathir Mohamad, who adopted a nationalist stance toward those pressures, was opposed openly by Deputy Prime Minister Anwar Ibrahim who aligned himself with neoliberal policies. Mahathir employed the relatively ruthless means of sacking Anwar and then using his legal system to bring charges of sodomy and corruption against his former ally, who was convicted of the corruption charges and incarcerated.

Within the framework of the liberal international political economy put into place and maintained by the powers, firms and individuals in the private sector have gained some power over outcomes (Strange, 1996). Some of the power stems from wealth that has been generated within the context of the liberal order. Other power grows from the use of violence, as drug-trafficking criminals in Mexico and Colombia have illustrated. Continuation of the former requires the persistence of effective states; whereas endurance of the latter relies upon the failure of states, including the United States itself, to suppress the activities.

States also possess power in relation to other states. Relative standings of states depend upon a number of different elements, but globalization processes, specifically those related to economic growth and industrialization, help to shape the power position of states. Japan and the East Asian 'tigers' have improved their respective standings among states, so much that even the recessions of the 1990s did not seriously disturb those standings, except possibly in the case of Indonesia (Lentner, 1999). Despite the downturn in Japan in the 1990s, its economy remains the second largest in the world. On the other hand, if one takes a longer view, the rise and decline of powers becomes apparent. For example, Britain ranked second in 1937 (Kennedy, 1987: Table 31) but only eighth in 1992 (Maddison, 1995: Table 1–8). Smaller countries undergo similar shifts in position over time, as the case of South Korea illustrates in its rise from a poverty-stricken country following the 1950–3 civil war to its place at the start of the twenty-first century as the world's eleventh largest economy.

Trying to measure power in terms of accumulated assets represents an important endeavor, but power generally needs to be connected to purpose. That is to say, one wants to know what objectives are or can be achieved with which resources. Purposes range from purely selfish acquisition of wealth to satisfy greed to such outrageous aims as 'creating a new man' in the mode of Stalin, Mao Zedong and Pol Pot. Among settled political purposes satisfied by well-formed and well-ordered states are security, identity and welfare. For the satisfaction of these three fundamental values, people have turned for the last several centuries to states to provide them. States make people safe, give them a sense of belonging to a group, and provide them with the means to achieve their own welfare and protect those unable to take advantage of those means.

Thus far, no substitute for the state in the service of these important purposes has been found. Neither firms nor criminals – entities with the wherewithal and access to the means of violence – serve the purpose of providing security to society as a whole; and isolated individuals cannot provide for their own security. Although families offer an important component of identity, they do not connect individuals to larger communities. Nongovernmental organizations offer another dimension of identity for many individuals, but they do not embody for most the emotional attachment or the institutionalization that the state does. Except in the context of broad national societal norms, such as those existing in Japan, firms do not offer the protection of welfare for those who fail, for reasons of health or age, to be in a position to provide for their own sustenance. Firms do not serve the broad welfare purposes of employees; in the economy, workers merely serve as instruments to achieve the purpose of the firm. In contrast, the very existence of modern states is justified by serving the welfare and other needs of its citizens.

CONCLUSION

Despite the prevailing academic discourse about globalization that tends to neglect politics, power as well as government and institutions continue to have immense relevance to the broad international processes occurring in the contemporary world. Although we live in an era of impressive technological, and to some extent social and political, change, evidence for fundamental transformation remains scant; and much of what purports to describe transformative processes relies largely on speculation rather than evidence.

About facts like computer technology, growing direct investment, and the increased speed, volume and novelty of financial transactions, there can hardly be any disagreement. On the other hand, observers can hold very different interpretative positions about the meaning of those facts. This chapter has presented a view that the world we live in shares more continuity than discontinuity with the one that came before. Such a view argues against a postmodern interpretation that finds discontinuity between conditions in the current world and those in the past. In my view, although globalization processes are real, they represent evolutionary change rather than revolutionary transformation.

Considered from the perspective of political science, the processes of integration depend upon existing power arrangements and the spread of liberal states. At the start of the twenty-first century, globalization remains a process rather than an accomplishment or even a project. Whether that process continues depends upon liberals remaining in power in both the leading states and other states joining the dominant coalition in the world, the continued cooperation of the members of that coalition, and the maintenance of the relative power position of that set of countries.

Looking at the competitors of the state in the current situation of the world, none provides any realistic basis for legitimation. Additionally, the problem of controlling violence persists as a fundamental one in achieving a just order. The state provides a solution to that problem while at the same time offering the positive advantages of affording the goods of security, identity and welfare.

A better order than the existing one may not lie outside the realm of imagination, but caution in conceiving it and in working toward it seem entirely to be called for.

NOTES

I am grateful to Philip G. Cerny and Mark Haugaard for useful suggestions to improve this chapter.

1 Democracy was restored to Nigeria in 1999 following Abacha's death.
2 For a comprehensive, brief overview of these efforts, see Group of Thirty (1997: Appendix A).

10 Capitalism as a System of Global Power

Elina Penttinen

Globalization has become a buzzword and affects us all. Some see it as a beneficial process resulting in prosperity all round, while others see it as causing further inequality and marginalization (Bauman, 1998: 1). Globalization is often understood as a process of liberalization of the economy in which states relinquish some of their authority according to free-market principles enforced by multilateral institutions, and in a situation within which new agents such as the International Monetary Fund, the World Bank and multinational corporations determine global politics, following neoliberal principles (Gill, 1997a). Globalization can also be seen as a process which involves further fragmentation and localization of interests, becoming a complex system of simultaneous integration and fragmentation of social systems (Ferguson and Mansbach, 1999).

My argument is that globalization represents a dominant discourse of the global market, which shapes the global order and which produces truth about individuals and their environment. This chapter speculates about how the Foucauldian notion of power can be used in the context of globalization of economy. The analysis consists of looking for elements in the globalization discourse that show how it can be seen as a Foucauldian technology of power, and further how it individualizes and totalizes within that discourse. This discourse of globalization of the economy is thus viewed as an institutional context within which certain subjectifications and objectifications of subjects are produced, constituting a technology of power that defines the truth of individuals and their environment.

The discourse of globalization is seen here as consisting of the discourse of integration and globalization of the market, economic liberalism and neoliberalism. It is argued that liberalism, taking neoliberal form, can be seen as representing a dominant discourse that is universalized, and which is legitimated on the grounds of an efficient and prosperous society generally beneficial for everyone. It is also argued that the neoliberal discourse is often contradictory to liberal principles, in the way that the principles are liberalizing the economy worldwide, while the processes often constrict economic activity.

My hypothesis is that globalization is a phenomenon that is not limited to international political or economic fields of such large and organized actors as states, transnational corporations or multilateral institutions, but is also a phenomenon which touches the individual by the production of global subjectifications. By employing the Foucauldian concept of power (Foucault, 1980a; 1983; 1988), the *problématique* of globalization can be approached from a perspective which lets us see how subjects are produced and how individual self-definitions are constituted within the context of globalized economy. Globalization, in this case, is no longer a process from 'above', but a process that is implemented in the everyday lives of individuals, affecting their sense of identity and self-esteem.

It has to be acknowledged here that Foucault (1983) was more interested in the process of how subjects are produced than in creating a theory of power. He analyses power by the analysis of produced individualizations, involving individualization as a process of becoming a subject, and rejects the stable and immobile notion of individual subjects assumed by liberal concepts of power (Pulkkinen, 1996: 89).[1] Foucault takes the Nietzschean idea of reality being the effect of power and focuses on the operation of power rather than on what power is as such (1996: 103–4). Foucault's theory of power can then be understood as anti-foundational and postmodern. He rejects the methods of modern epistemology, which involve the search for the true (primary) origin of particular phenomena, through which the (secondary) outside is explained. It is inherent that things are in constant motion. Foucault refuses to look for foundations, or to use valorized dichotomies, and rejects the idea that history can be written as a story of progress (1996: 46–8). To Foucault modern science, the valorized concept of truth, and even the concept of man, are effects of power, representing a system of thought and constituting a discursive formation through which individuals are subjectified (Haugaard, 1997a). In this chapter Foucault's concept of power is understood as a means to analyze how subjects are formed by certain discursive formations as in the case of the discourse of globalization.

Foucault (1980a) defines power as a technology which normalizes, produces subjects and becomes visible at the level of the individual body. Foucault's concept of power is a form of positive power, as it is productive and not merely repressive or coercive (Haugaard, 1997a). Foucault's definition of power differs greatly from definitions of power that focus on power over others and which assume clear agency.[2] To Foucault power takes the form of an anonymous network, something which is subordinate to relationships and constitutes them. Foucault's theory of power then differs from a classic scenario of rational actors (usually called A and B) and their relations of power. To Foucault these As and Bs are constructed by historically specific discursive practices, and thus the question is not simply about the relations of agents and their interests, but about how the discursive practices that constitute these subjects are formed (Haugaard, 1997b).

Thus, at the center of Foucault's theory of power is the individual, who is subjectified and objectified as a subject by certain powers constituting the reality and the relations of individuals. Power in Foucauldian terms, then, is not a possession, something which one could have more or less of, but something which exists everywhere in individual actions and normalizing practices. Therefore, power not only consists in the possibility for one to influence the actions of others against their wills, but is produced both by the dominant and by the dominated through identity-constituting discursive practices (Foucault, 1983). It is inherent in Foucault's theory that an individual does not simply reproduce power relations but may also reject and struggle against the way she or he is made into a subject. Individualizations are then never exhaustive or complete, so there is room for resistance against imposed subjectifications and for the development of alternative and plural identities (Ransom, 1997: 48–9).

Power is therefore always exercised in an environment of free will, meaning that individuals are not forced to subject themselves to the technologies of power, but at some level choose to do so. Therefore, there remains always a possibility for counterpower. Although the structure of relationships may be constituted by the dominating discursive formation as in the case of categories such as legal/illegal, sane/insane or sick/healthy, these categorizations can also be resisted. The individual may accept or reject these definitions by submitting to them or by struggling against them. It is actually through resistance that the normalizing practices become visible and can be denaturalized. Power to Foucault is thus a technology which normalizes, defining that which is considered normal and true, objectifying subjects to certain identities and defining their environment (Foucault, 1983; 1988).

It is also central to Foucault that there is no escape or emancipation from power and that power as such cannot be reduced or abolished. Foucault (1988) does talk of liberation from power, yet he does not mean the end of power, but rather the transformation of power relations. This is often misconceived in Foucault's method, since it seems to be pointless to resist power if it will prevail anyway. But it is inherent in Foucault's concept of power that power as such is not negative, and therefore liberation from power is not the objective. Foucault implies that the relations of power can be modified. This does not mean the end of power but its emergence in new forms. Saying that power cannot be escaped can paradoxically be understood as the empowerment of each individual (Ransom, 1997: 57–8). Since both the dominant and the dominated are in the process of producing prevalent power relations, it means that neither group has more or less power. There is power, but it is anonymous and ubiquitous in individual minds and the environment. Therefore, the perceptions that individuals have of themselves and their environment are also those which determine and reproduce the relations of power.

As we approach globalization from a Foucauldian perspective the question concerns how that particular discourse has emerged and been institutionalized. How are subjects produced by it, and what are its limits and legitimations? Global capitalism can be seen then as constituting a dominating discourse that is legitimated by economic liberalism, which is both a totalizing and an individualizing discourse at one and the same time as it extends to all fields of life, and affects the way individuals define the limits of the possible. This system of dominating discourse of the global market can be explained by Stewart Clegg's (1989: 187–239) third circuit of power, which is defined as a deep system of meaning that produces individuals as subjects. Resistance to this deep system of meaning may happen at the level of the second circuit of power through which the system of meaning, which has produced the power relations, could be redefined by individual empowerment (1989: 218–23). This deep system of meaning in the context of globalization is the institutionalized discourse of global capitalism, by which subjectifications are produced. The subjectifications of the global market could thus be contested by a person's becoming individually aware of the system of meaning through which one's subjectivity is constituted.

The principal ideology of the dominating discourse of globalization can be seen as the integration of the global market based on principles of economic liberalism. Globalization involves rivalry among states and transnational firms as principles of liberalism and neoliberal practices are used to shape the globalized system. According to Stephen Gill (1997a) globalization is based on neoliberalism, resulting in the competitive state becoming more and more privatized, moving away from the welfare state structure. This process is produced mainly through preclusive discourse, meaning that the discourse is presented as if there were no alternatives to it. Falk (1997) argues that this is a response to the market forces. Still the 'no alternative' discourse is only a part of the discursive practice for 'marketing' neoliberal globalization. It is also grounded in classical liberalism, drawing on Adam Smith, promising growth and prosperity to all. Conflict between the discourses arises from discrepancy between theory and practice, meaning the difference between the discourse that legitimizes the integration of global market and the practices by which it is actually implemented (Gill, 1995). Growth and prosperity for all turns into growth and prosperity for the privileged few in a system of global capitalism, in which transnational firms aim to maximize their financial gains by the implementation of neoliberal policies.

DOMINATING DISCOURSE OF GLOBALIZATION

Since the end of the Cold War economic liberalism has been seen by many as the dominant discourse to which no real alternatives can, or should, be presented (Richardson, 1997). The world has become a global marketplace, in which market forces are said to determine the policies of states, and in which states need to form their policies taking into account the new trans-national non-territorial actors that have become relevant in the international arena. Although globalization has a long lineage (Gill, 1997b), it can be argued that the current global economy has emerged since the 1970s after which national economies have become subordinate to the transnational corporations and financial institutions (Hirst, 1997a). It seems that the international system has given way to a global system which is determined by a hegemonic discourse of the global market. This type of globalization is 'represented in the OECD countries as inevitable, if not desirable' and 'reflected and reinforced worldwide by the global spread of transnational media corporations, which are often controlled by politically conservative neoliberals' (Gill, 1997b). This discourse is about the organization of the world order according to market discipline, the commodification of the state, and the implementation of neoliberal policies, such as structural adjustment policies, by international financial institutions.

Korten (1996) has argued that the principles of Adam Smith cannot be invoked as the grounds for integration of the global market, since they were aimed at the state-regulated domestic level, having in mind a local market of buyers and sellers. The implementation of *laissez-faire* was to be protected by the state (Gill, 1997b). Therefore these principles cannot, and should not, be employed at the global level, where the financial gains will not be territorially bound or cannot be regulated by governments (Korten, 1996).

Nevertheless it can be argued that the institutionalization of neoliberal globalization is linked with how truths are produced by the discourse of economic liberalism. Smithian principles prescribe the good and efficient society, one which will benefit all individually and globally. These principles are normative in the definition of both individual and environment. The principles of economic liberalism are conveyed in such a way that the individual internalizes them as truth about himself or herself, becoming a subject of globalization discipline. The individualization of Smith is *homo economicus*, the rational individual who acts according to her or his self-interests and seeks financial gains. This rational individual is also assumed to have clear interests and a stable identity. The processes of becoming an individual, therefore, do not comprise an issue in liberal discourse.

The normalizations produced by Smithian liberalism include the notion that 'sustained *economic growth* as measured by Gross National Product is the foundation of human progress and is essential to alleviate poverty and protect [the] environment'. It is also assumed that 'free markets . . . result in the most efficient and socially optimal allocation of resources', and that 'economic globalization – moving toward a single integrated world market . . . spurs competition, increases economic efficiency and growth, and is generally beneficial to everyone', and also that 'localities achieve economic success by abandoning goals of self-sufficiency and aspiring to become *internationally competitive* in providing conditions that attract outside investors' (Korten, 1996: 184). These basic principles describe the received 'truths' about the global economy. These assumptions are based on the concept of the rational individual who is motivated by self-interest and who seeks financial gains. It is also assumed that 'competitive behavior is more rational for the individual and the firm and more beneficial to society than cooperative behavior', and finally that 'human progress is measured by the increases that humans consume, and those who consume the most contribute the most to that progress' (1996: 185).

These elements of liberalism constitute what can be called a grand narrative. Lyotard has argued that Marxism was the last grand narrative, since it included the Faustian dream of progress and the development of the individual (Benhabib, 1990). The above-mentioned tenets of liberalism also tell the story of progress and development; thus, liberalism can also be seen as constituting a grand narrative. This requires that individuals internalize these liberal principles and begin to reproduce them in their actions. Economic liberalism in its classical and theoretical form is a narrative of growth, progress and prosperity. It is based on reductionist argumentation, and accepts modern epistemology as the way to produce universal truths (Pulkkinen, 1996: 48).

An important aspect of liberal doctrine is the freedom to pursue one's economic interest and the freedom to choose (Eccleshall et al., 1994). This freedom results in economic growth and development, and therefore government regulations should be minimized in order that individuals can pursue their interests freely within local markets (Richardson, 1997). At the core of liberal doctrine is the individual, and subjectifications are produced in the following ways: first, the individual is responsible for his or her own wellbeing, since the normal individual acts rationally according to his or her self-interests, meaning financial gains; and second, the one who does act according to these principles will achieve economic prosperity and wellbeing.

Liberal economic doctrine has individualizing and totalizing elements, since it is grounded in individual self-definition and behavior, and it is used to legitimize the integration of the international market into the global market. Liberal doctrine offers the prospect that global capitalism will result in benefits to all who participate and internalize its message, and that the benefits will at least 'trickle down' to Third World countries (Richardson, 1997). Instead of accepting the concepts of the individual and the global market as legitimated universal truths, these can be analyzed as parts of a normative and totalizing discourse that represents Clegg's (1989) deep system of meaning. Thus, the truths conveyed apply only within a specific and progress-oriented discursive field, producing a regime of truth that also provides the possibility for resistance through individual empowerment (Foucault, 1980a).

The contradiction between neoliberal practices and Smithian principles may be seen in that the principles are used not to promote competition, but to protect the rights of multinational firms to achieve monopolies. For example, Caves (1995: 142–3) explains that, in a situation of several companies producing the same product, remaining separate and competing for the market would not be as profitable as banding together and forming a multinational corporation. As mentioned briefly above, Korten (1996: 186) has argued that Smith had in mind a local market of buyers and sellers, and that he presupposed that capital would be located in a particular place. This does not happen in the case of the transnational corporations. The financial gains do not reach the population but go to the transnational firm. In such a system individuals who become subjects of the globalization discourse can best fulfill their function as consumers of the products produced by transnational corporations. The individual, then, becomes objectified in the role of consumer or worker by the neoliberal discourse (Gill, 1995). According to the neoliberal discourse, states should become commodified and marketized in their outlook and give way to the 'market discipline', according to which 'the virtues of prudence, responsibility, good governance, and social progress will arise' (Gill, 1997b).[3] This governance without governments, that is the market discipline, can be seen as 'governmentality' of neoliberal globalization.

GOVERNMENTALITY OF THE GLOBAL MARKET

The concept of governmentality according to Foucault (1991) includes mental and practical levels of governance. Governmentality is a result of mentality and the organization of conduct that composes the 'art of governance'. Foucault explains that state governance has evolved from pastoral power, taking the functions and individualizing practices of the Church and extending them to a form that totalizes governance. The pastoral power of the Church was based on the idea of the good shepherd, who had complete knowledge of the flock, who took care of the flock and watched over each of them individually and collectively. The pastoral power was a form of ultimate kindness in which the good shepherd, through perfect knowledge, could attend to the flock's needs (Foucault, 1988). The difference between pastoral power and the power of the nation-state was that whereas pastoral power was concerned with the salvation of the individual in the next world, state power was concerned with the salvation of the individual in this world. Foucault explains how the nation-state took the tasks previously performed by the Church – including education, hospitals and welfare – and incorporated these within the governance of the state. Then, state governance was effected both at the level of the state and at the level of the individual, aiming at perfect knowledge of each individually and collectively (Foucault, 1983).

What does this continuous governmentality, or power/knowledge relationship, have to do with the governance of the global market? Are there implications of this type of governance for the global or transnational level? What aims and intentions does market force governance represent, and how is knowledge of the individual acquired? Ferguson and Mansbach (1999) argue that in the current globalized system state functions have been reduced and that states are unable to provide security for the individual against 'shocks of globalization'. Not only are states less able to protect their citizens, but they are also eager to remove obstacles to globalization, resulting in a situation in which relations among governments are replaced by reliance on market force governance. In such a situation, individual identities and loyalties shift away from the state as the state's ability to provide welfare and other functions is reduced. Instead, these functions are increasingly assumed by the private sector. Conversely, states attempt to retrieve their authority by creating international organizations, which they in turn control.

According to Gill, the global governance that is shaping the present world order is based on the hegemonic ideology of 'transnational liberalism'. Gill refers to transnational liberalism as 'the economic doctrine and political ideology primarily associated with the most powerful elements of internationally mobile capital' (1990: 23). This ideology of transnational liberalism takes the form of disciplinary neoliberalism linked to economic globalization and the structure of the capitalist state. Disciplinary neoliberalism has become a form of 'new constitutionalism', meaning the development of 'new legal and constitutional practices, linked to the reconstitution of capital (and labour) on a world scale' (Gill, 1995: 1). The contradiction lies at the level of ideology of economic liberalism that stresses private property and the need for a system of an integrated world market, relying on the liberal principles of life, liberty and property (1995: 22).

Gill argues that the structural power of capital shapes the present world order at both macro- and micro-levels, shaping the way in which individuals perceive their options and form their expectations. Finally, the power of capital institutionalizes these patterns of actions so that the 'limits of the possible' are set. Gill stresses the development of the neoliberal state but also the development of the global market as the decisive factors. He argues that, although governments have invested in and been the innovators of the new technologies of surveillance, the capitalist enterprises have also become interested in them in order to maximize their profits and eliminate risks. Gill argues that it has been the governments that have helped the population to conform to these methods of surveillance, for example, by legitimating databases on individuals that are now used by private corporations, credit-rating agencies and other such institutions (Gill, 1995).

Governmentality of global governance is well described in the report *Our Global Neighbourhood* produced by the Commission on Global Governance (1995). Global governance is defined in the report as a form of intergovernmental relationships, including nongovernmental organizations, citizens' movements and multinational corporations (1995: 3). As the central actor of global governance the report sees the UN, which should serve as the principal mechanism by which states and other actors could aim at the 'multilateral management of global affairs' (1995: 6). The report speaks the language of 'global values' and the neighborhood ethics of the 'global village'. The problem arises with defining those who belong to the global village and those who are defined as 'strangers' to it (Baxi, 1996). The report focuses on the global market as the defining factor of the global village, defining the world as a global marketplace and claiming consumerism as the highest form of activity.

Global governance can also be defined as governance without governments, a system that is regulated and governed by market forces lacking central authority. Rosenau (1992: 2) defines governance without governments as a set of functions that are performed in the absence of central authority, explicit organization or institutions. Rosenau argues that in the present system governance without governments exists already, as the world is marked by global interdependencies that have become apparent in the areas of global economy, information technology and environment.

The question then is, how is global governance institutionalized? How is the discourse produced and practiced, and how is it legitimated and subjectified? It is clear that with a concept such as global governance we are dealing with a discourse that extends to both micro- and macro-levels. It is a type of discourse that challenges state authority as a principal actor, challenging both the industrialized countries and the Third World countries. Yet it can be argued that this discourse does not challenge the ideology of the Western countries but brings the ideology to an even more comprehensive level. The dominant actors at the global level are obviously the capitalist states, transnational corporations, financial institutions and multilateral organizations, which reflect and reproduce the dominating discourse of globalization and the accompanying individualizations. The dominating individualization, which is the rational self-interested actor seeking financial gains, is normalized as a universal truth and applied in a global context that also includes other than Western societies. The ensuing problem is that, although governance without governments aims at worldwide development through economic growth and competition, in practice the aims of the major actors are not to increase economic growth in developing countries, but to increase their own profits on a global scale.

An example which reflects the institutionalization of neoliberal governmentality is the intellectual property rights regime. Farrands (1996) argues that intellectual property rights were previously based on territory, but have been detached, and are used more and more by corporations and by international institutions. As a result, the political space of power/knowledge relations changes from the state-centered model to a transnational one. This entails a discursive transformation by which changes in political space are legitimated, allowing some institutions or actors access to knowledge while denying it to others. The mentality of global governance reflects the aims of the dominating agents, shaping the macro-structure so that patenting of ideas becomes possible and interests of transnational corporations are protected against individuals. At the micro-level this means acceptance of a governmentality that means both liberation and restrictions, and subjectification into practices which normalize differences in access to knowledge.

GOVERNMENTALITY OF THE INDIVIDUAL

The discourse of neoliberal globalization constitutes the governmentality of the individual within the global market. Accordingly, the discourse of global capitalism is an individualizing process, which can be seen as producing global subjectifications. To be a subject according to Foucault (1983) can mean either to be subject to someone else by dependence or control, or to be subject to knowledge practices which subjectify or objectify the subject. Subjectification to the global market means, then, subjectification to certain practices that are produced through discourses of economic liberalism and neoliberalism. The grounds for identity and loyalty have previously been the nation-state (Ferguson and Mansbach, 1999), but in the globalized system in which state functions have been reduced and states become privatized, an individual becomes directly subjectified by the global market discipline. This means that an individual begins to define his or her identity according to the implicit normalizations of the global market and to reproduce them in his or her behavior, producing mainly subjects as consumers or objects of consumption.

According to Foucault (1991: 92) government means governance of the individual and family. Governance was first produced at the level of the family in order to function at the level of the state. Governance of the state therefore comprised primarily individual behavior. In the sixteenth century governance meant the government of micro-economy, i.e., the family. Government of the family meant the ordering of things in such a way that the family would prosper as a result of individual behavior. State governance was applied to these micro-economies by the police so that individual behavior was guided according to good governance, taking an individualizing and totalizing form. Governance was understood as 'the right disposition of things, arranged so as to lead to a convenient end' (1991: 93). Things actually meant men in their relations and links to wealth, customs, habits, ways of thinking, acting, etc. Thus governance as the right disposition of things brought together both the totalizing level of ordering the state on the one hand and the individualizing level of guiding each individual to behave in the appropriate manner on the other.

The governance of the global market differs greatly from the governance of the family, or state, as described above. The governmentality of global capitalism is totalizing not in the sense that it actively enforces the policing of families, or in the sense that the prosperity of the individual is the aim of governance, but in the sense that individuals accept the governmentality of global economy and act according to its principles.

GLOBAL CONSUMER SUBJECT

In addition to the type of individualization legitimated by Smithian economic liberalism, governmentality of the global market is produced by the normalization of consumer culture. Zygmunt Bauman (1998) argues that consumer culture has become the defining factor of subjectivities in a globalized world. This consumer society is a system in which the things consumed become secondary to the sensations produced by the act of consumption. The store, the mall, the internet site supersede the product being sold to become the focus of such a culture and to stimulate the process of continuous consumption. In this system consumption is about instant sensations, about desire for desire, being on the move, and aiming for the promised bliss to be experienced in the act of consumption.

Jean Baudrillard (1988) has also analyzed consumer culture, defining consumption as the basis of the social order. He argues that consumer objects should be analyzed into linguistic categories rather than by Marxist or liberal economics, which he sees as different sides of the same coin as both are based on the concept of humanity as labor. Consumer objects should be analyzed instead as a classification system in which a sign is understood as separate from its referents. This composite organization of signs, which are defined as floating signifiers without linguistic referents, constitutes a code that produces individual and group behavior. Baudrillard's (1988) main argument was that referent takes the form of an alibi to the signifier in the same way that use value is an alibi for exchange value in Marxist theory. The signifieds are taken from the social and redeployed as floating signifiers, having no actual referent. Individuals are then bombarded by these signifiers which are self-referential, and which constitute a 'hyper-reality'. The floating signifiers, such as brand names, produce the false message of consumption as the highest form of activity. Problems arise in the contradiction that the word 'consume' deploys. To consume means to devour, to destroy and to use up, but Baudrillard claims that the kind of consumption that is induced by the self-referential signifiers cannot yield satisfaction as would using something up or destroying it. If consumption were only the act of devouring, then the appetite would be satisfied at some point, but consumer objects are represented in such a way that the individual needs to consume more and more without ever being totally satisfied. In order to assert and reassert her or his existence in the world an individual needs to go on consuming, and as in Bauman's description of consumer society, there cannot be any moment of satisfaction or fulfillment, but a continuing search for new sensations.

Consumer society is also linked to the idea of modernity. Levels of development and growth are measured according to consumption. The modern citizen is also defined as a consumer. Yet it can be argued that individualization of consumer subject in the globalized consumer society is about some other instance benefiting from it. Baudrillard (1988: 29–55) has argued that the needs that are produced by the consumer society are created by the system of production and so do not actually exist. According to Baudrillard (1988) a normalization of consumers is imposed by the productive system, which also produces the need for its products, or rather the need for the sensation acquired from consuming the product. Although consumption is represented as an act which brings happiness, pleasure and a sense of self, it is also represented as an obligation, or as a duty, through which existence in consumer society can be maximized.

But not everyone can exist as a consumer. The world is divided into those who consume and those who dream of consumption. Globalization is about the universalization of consumer society as a norm. What is silenced is that the world's wealth and impoverishment stem from the same source (Bauman, 1998). What is forgotten in the praise for economic development and integration of the market is that the normalization of globalization discourse results in further marginalization between the industrial and developing countries, and as described by Gill (1997b) in 'the destruction or restructuring of other civilizational forms'. As a result, indigenous cultures of Third World countries that are not based on consumer culture are undermined and defined by its absence, and are placed in the position of otherness. When they begin to define themselves as consumers in the system of the global market, they are placed in an unequal position in which they do not have the opportunity to consume as the Western world does. They cannot gather sensations or participate in the 'fun system' as do their counterparts in developed countries. This may result in the loss of sense of self and definition of one's identity by one's lack. The marginalized of the global market are also often those who keep the consumer culture running, as the many transnational corporations use women and children of Third World countries as sweatshop labor. The structural adjustment policies that are imposed on these countries then seem to benefit the global giants rather than the developing countries, which are forced to reform their economies in neoliberal terms (Pettman, 1996: 160–8).

An example of this process is well illustrated by the case of Ladakh people in the Himalayas (Nordberg-Hodges, 1996). The Ladakh people were an isolated, self-sufficient group, who perceived themselves as prosperous, and were proud of their own way of life. Two decades ago they were first exposed to tourism and to the ideology of development as defined by the West. Before the Ladakhis were exposed to progress they were content with their subsistence economy, but as they compared themselves with tourists they noticed that they were poor, for they did not have the money to spend as the tourists did. Once the Ladakhis received electricity, they soon also received the media, which brought them more images of what they were not and did not have. The culture presented to them was defined as progress, and the Ladakhis began to define their own culture and knowledge as backward, having no value compared to the Western, global culture. But as they assimilated the Western ideology, their wealth did not increase. On the contrary, they had to accept low-paid jobs, or were often unemployed, resulting not only in their impoverishment, but in the loss of their knowledge and culture.

Consumer society can also be seen as a communicative process in the way in which the subjectifications are currently being produced in the postmodern period, and as being not merely a homogenizing Western discourse based on the universalization of neoliberal practices but a further dimension as well. Ashley (1997) argues that the needs and the objects consumed are given different meanings by consumers themselves. The commodity economy becomes a communicative field of social interaction in which consumption is given new signification by different social groups. In addition to goods, ideologies, cultures and even gender also become objects of consumption. When new marketing strategies are developed, these different social groups are taken into account and specific products can be marketed to specific groups of people. Whether this means liberation from homogenizing mass culture of consumption is still highly arguable. My argument is that this process portrays an even deeper commodification of the individual, as the differences between social groups are specified and commodified in themselves. Although the diversity of individuals is acknowledged, consumption is still portrayed as the primary means to assert existence, and specified difference as diversity itself becomes commodified.

GLOBAL CONSUMER OBJECT

The discourse of global capitalism does not end merely in producing individuals as consumers but also extends to producing individuals as consumer objects. This means that an individual body, or a body part, may become an object of consumption. Thus, the body of a person becomes objectified as a commodity that can be bought and sold in the global market. The dominant discourse of neoliberal globalization is thus inscribed on the body of the individual, taking the form of bio-power.

The ways in which the human body is objectified as a commodity are, for example, sales in body parts, genetic engineering and reproductive technology. These tendencies confirm a discourse of commodification of the body based on 'value free'[4] technology and science. The sales of body parts to the West have become numerous from Third World countries, including everything from blood for transfusion, cells, genes and tissues to organs. An important aspect of these sales in body parts is that many donors, for example in India, receive more money for an organ than they would be paid for a lifetime of work (Kimbrell, 1997). This way the donors may begin to define their bodies as property, which has exchange value, and the body, or its part, becomes a commodity that can be bought and sold in the global market. The human body could then be defined as 'profit-generating property' (Mies, 1993).

If the human body could be defined as private property, that would facilitate the definition of donors as sellers and the receivers as buyers. Arguments have been evinced that individuals should face up to the tendencies of globalization that imply the commodification of the body as a consumer object and acknowledge the benefits produced by it. According to these arguments, the benefits that arise from the definition of the body as property are that the owner of the body has a legal right to the profit made by it, and the misuse of the body parts could be prevented. An example of misuse is the case of John Moore, a leukemia patient whose blood cells were taken without his knowledge and developed by a pharmaceutical company, with the aid of his physician, into a patented MO cell line. Moore had not given his consent and did not receive any profits from this 'involuntary' donation to the pharmaceutical company. If all legal obstacles were removed from defining body as property and the individual as its owner, then individuals could gain from the profits made by the company using and patenting the particular cell or gene (Mies, 1993).

The effects of the global market have also become apparent in the acceptance of patenting genes from human and animal cell lines. Projects such as the Human Genome Diversity Project (HGDP) convey the message of human genes as material for the global market, and thus subjectify humans as patentable objects. According to Kimbrell (1997) the HGDP was developed on the initiative of European and North American scientists in 1990. The aim of the project was to search for genes from the 'endangered' indigenous communities by collection of blood, tissues and hair samples which were then to be transformed and the manipulations patented. The products of this project were to be used by northern transnational pharmaceutical corporations for profit. This would have resulted in a situation in which Third World countries would have needed to buy back what they had originally produced.[5] This project was condemned as immoral and unethical by many leaders of religious and indigenous communities who called it a form of 'genetic slavery' that would have legitimized the reduction of human cell lines and genes into patented objects for sale in the global market for immense profits.

The subjectification of the dominant discourse of globalization can thus be understood as being inscribed on the body of the individual in the process of commodification of body parts and by the discourse of the body as property. It can be concluded from the ideology of the global market that the determining factor of the value of life is the profit generated. Thus, human life and other life forms are reduced to commodities, or commercial material, which can be bought, sold or replaced in the global market. This process is facilitated by the advanced science and technology that are claimed to be value free, but which nevertheless reflect, reproduce and legitimate the discourse and ideology behind globalizing and modernizing processes and the inherent value worlds.

CONCLUSION

The discourse of global capitalism can be understood as a technology of power which is legitimated through the liberal ideology of development, growth and progress. It seduces the individual to give himself or herself up to a definition of consumer subject and object, promising pleasure, happiness, wealth and success. But this discourse is not only about the benefits that result from adhering to the market discipline, but about the obligation to do so. The dominating discourse of the global market is represented as the only alternative, as the modern alternative; and other cultural forms are seen as backward. The way to global efficiency and growth, then, is through subjectifying to the global governance of the market.

The consumer subject is produced by the discourse of consumer society in which consumption of commodities is secondary to the sensations gained from the act of consumption, and from the symbolic value added to the consumer goods. The consumer subjectifications benefit the dominant actors in the power relations produced by the discourse of global capitalism, as continuing consumption is universalized and normalized as a means to assert one's identity. Freedom of choice for individuals in the global market becomes an obligation as the choice itself is no longer a choice (Bauman, 1998). Then the principles of economic liberalism are applied only at the macro-level, and the individual is placed in an object position. The subjectification extends to the objectification of the subject by discourse that legitimizes the commodification of the body.

The role of an individual is crucial to the system of global capitalism, since it is the consumers, workers and savers who reproduce the discourse by subjectifying to it. If these subjectifications were to alter, then the totalizing discourse could also be transformed. It is therefore important to become aware individually of the identity constituting practices of global economy in order to change them. Resistance to this dominating discourse could be effected by a reversal of the discourse, by redefining the subjectification at the subject level. The voice of the subject could be reasserted simultaneously by the discourse and outside the discourse. The incomplete and inadequate nature of the individualizations produced by the global market could be thus highlighted, and opened up for the emergence of competing discourses that define globalization from multiple perspectives. It is then important to ask oneself what kind of powers are involved in constituting one's identity and actions in order to begin to challenge the discourse at the individual level. As a result, the discourse of globalization could be challenged by multiple alternative discourses which coexist and blend with each other, bringing the normalizations produced into focus and potentially leading to a transformation to the dominant system of thought.

NOTES

I am indebted to participants of the RC 36 roundtable meeting, and especially to Mark Haugaard and Howard Lentner for their comments, criticism and help in rewriting this chapter. I am also grateful to the anonymous reviewers for pointing out serious weaknesses. Special thanks to Professor Jyrki Käkönen for his support and the University of Tampere for funding my research. This chapter is based on work done earlier at the University of Turku.

1 According to the liberal concept, power is understood in economic terms. The relations of power can be reduced to the relation of the power between two agents, whose identities are perceived as stable. The language of power is that of actions and intentions; the person who has power can act according to her or his intentions and the one without power has to give up her or his intentions. The liberal notion of power overlooks completely the becoming of an individual and does not give

answers on how the authority relations experienced by individuals work to constitute their identities (Pulkkinen, 1996: 90–1).

2 For a fuller discussion on definitions of power in comparison to Foucault's concept of power see the chapters by Clegg, Goehler, and Haugaard.

3 However, Stephen Gill argues that this neoliberal discourse will not go unchallenged and discusses how many Third World countries and NGOs have begun to resist the dominating discourse.

4 Mies (1993) argues that modern epistemology is a masculinist and colonizing discourse that legitimizes the exploitation of resources on the basis of reductionist argumentation and on binary opposition of the knower and the object of knowledge.

5 See also the case of the Neem tree (Shiva and Holla-Bhar, 1996).

Epilogue

The analyses of power contained in this work are quite unlike modern 'advice books', such as *The 48 Laws of Power* (1998) by Robert Greene and Joost Elffers, or classic handbooks like Machiavelli's *The Prince*. Such guides do not give insight into the position, function, structure and dynamics of power in communities, organizations, states and societies. In fact, they provide neither a sociology of power nor a coherent theory about power.

The book you have just read is different, for it offers a state of the art overview of social scientific research on power. Still, there is not a complete and satisfactory theory of power, although the authors of the chapters of this work have contributed to theory construction and have demonstrated an intellectual shift in developing novel theoretical notions about power. Furthermore, they have noted new global conditions that lead to rethinking power as a key concept in the social sciences.

An epilogue provides the opportunity to reflect upon the issues of this book, particularly to link some conclusions and trends to an ongoing research program. Based upon earlier work by the International Political Science Association (IPSA) Research Committee on Political Power, attention is focused upon certain trends discussed in the last 10 years. Moreover, potential future developments of the main themes advanced are outlined by our authors.

The activities of the IPSA Research Committee on Political Power reflect changes in the literature on power. Following the 'classical discussion' on power by Hunter, Dahl, Mills, Bachrach and Baratz, and Lukes – referred to by several authors in this book – research on power a decade ago focused primarily on actors. Those studying power posed such questions as the following: Who are the relevant actors in power relations? How do those actors themselves perceive their power and that of competing actors? In policy research, attention shifted in the 1980s from 'who governs?' to 'how to govern?' while, in social and political theory, Foucault's work became influential.

As this book has explained, power analysis reflects a deep shift in social theory (Part I). Understanding the dynamics of power in different practices, particularly in multilevel governance, requires knowledge of the exercise of power, structural power and systemic power (Part II). The analysis of contemporary power in the international system, which often functions as a context for individuals, organizations, networks of private and public actors, and states, has produced a great variety of continuities and discontinuities (Part III). When reflecting on these three parts it is important to bear in mind that 'theories, practices and globalizations' are not separate 'dimensions' or 'faces' of power but, rather, form an integral whole.

What type of research agenda on power can be deduced from current developments in the field of political and social power analysis? In attempting to answer such a question one of the main issues which we have to deal with concerns the question of paradigm shifts. If it is the case that the discourse of power has been radically changed since Lukes's *Power* (1974), is such a change likely again? It is difficult to answer this definitively because, as Thomas Kuhn argued, paradigm shifts are, by their very nature, unpredictable. However, Kuhn's work also tells us that paradigm shifts are likely if a theory has run into conceptual difficulty and if there are new data. If we look back to 1974, and the changes since then, both these elements were present. Lukes's concept of three-dimensional power was in severe conceptual difficulty. The whole idea of 'false consciousness' was theoretically indefensible within the tradition of remaining open to falsification that characterizes good scientific practice. On the empirical side, the events of 1989 fundamentally changed the global order. Consequently, between conceptual problems of the third dimension of power and a radical change in the world of politics, the conditions were ripe for a paradigm shift. If we look at the position now there are both similarities and differences to circumstances then. On a theoretical level there is no theoretical impasse. In fact, power analysts are still trying to come to grips with the implications of the new paradigm. On the other hand, however, empirical events are changing rapidly: we do not know if the nation-state will survive, if there will be global governance, if neoliberalism can remain a dominant discourse or if the future lies in the direction of American hegemony. In short, on a theoretical level a new paradigm shift appears unlikely but, on the other hand, it may be the case that events in the 'world out there' will render our present conceptual tools inadequate.

However, for the moment, these events have not occurred. As a consequence, we, the editors of this book (and also the members of the IPSA Research Committee on Political Power), would like to invite you, our readers, to help us work out the full implications of the present paradigm.

References

Aarts, Kees (1991) 'Collectieve actie: een overzicht van recentelijke Nederlandse literatuur', *Acta Politica*, (3): 327–55.

Albrow, Martin (1996) *The Global Age: State and Society Beyond Modernity*. Cambridge: Polity.

Aldrich, Howard E. (1979) *Organizations and Environments*. Englewood Cliffs, NJ: Prentice-Hall.

Allen, Amy (1999) *The Power of Feminist Theory: Domination, Resistance, Solidarity*. Boulder: Westview.

Alvesson, Mats (1996) *Communication, Power and Organization*. Berlin: de Gruyter.

Aman, Alfred C. Jr (1999) 'Administrative law for a new century', in Aseem Prakash and Jeffrey A. Hart (eds), *Globalization and Governance*. London: Routledge. pp. 263–84.

Andersen, Martin-Arne and Lauritsen, Jan-Ståle (1990) *Organisasjonsarkivet*. Rapport 86. Tromsø: Norsk sammfunnsvitenskapelig datatjeneste.

Anderson, Perry (1983) *In the Tracks of Historical Materialism*. London: Verso.

Anderson, Perry (1985) *Western Marxism*. London: New Left.

Arendt, Hannah (1958) *The Human Condition*. Chicago: University of Chicago Press.

Arendt, Hannah (1970) *On Violence*. London: Allen Lane, Penguin. New York: Harcourt, Brace & World.

Arts, Bas (1998) *The Political Influence of Global NGOs: Case Studies on the Climate and Biodiversity Conventions*. Utrecht: International Books.

Arts, Bas and van Roozendaal, Gerda (eds) (1999) *The Influence of NGOs on International and Transnational Politics*. Nijmegen: Nijmegen University Press.

Arts, Bas and Verschuren, Piet (1999) 'Assessing political influence in complex decision-making: an instrument based on triangulation', *International Political Science Review*, 20 (4): 411–24.

Ashley, David (1997) *History without a Subject: the Postmodern Condition*. Boulder, CO: Westview.

Axford, Barrie (1995) *The Global System: Economics, Politics and Culture*. New York: St Martin's.

Baakman, Nikolaas (1993) 'De Socio-genese van beleidsinstrumenten', in J. Hans, Th.A. Bressers (eds), *Beleidsinstrumenten bestuurskundig beschouwd*. Den Haag: VUGA. pp. 173–89.

Bacevich, Andrew J. (1999) 'Policing utopia: the military imperatives of globalization', *The National Interest*, 56 (Summer): 5–13.

Bachrach, Peter and Baratz, Morton S. (1962) 'Two faces of power', *American Political Science Review*, 56: 947–52.

Bachrach, Peter and Baratz, Morton S. (1963) 'Decisions and nondecisions: an analytical framework', *American Political Review* 57: pp. 632–42.

Ball, Terence (1988) 'The changing face of power,' in Terence Ball (ed.), *Transforming Political Discourse*. Oxford: Basil Blackwell. pp. 80–105.

Banfield, Edward C. (1961) *Political Influence*. New York: Free Press.

Barbalet, Jack M. (1985) 'Power and resistance', *British Journal of Sociology*, XXXVI (1): 521–48.

Barbalet, Jack M. (1987) 'Power, structural resources and agency', *Perspectives in Social Theory*, 8: 1–24.

Barnes, Barry (1988) *The Nature of Power*. Cambridge: Polity.

Barry, Brian (1991) *Democracy and Power*. Oxford: Clarendon.

Baudrillard, Jean (1988) *Selected Writings*, ed. Mark Poster. Palo Alto, CA: Stanford University Press.

Bauman Zygmunt (1988) *Legislators and Interpreters*. Cambridge: Polity.

Bauman, Zygmunt (1989) 'Hermeneutics and modern social theory', in D. Held and J.B. Thompson (eds), *Social Theory of Modern Societies: Anthony Giddens and His Critics*. Cambridge: Cambridge University Press.

Bauman, Zygmunt (1991) *Modernity and Ambivalence*. Cambridge: Polity.

Bauman, Zygmunt (1998) *Globalization: the Human Consequences*. Cambridge: Polity.

Baxi, Upendra (1996) 'Review essay, "global neighbourhood" and the "universal otherhood": notes on the Report of the Commission on Global Governance', *Alternatives*, 21 (4): 525–49.

Beck, Ulrich (1992) *Risk Society: Towards a New Modernity*. London: Sage.

Beck, Ulrich (1994) 'The reinvention of politics: towards a theory of reflexive modernization', in U. Beck, A. Giddens and S. Lash (eds), *Reflexive Modernization: Politics, Tradition and Aesthetics in the Modern Social Order*. Oxford: Polity.

Beck, Ulrich (1996a) 'Risk society and the provident state', in S. Lash, B. Szerszynski and B. Wynne (eds), *Risk, Environment and Modernity: Towards a New Ecology*. London: Sage. pp. 27–43.

Beck, Ulrich (1996b) 'World risk society as cosmopolitan society? Ecological questions in a framework of manufactured uncertainties', *Theory, Culture and Society*, 13 (4): 1–32.

Beck, Ulrich (1998) 'Politics of risk society', in J. Franklin (ed.), *The Politics of Risk Society*. Cambridge, Oxford: Polity.

Beetham, David (1991) *The Legitimation of Power*. London: Macmillan.

Bell, Roderick, Edwards, David V. and Wagner, R. Harrison (eds) (1969) *Political Power: a Reader in Theory and Research*. New York: Free Press.

Benhabib, Seyla (1990) 'Epistemologies of postmodernism: a rejoinder to Jean-François Lyotard', in Linda J. Nicholson (ed.), *Feminism/Postmodernism*. New York: Routledge. pp. 107–30.

Benson, J. Kenneth (1975) 'The interorganizational network as a political economy', *Administrative Science Quarterly*, 20: 229–49.

Bentley, Arthur F. (1908) *The Process of Government: a Study of Social Pressures*. Chicago: University of Chicago Press.

Berger, Peter L. and Luckmann, Thomas (1966) *The Social Construction of Reality*. New York: Doubleday.

Berndtson, Erkki (1985) 'The party system and the future of the state in advanced capitalist countries', *International Political Science Review*, 6 (1): 65–80.

Biersteker, Thomas J. (1993) 'Constructing historical counterfactuals to assess the consequences of international regimes: the global debt regime and the course of the debt crisis of the 1980s', in Volker Rittberger (ed.), *Regime Theory and International Relations*. Oxford: Clarendon. pp. 315–38.

Birnbaum, Norman (1977) 'On the possibility of a new politics in the West,' in Norman Birnbaum (ed.), *Beyond the Crisis*. New York: Oxford University Press. pp. 199–232.

Blau, Peter M. (1964) *Exchange and Power in Social Life*. New York: Wiley.

Bodansky, David (1993) 'The United Nations Framework Convention on Climate Change: a commentary', *Yale Journal of International Law*, 18: 453–559.

Bos, J. and Geurts, P.A.Th.M. (1994) 'Procesmethode', in L.W.J.C. Huberts and J. Kleinnijenhuis (eds), *Methoden van invloedsanalyse*. Amsterdam/Meppel: Boom. pp. 61–82.

Boschi, Renato (1997) 'The corporatist heritage and new patterns of interest representation in Brazil'. Paper presented at the XVIIth IPSA World Congress, Seoul, 17–21 August.

Boulding, Kenneth E. (1989) *Three Faces of Power*. Newbury Park, CA: Sage.

Bourdieu, Pierre (1979) 'Symbolic power', *Critique of Anthropology*, 4: 77–85.

Bourdieu, Pierre (1985) *Sozialer Raum und 'Klassen'*. Frankfurt am Main: Suhrkamp. pp. 7–46.

Bourdieu, Pierre (1986) 'The forms of capital', in John G. Richardson (ed.), *Handbook of Theory and Research for the Sociology of Education*. Westport, CT: Greenwood.

Bourdieu, Pierre (1989) 'Social space and symbolic power', *Sociological Theory*, 7: 14–25.

Bourdieu, Pierre (1990) *The Logic of Practice*. Cambridge: Polity.

Braam, Gerard P.A. (1973) *Invloed van bedrijven op de overheid: Een empirische studie over de verdeling van maatschappelijke invloed*. Meppel: Boom.

Braudel, Fernand, Aymard, Maurice, Dupaquier, Jacques, Gourou, Pierre and Pallottino, Massimo (1992) *Eurooppa*. Tampere: Vastapaino.

Braverman, Harry (1974) *Labor and Monopoly Capital: the Degradation of Work in the Twentieth Century*. New York: Monthly Review.

Bull, Hedley (1977) *The Anarchical Society*. London: Macmillan.

Burawoy, Michael (1979) *Manufacturing Consent: Changes in the Labor Process under Capitalism*. Chicago: University of Chicago Press.

Burchell, Graeme, Gordon, Colin and Miller, Peter (eds) (1991) *The Foucault Effect*. London: Harvester Wheatsheaf.

Burke, Tim (1982) 'Friends of the Earth and the conservation of resources', in Peter Willets (ed.), *Pressure Groups in the Global System*. London: Pinter. pp. 105–24.

Butler, Judith (1990) *Gender Trouble: Feminism and the Subversion of Identity*. London: Routledge.

Caldwell, Lynton K. (1990) *International Environmental Policy: Emergence and Dimensions*. Durham, NC: Duke University Press.

Callon, Michel (1980) 'Struggles and negotiations to define what is problematic and what is not: the socio-logic of translation', in Karen D. Knorr-Cettina, R. Krohn and Richard D. Whitley (eds), *The Social Processes of Scientific Investigation: Sociology of the Sciences Yearbook*, (vol. 4). Dordrecht: Reidel. pp. 197–219.

Callon, Michel (1986) 'Some elements of a sociology of translation: domestication of the scallops and the fishermen of St Briene Bay', in J. Law (ed.), *Power, Action and Belief: a New Sociology of Knowledge?* Sociological Review Monograph 32. London: Routledge and Kegan Paul.

Callon, Michel and Latour, Bruno (1981) 'Unscrewing the big leviathan: how actors macrostructure reality and sociologists help them to do so', in Karen D. Knorr-Cettina and Aaron Cicourel (eds), *Advances in Social Theory and Methodology: Towards an Integration of Micro- and Macro-Sociologies*. London: Routledge and Kegan Paul. pp. 227–303.

Callon, Michel and Law, John (1982) 'On interests and their transformation', *Social Studies of Science*, 1: 615–25.

Callon, Michel, Courtial, Jean P., Turner, William A. and Bauin, S. (1983) 'From translations to problematic networks: an introduction to co-word analysis', *Social Science Information*, 22: 199–235.

Callon, Michel, Law, John and Rip, Arie (eds) (1986) *Mapping out the Dynamics of Science and Technology: Sociology of Science in the Real World*. London: Macmillan.

Cassirer, Ernst (1923–9) *Philosophie der symbolischen Formen*, 3 vols, 2nd edn. Darmstadt: Wissenschaftliche Buchgesellschaft.

Castells, Manuel (1996) *The Information Age: Economy, Society and Culture. Volume I: The Network Society*. Malden, MA: Blackwell.

Castells, Manuel (1997) *The Information Age: Economy, Society and Culture. Volume II: Power and Identity.* Malden, MA: Blackwell.

Castells, Manuel (1998) *The Information Age: Economy, Society and Culture, Volume III: The End of Millennium.* Oxford: Blackwell.

Caves, Richard E. (1995) 'The multinational enterprise as an economic organization', in Jeffry A. Frieden and David A. Lake (eds), *International Political Economy: Perspectives on Global Power and Wealth.* 3rd ed. New York: St Martin's Press.

Cerny, Philip G. (1990) *The Changing Architecture of Politics: Structure, Agency and the Future of the State.* London: Sage.

Cerny, Philip G. (1993) 'Plurilateralism: structural differentiation and functional conflict in the post-Cold War world order', *Millennium: Journal of International Studies,* 22 (1): 27–51.

Cerny, Philip G. (1995) 'Globalization and the changing logic of collective action', *International Organization,* 49 (4): 595–625.

Cerny, Philip G. (1997) 'Paradoxes of the competition state: the dynamics of political globalization', *Government and Opposition,* 32 (2): 251–74.

Cerny, Philip G. (1998) 'Neomedievalism, civil wars and the new security dilemma: globalization as durable disorder', *Civil Wars,* 1 (1): 36–64.

Cerny, Philip G. (1999a) 'Globalization, governance and complexity', in A. Prakash and J.A. Hart (eds), *Globalization and Governance.* London: Routledge, pp. 184–208.

Cerny, Philip G. (1999b) 'Globalization and the erosion of democracy', *European Journal of Political Research,* 36 (1): 1–26.

Cerny, Philip G. (1999c) 'Reconstructing the political in a globalizing world: states, actors, institutions and governance', in Frans Buelens (ed.), *Globalization and the Nation-State.* Cheltenham: Edward Elgar for the Belgian-Dutch Association for Institutional and Political Economy.

Cerny, Philip G. (2000a) 'Embedding global financial markets: securitization and the emerging web of governance', in K. Ronit and V. Schneider (eds), *Private Organizations, Governance and Global Politics.* London: Routledge.

Cerny, Philip G. (2000b) 'The new security dilemma: divisibility, defection and disorder', *Review of International Studies,* 26: 4.

Cerny, Philip G. and Evans, M. (1999) 'New Labour, globalization and the competition state'. Center for European Studies, Harvard University, Working Paper Series #70.

Chandler, Alfred D. Jr (1992) *Scale and Scope: the Dynamics of Industrial Capitalism.* Cambridge, MA: Harvard University Press.

Christensen, Tom and Egeberg, Morten (1979) 'Organized group–government relations in Norway', *Scandinavian Political Studies,* 2: 239–59.

Christiansen, Peter Munk and Rommetvedt, Hilmar (1999) 'From corporatism to lobbyism? Parliaments, executives, and organized interests in Denmark and Norway', *Scandinavian Political Studies,* 22: 195–220.

Clegg, Stewart R. (1989) *Frameworks of Power.* London: Sage.

Clegg, Stewart R. (1994) 'Power and the resistant subject', in John Jermier, Walter Nord and David Knights (eds), *Resistance and Power in Organizations: Agency, Subjectivity and the Labour Process.* London: Routledge.

Clegg, Stewart R. and Rura-Polley, T. (1998) '"Pfeffer and Salancik", in M. Warner (ed.), *The IEBM Handbook of Management Thinking'.* London: International Thomson Business Press. pp. 537–43.

Climate Action Network (1992) *No Joint Implementation and Emissions Trading.* Geneva.

Climate Action Network (1994) *Joint Implementation from a European NGO Perspective.* Brussels.

Cohen, Ira (1989) *Structuration Theory: Anthony Giddens and the Constitution of Social Life,* London: Macmillan.

Cohen, Margot and Sigli (1998) 'Deport and deter: Indonesian illegal workers get a harsh send-off from Malaysia,' *Far Eastern Economic Review, Interactive Edition E-Newsletter Version 1.1*, 161 (17), 23 April.

Collinson, David (1994) 'Strategies of resistance: power, knowledge and subjectivity in the workplace', in John Jermier, Walter Nord and David Knights (eds), *Resistance and Power in Organizations: Agency, Subjectivity and the Labour Process*. London: Routledge.

Commission on Global Governance (1995) *Our Global Neighbourhood*. Oxford: Oxford University Press.

Cooke, Maeve (1994) *Language and Reason: a Study of Habermas' Pragmatics*. Cambridge, MA: MIT Press.

Cox, Robert and Jacobson, Harold Karan (eds) (1973) *The Anatomy of Influence*. New Haven, CT: Yale University Press.

Crepaz, M.M.L. (1994) 'From semisovereignty to sovereignty: the decline of corporatism and rise of Parliament in Austria', *Comparative Politics*, 27: 45–65.

Crozier, Michel (1963) *The Bureaucratic Phenomenon*. London: Tavistock.

Crozier, Michel and Friedberg, Erhard (1977) *L'Acteur et le système: les contraintes de l'action collective*. Paris: Editions du Seuil.

Cutler, A. Claire (1995) 'Global capitalism and liberal myths: dispute settlement in private international trade relations', *Millennium: Journal of International Studies*, 24 (3): 377–97.

Dahl, Robert A. (1957) 'The concept of power', *Behavioral Science*, 2: 201–15.

Dahl, Robert A. (1961) *Who Governs? Democracy and Power in an American City*. New Haven, CT: Yale University Press.

Dahl, Robert A. (1968) 'Power', in David L. Sills (ed.), *International Encyclopedia of the Social Sciences, Vol. 12*. New York: Macmillan.

Dahl, Robert A. (1989) *Democracy and Its Critics*. New Haven, CT: Yale University Press.

Dahl, Robert A. (1993) 'Americans struggle to cope with a new political order that works in opaque and mysterious ways', *Public Affairs Report* (Institute of Governmental Studies, University of California Press), 34 (5): 1, 4–6.

Damgaard, Erik (1994) 'The strong parliaments of Scandinavia', in Gary W. Copeland and Samuel C. Patterson (eds), *Parliaments in the Modern World*. Ann Arbor: Michigan.

De Jong, Mart-Jan (1997) *Grootmeesters van de sociologie*. Amsterdam: Boom.

Dinan, Desmond (1999) *Ever Closer Union: an Introduction to European Integration*, 2nd edn. London: Macmillan.

Douglas, Ian R. (1999) 'Globalization as governance: toward an archaeology of contemporary political reason', in Aseem Prakash and Jeffrey A. Hart (eds), *Globalization and Governance*. London: Routledge, pp. 134–60.

Dowding, Keith (1991) *Rational Choice and Political Power*. Aldershot: Edward Elgar.

Dowding, Keith (1996) *Power*. Buckingham: Open University Press.

Dowding, Keith and Dunleavy, Patrick (1995) 'Rational choice and community power structures', *Political Studies*, XLIII: 265–77.

Eccleshall, Robert, Geoghegan, Vincent, Jay, Richard, Kenny, Michael, MacKenzie, Ian and Wilford, Rick (1994) *Political Ideologies: an Introduction*. London: Routledge.

Eco (1993) *NGO Journal 'Eco': a Special Joint Implementation Insert*. INC8, Geneva, August.

Edelman, Murray (1964) *The Symbolic Uses of Politics*. Urbana, IL: University of Illinois Press.

Edelman, Murray (1971) *Politics as Symbolic Action: Mass Arousal and Quiescence*. Chicago: Markham.

Egeberg, Morten (1981) *Stat og organisasjoner*. Bergen: Universitetsforlaget.
Egeberg, Morten, Olsen, Johan P. and Saetren, Harald (1978) 'Organisasjonssamfunnet og den segmenterte stat', in Johan P. Olsen (ed.), *Politisk organisering*. Bergen: Universitetsforlaget. pp. 115–42.
Elias, Norbert (1969) *Über den Prozess der Zivilisation: Soziogenetische und Psychogenetische Untersuchungen*, vols I and II. Bern: Francke.
Elias, Norbert (1971) *Wat is Sociologie?* Utrecht, Antwerpen: Het Spectrum.
Elias, Norbert (1987) 'Wandlungen der Wir-Ich-Balance', in Norbert Elias (ed.), *Die Gesellschaft der Individuen*. Frankfurt am Main: Suhrkamp. pp. 207–315.
Elias, Norbert (1994) *The Civilizing Process: The History of Manners and State Formation and Civilization*. Oxford: Blackwell.
Elias, Norbert and Scotson, John L. (1965) *The Established and the Outsiders: A Sociological Enquiry into Community Problems*. London: Frank Cass.
Ellwood, David, van Elteren, Mel, Gidley, Mick, Kroes, Rob, Nye David E., and Rydell, Bob (1994) 'Questions of cultural exchange: the NIAS statement on the European reception of American mass culture', *American Studies International* 32 (2): 32–44.
Emmerson, Donald K. (1998) 'Americanizing Asia?', *Foreign Affairs*, 77 (3): 46–56.
Espeli, Harald (1998) *Lobbyvirksomhet på Stortinget*. Oslo: Tano Aschehoug.
Everdell, William R. (1997) *The First Moderns: Profiles in the Origins of Twentieth-Century Thought*. Chicago: University of Chicago Press.
Everts, Philip P. (1985) *Controversies at Home: Domestic Factors in the Foreign Policy of the Netherlands*. Dordrecht: Martinus Nijhoff.
Falk, Richard (1997) 'The critical realist tradition and the demystification of interstate power', in Stephen Gill and James H. Mittelman (eds), *Innovation and Transformation in International Studies*. Cambridge: Cambridge University Press.
Farrands, Chris (1996) 'The globalization of knowledge and the politics of global intellectual property: power, governance and technology', in Eleanore Kofman and Gillian Youngs (eds), *Globalization: Theory and Practice*. London: Cassell. pp. 175–87.
Farsund, Arild Aurvåg (1997) 'Den globale utfordring: CO$_2$ målsettingen og klimapolitikken', in Jan Erling Klausen and Hilmar Rommetvedt (eds), *Miljøpolitikk: Organisasjonene, Stortinget og forvaltningen*. Oslo: Tano Aschehoug. pp. 74–93.
Framework Convention on Climate Change (FCCC) (1995) *Conclusion of Outstanding Issues and Adoption of Decisions: Activities Implemented Jointly under the Pilot Phase* FCCC/CP/1995/L.13, 6 April.
Feld, Werner J. and Jordan, Robert S. (1983) *International Organizations: a Comparative Approach*. New York: Praeger.
Feldstein, Martin (1998) 'Refocusing the IMF,' *Foreign Affairs*, 77 (2): 20–33.
Ferguson, Yale H. and Mansbach, Richard W. (1999) 'Global politics at the turn of the millennium: changing bases of "us" and "them"', in Davis Bobrow (ed.), Special Issue of *International Studies Review* 1 (2): pp. 77–107.
Flyvberg, Bent (1998) *Rationality and Power: Democracy in Practice*. Chicago: Chicago University Press.
Foucault, Michel (1977) *Discipline and Punish: the Birth of the Prison*. Harmondsworth: Penguin.
Foucault, Michel (1978) *The History of Sexuality. Volume 1: An Introduction*. Harmondsworth: Penguin.
Foucault, Michel (1980a) 'Body power', in Colin Gordon (ed.), *Power/Knowledge: Selected Interviews and Other Writings 1972–1977*. New York: Harvester.
Foucault, Michel (1980b) *Power/Knowledge: Selected Interviews and Other Writings 1972–1977*, ed. C. Gordon. Brighton: Harvester.
Foucault, Michel (1983) 'Afterword: the subject and power', in Hubert L. Dreyfus

and Paul Rabinow (eds), *Michel Foucault: Beyond Structuralism and Hermeneutics.* Chicago: University of Chicago Press. pp. 208–25.

Foucault, Michel (1986) *The History of Sexuality. Volume 2: The Use of Pleasure.* Harmondsworth: Penguin.

Foucault, Michel (1988) 'On power', in Lawrence D. Kritzman (ed.), *Michel Foucault: Politics, Philosophy, Culture, Interviews and Other Writings 1977–1984.* New York: Routledge. pp. 96–109.

Foucault, Michel (1990) *The History of Sexuality. Volume 3: The Care of the Self.* Harmondsworth: Penguin.

Foucault, Michel (1991) *The Foucault Effect: Studies in Governmentality,* eds Graham Burchell, Colin Gordon and Peter Miller. Exeter: Wheatons.

Friedman, Thomas L. (1999) 'A manifesto for the fast world. From supercharged financial markets to Osama bin Laden, the emerging global order demands an enforcer. That's America's new burden', *The New York Times Magazine,* 28 March.

Friman, H. Richard and Andreas, Peter (eds) (1999) *The Illicit Global Economy and State Power.* Lanham, MD: Rowman and Littlefield.

Frouws, Jaap (1994) 'Mest en Macht: Een politiek-sociologische studie naar belangenbehartiging en beleidsvorming inzake de mestproblematiek in Nederland vanaf 1970'. Dissertation, WAU, Wageningen.

Frouws, Jaap and van Tatenhove, Jan (1993) 'Agriculture, environment and the state: the development of agro-environmental policy-making in the Netherlands', *Sociologia Ruralis,* 2: 220–39.

G77 and China (1995) *Position on Proposals from the Co-chairs of Working Group I. Matters relating to Commitments. Criteria for Joint Implementation. Draft Decision of the Committee,* 15 February.

Gaddis, John Lewis (1997) *We Now Know: Rethinking Cold War History.* New York: Oxford University Press.

Garfinkel, Harold (1984) *Studies in Ethnomethodology.* Cambridge: Polity.

Gaventa, John (1980) *Power and Powerlessness: Quiescence and Rebellion in an Appalachian Valley.* Urbana, IL: University of Illinois Press.

Geras, Norman (1987) 'Post-Marxism?', *New Left Review,* 163: 40–82.

Geras, Norman (1988) 'Post-Marxism: a rejoinder', *New Left Review,* 169: 34–62.

Gibbins, John R. and Reimer, Bo (1999) *The Politics of Post-Modernity: an Introduction to Contemporary Politics and Culture.* London: Sage.

Giddens, Anthony (1968) '"Power" in the recent writings of Talcott Parsons', *Sociology,* 2: 257–72.

Giddens, Anthony (1979) *Central Problems in Social Theory: Action, Structure and Contradiction in Social Analysis.* London: Macmillan.

Giddens, Anthony (1981) *A Contemporary Critique of Historical Materialism. Volume 1: Power, Property and the State.* London: Macmillan.

Giddens, Anthony (1984) *The Constitution of Society: Outline of the Theory of Structuration.* Cambridge: Polity.

Giddens, Anthony (1985) *The Nation-State and Violence.* Cambridge: Polity.

Giddens, Anthony (1991) *The Consequences of Modernity.* Cambridge: Polity.

Gill, Stephen (1990) *American Hegemony and the Trilateral Commission.* Cambridge: Cambridge University Press.

Gill, Stephen (1995) 'The global panopticon? The neoliberal state, economic life, and democratic surveillance', *Alternatives,* 2 (1): 1–49.

Gill, Stephen (1997a) 'Transformation and innovation in the study of world order', Stephen Gill and James H. Mittelman (eds), *Innovation and Transformation in International Studies.* Cambridge: Cambridge University Press. pp. 5–24.

Gill, Stephen (1997b) 'Globalization, democratization and indifference', in James H. Mittelman (ed.), *Globalization: Critical Reflections.* Boulder, CO: Lynne Rienner. pp. 205–28.

Godfroij, Arnold (1989) 'Netwerken van Organisaties', in P. van de Bunt and K.J. Nijkerk (eds), *Handboek Organisaties*. Alphen aan den Rijn.

Goehler, Gerhard (1997) *Institution – Macht – Repräsentation: Wofür politische Institutionen stehen und wie sie wirken*. Baden-Baden: Nomos.

Goehler, Gerhard (1998) 'Rationalität und Symbolizität der Politik', in M. Th. Greven and R. Schmalz-Bruns (eds), *Politische Theorie – heute*. Baden-Baden: Nomos. pp. 255–74.

Goehler, Gerhard and Speth, Rudolf (1998) 'Symbolische Macht: Zur institutionen-theoretischen Bedeutung von Pierre Bourdieu', in R. Blänkner and B. Jussen (eds), *Institutionen und Ereignis*. Göttingen: Vandenhoeck and Ruprecht. pp. 17–48.

Goffman, Erving (1961) *The Presentation of Self in Everyday Life*. Harmondsworth: Penguin.

Goldthorpe, John H., Lockwood, David, Bechofer, Frank, and Platt, Jennifer (1969) *The Affluent Worker in the Class Structure*. Cambridge: Cambridge University Press.

Gomez, Edmund Terence and Jomo, K.S. (1997) *Malaysia's Political Economy: Politics, Patronage and Profits*. Cambridge: Cambridge University Press.

Goudsblom, Johan (1974) 'Norbert Elias', in Leonardus Rademaker and Errit Petersma (eds), *Hoofdfiguren uit de sociologie. Deel 2: de Modernen*. Utrecht: Het Spectrum. pp. 94–109.

Goverde, Henri (1987) *Macht over de Markerruimte*. Nijmegen: Geografisch en Planologisch Instituut.

Goverde, Henri, Wisserhof, Johan, Dijkstra, Erik and Tilmans, Raymond (1997) *Bestuurlijke evaluatie Strategische Groenprojecten Natuurontwikkeling*. IBN-rapport 269, Wageningen, IBN-DLO.

Gramsci, Antonio (1971) *Selections from the Prison Notebooks*. London: Lawrence and Wishart.

Greco, M. (1993) 'Psychosomatic subjects and "the duty to be well": personal agency within medical rationality', *Economy and Society*, 22 (3): 357–72.

Greene, Robert and Elffers, Joost (1998) *The 48 Laws of Power*. New York: Viking.

Greenspan, Alan (1998) 'On Asian financial crisis: a testimony before the Sub-committee on Foreign Operations of the Committee on Appropriations'. US Senate, 3 March.

Group of Thirty (1997) *Global Institutions, National Supervision and Systemic Risk: A Study Group Report*. Washington, DC: Group of Thirty.

Gundelach, Peter (1982) 'Grass-roots organizations, societal control and dissolution of norms', *Acta Sociologica*, 25: 57–65.

Guzzini, Stefano (1993) 'Structural power: the limits of neo-realist power analysis', *International Organization*, 7 (3): 443–78.

Habermas, Jürgen (1976) 'Hannah Arendts Begriff der Macht', in Jürgen Habermas, *Politisch-philosophische Profile*. Frankfurt am Main: Suhrkamp. pp. 228–48. English translation: 'Hannah Arendt: on the concept of power', in *Philosophical-Political Profiles*, 1983. Cambridge, MA: MIT Press. pp. 168–89.

Habermas, Jürgen (1977) 'Hannah Arendt's communications concept of power', *Social Research*, 44: 2–24.

Habermas, Jürgen (1979) *Communication and the Evolution of Society*. London: Heinemann.

Habermas, Jürgen (1981) *Theorie des kommunikativen Handelns*. Frankfurt am Main: Suhrkamp. English translation *The Theory of Communicative Action*, 2 vols, 1984 and 1987. Cambridge: Polity.

Habermas, Jürgen (1992) *Faktizität und Geltung*. Frankfurt am Main: Suhrkamp.

Hajer, Maarten (1995) *The Politics of Environmental Discourse: Ecological Modernization and the Policy Process*, Oxford: Clarendon.

Hallenstvedt, Abraham and Trollvik, Jan (eds) (1993) *Norske organisasjoner*. Oslo: Fabritius.

Hanf, Kenneth (1978) 'Introduction', in K. Hanf and F.W. Scharpf (eds) *Interorganizational Policy Making: Limits to Coordination and Central Control.* London: Sage.

Hanf, Kenneth and Scharpf, F.W. (1978) (eds) *Interorganizational Policy Making: Limits to Coordination and Central Control.* London: Sage.

Hardy, Cynthia and Clegg, Stewart R. (1996) 'Some dare call it power', in Stewart R. Clegg, Cynthia Hardy and Walter R. Nord (eds), *Handbook of Organization Studies.* London: Sage. pp. 622–41.

Hastings, Adrian (1997) *The Construction of Nationhood: Ethnicity, Religion and Nationalism.* Cambridge: Cambridge University Press.

Haugaard, Mark (1992) *Structures, Restructuration and Social Power.* Aldershot: Avebury.

Haugaard, Mark (1997a) *The Constitution of Power: a Theoretical Analysis of Power, Knowledge and Structure.* Manchester: Manchester University Press.

Haugaard, Mark (1997b) 'Power, knowledge and capital'. Paper presented at the IPSA World Congress, Seoul.

Haugaard, Mark (1999) 'Power, social and political theories of', in *Encyclopedia of Violence, Peace, and Conflict.* San Diego, CA: Academic Press.

Heilbroner, Robert L. (1990) 'The future of capitalism,' in Nicholas X. Rizopoulos (ed.), *Sea Changes: American Foreign Policy in a World Transformed.* New York: Council on Foreign Relations Press.

Heinz, John P., Laumann, Edward O., Nelson, Robert L., and Salisbury, Robert H. (1993) *The Hollow Core: Private Interests in National Policy Making.* Cambridge, Massachusetts: Harvard.

Held, David (1995) *Democracy and the Global Order: from the Modern State to Cosmopolitan Governance.* Cambridge: Polity.

Helleiner, Eric (1994) *States and the Reemergence of Global Finance: from Bretton Woods to the 1990s.* Ithaca, NY: Cornell University Press.

Heller, Hermann (1934) *Staatslehre.* Leiden: Sijthoff.

Heller, Hermann (1971) 'Politische Demokratie und soziale Homogenität', in *Gesammelte Schriften*, vol. 2 (1928). Leiden: Sijthoff. pp. 421–33.

Higgott, Richard (1997) 'Mondialisation et gouvernance: l'émergence du niveau régional', *Politique Étrangère*, 66 (2): 277–92.

Hindess, Barry (1996) *Discourses of Power: from Hobbes to Foucault.* Oxford: Blackwell.

Hinsley, F.H. (1966) *Sovereignty.* London: Watts.

Hirst, Paul (1997a) 'Challenges of globalization to the nation state', *Politiikka*, 39 (1): 3–13.

Hirst, Paul (1997b) *From Statism to Pluralism: Democracy, Civil Society and Global Politics.* London: UCL Press.

Hirst, Paul and Thompson, Grahame (1996) *Globalization in Question? The International Economy and the Possibilities of Governance.* Oxford: Polity.

Hobsbawm, E.J. (1972) *Bandits*, rev. edn. Harmondsworth: Penguin.

Hocking, Brian and Smith, Michael (1990) *World Politics: an Introduction to International Relations.* New York: Harvester/Wheatsheaf.

Huberts, Leo (1988) *De politieke invloed van protest en pressie: Besluitvormings-processen over rijkswegen.* Leiden: DSWO.

Huberts, Leo (1989) 'The influence of social movements on government policy', *International Social Movement Research*, 2: 395–426.

Huberts, Leo (1994) 'Intensieve procesanalyse', in L.W.J.C. Huberts and J. Kleinnijenhuis (eds), *Methoden van invloedsanalyse.* Meppel: Boom. pp. 38–60.

Huberts, Leo and Kleinnijenhuis, J. (1994) *Methoden van invloedsanalyse.* Meppel: Boom.

Hunter, Floyd (1953) *Community Power Structures.* Chapel Hill, NC: University of North Carolina Press.

Hunter, Ian (1993) 'Subjectivity and government', *Economy and Society*, 22 (1): 123–34.

Huntington, Samuel P. (1991) *The Third Wave: Democratization in the Late Twentieth Century*. Norman, OK: University of Oklahoma Press.

Huntington, Samuel P. (1993) 'Democracy's Third Wave,' in Larry Diamond and Marc F. Plattner (eds), *The Global Resurgence of Democracy*. Baltimore: Johns Hopkins University Press.

Hurrell, Andrew and Kingsbury, Benedict (eds) (1992) *The International Politics of the Environment: Actors, Interests, and Institutions*. Oxford: Clarendon.

Jenkins, Craig (1983) 'Resource mobilization theory and the study of social movements', *Annual Review of Sociology*, 9: 527–53.

Jomo, K.S. (1998) 'Notes for a talk, "Malaysia"', at Institute for Malaysian and International Studies, Universiti Kebangsaan Malaysia, Bangi, 16 March.

Jordan, Grant and Schubert, Klaus (1992) 'A preliminary ordering of policy network labels', *European Journal of Political Research*, 21: 7–27.

Kaplan, R.D. (1997) *The Ends of the Earth: a Journey at the Dawn of the 21st Century*. London: Macmillan.

Kapstein, Ethan B. (1994) 'Governing global finance', *The Washington Quarterly*, 17 (Spring): 77–87.

Kennedy, Paul (1987) *The Rise and Fall of Great Powers: Economic Change and Military Conflict from 1500 to 2000*. New York: Random House. London: Unwin Hyman.

Kennedy, Paul (1999) 'Will the next century be American too?', *New Perspectives Quarterly*, 16 (1): 53–7.

Keohane, Robert O. and Nye, Joseph S. (1989) *Power and Interdependence: World Politics in Transition*, 2nd edn. Glenview, IL: Scott, Foresman.

Kickert, Walter, Klijn, Erik-Hans and Koppenjan, Joop (eds) (1997) *Managing Complex Networks: Strategies for the Public Sector*. London: Sage.

Kimbrell, Andrew (1997) 'Biocolonization: the patenting of life and the global market in body parts', in Jerry Mander and Edward Goldsmith (eds), *The Case against the Global Economy*. San Francisco: Sierra. pp. 131–45.

Kimmelman, Michael (1999) 'A century of art: just how American was it?', *The New York Times*, 18 April.

Klausen, Jan Erling and Rommetvedt, Hilmar (eds) (1997) *Miljøpolitikk: Organisasjonene, Stortinget og forvaltningen*. Oslo: Tano Aschehoug.

Klijn, Erik-Hans (1997) 'Policy networks: an overview', in Walter Kickert, Erik-Hans Klijn and Joop Koppenjan (eds) (1997) *Managing Complex Networks: Strategies for the Public Sector*. London: Sage. pp. 14–34.

Knights, David and Vurdubakis, Theo (1993) 'Power, resistance and all that', in John M. Jermier, David Knights and Walter R. Nord (eds), *Resistance and Power in Organizations*. London: Routledge. pp. 167–98.

Korten, David C. (1996) 'The mythic victory of market capitalism', in Jerry Mander and Edward Goldsmith (eds), *The Case against the Global Economy*. San Francisco: Sierra. pp. 183–91.

Kuhn, Thomas (1962) *The Structure of Scientific Revolutions*. Chicago: University of Chicago Press.

Kuypers, Gijsbert (1973) *Grondbegrippen van politiek*. Utrecht: Het Spectrum.

Kvavik, Robert B. (1976) *Interest Groups in Norwegian Politics*. Oslo: Universitetsforlaget.

Laclau, Ernesto (1980) 'Nonpopulist rupture and discourse', *Screen Education*, 34: 87–93.

Laclau, Ernesto (1983a) 'The impossibility of society', *Canadian Journal of Political and Social Theory*, 7: 21–4.

Laclau, Ernesto (1983b) '"Socialism", the "people", "democracy": the transformation of hegemonic logic', *Social Text*, 7: 115–19.

Laclau, Ernesto and Mouffe, Chantal (1985) *Hegemony and Socialist Strategy*. London: Verso.

Laclau, Ernesto and Mouffe, Chantal (1987) 'Post-Marxism without apologies', *New Left Review*, 166: 77–106.

Lake, David A. (1999) 'Global governance: a relational contracting approach', in Aseem Prakash and Jeffrey A. Hart (eds), *Globalization and Governance*. London: Routledge. pp. 30–53.

Landshut, Siegfried (1968) 'Der politische Begriff der Repräsentation', in H. Rausch (ed.), *Zur Theorie und Geschichte der Repräsentation und der Repräsentativverfassung* (1964). Darmstadt: Wissenschaftliche Buchgesellschaft. pp. 482–97.

Lasswell, Harold D. (1936) *Politics: Who Gets What, When and How?* New York: Meridian, 1958.

Lasswell, Harold D. and Kaplan, Abraham (1950) *Power and Society*. New Haven, CT: Yale University Press.

Law, John (1996) *Organizing Modernity*. Oxford: Polity.

Lentner, Howard H. (2000) 'Globalization and power,' in Michael G. Schechter and Preet Aulakh (eds) *Rethinking Globalization(s): from Corporate Transnationalism to Local Interventions*. New York: St Martin's Press. pp. 56–72.

Lentner, Howard H. (1999) 'Implications of the economic crisis for East Asian foreign policies', *The Journal of East Asian Affairs*, 13 (1): 1–32.

Leroy, Pieter and van Tatenhove, Jan (2000) 'Political modernization theory and environmental politics', in Gert Spaargaren, Arthur P.J. Mol and Frederick H. Buttell (eds), *Environment and Global Modernities*. London: Sage.

Levi, Margaret (1981) 'The predatory theory of rule', *Politics and Society*, 10 (4): 431–65.

Levine, S. and White, P.E. (1961) 'Exchange as a conceptual framework for the study of interorganizational relationships', *Administrative Science Quarterly*, 5: 583–601.

Lewin, Leif (1994) 'The rise and decline of corporatism: the case of Sweden', *European Journal of Political Research*, 26: 59–79.

Lieshout, Robert H. (1993) *Anarchie en Hierarchie: Een theorie van internationale betrekkingen en buitenlandse politiek*. Bussum: Coutinho.

Lijphart, Arendt and Crepaz, Markus M.L. (1991) 'Corporatism and consensus democracy in eighteen countries: conceptual and empirical linkages', *British Journal of Political Science*, 21: 235–56.

Littler, Craig and Salaman, Graeme (1982) 'Bravermania and beyond: recent theories of the labour process', *Sociology*, 16: 251–69.

Lockwood, David (1964) 'Social integration and system integration', in G.K. Zollschan and W. Hirsch (eds), *Explorations in Social Change*. Boston: Houghton Mifflin. pp. 244–57.

Lowi, Theodore J. (1984) 'Why is there no socialism in the United States?', *International Political Science Review*, 5 (4): 369–80.

Luhmann, Niklas (1988) *Macht* (1975), 2nd edn. Stuttgart: Enke.

Lukes, Steven (1974) *Power: a Radical View*. London: Macmillan.

Lyotard, Jean-François (1986) *The Postmodern Condition: a Report on Knowledge*. Manchester: Manchester University Press.

Maddison, Angus (1995) *Monitoring the World Economy, 1829–1991*. Paris: Development Centre of the Organization for Economic Cooperation and Development.

Malecki, Edward S. (1990) 'Learning lessons from our critics: post-modern insights into the study of power'. Paper presented at the Annual Meeting of the American Political Science Association, San Francisco.

Mann, Michael (1986) *The Sources of Social Power. Volume 1: A History of Power from the Beginning to A.D. 1760*. Cambridge: Cambridge University Press.

March, James G. and Simon, Herbert A. (1958) *Organizations*. New York: Wiley.

Marin, Bernd and Mayntz, Renate (eds) (1991) *Policy Networks: Empirical Evidence and Theoretical Considerations*. Boulder, CO: Westview.

Marsh, David and Rhodes, Roderick (eds) (1992) *Policy Networks in British Government*. Oxford: Clarendon.

Martin, Hans-Peter and Schumann, Harold (1997) *The Global Trap: Globalization and the Assault on Democracy and Prosperity*. London: Zed.

Marx, Karl and Engels, Friedrich (1970) *The German Ideology*. Moscow: International Publishing Company.

May, Christopher (1997) 'Knowing, owning, enclosing: a global political economy of intellectual property rights.' PhD dissertation, Nottingham Trent University.

Mayer, Arno J. (1981) *The Persistence of the Old Regime: Europe to the Great War*. London: Croom Helm.

McCormick, John (1989) *The Global Environmental Movement*. London: Belhaven.

McKinley, Alan and Starkey, Ken (eds) (1998) *Foucault, Management, and Organization Theory*. London: Sage.

Melucci, Alberto (1985) 'The symbolic challenge of contemporary movements', *Social Research*, 52: 789–816.

Mennell, Stephen and Goudsblom, Johan (1998) *Norbert Elias: On Civilization, Power and Knowledge*. Chicago: University of Chicago.

Merriam, Charles E. (1964) *Political Power*. New York: Collier.

Mies, Maria (1993) 'New reproductive technologies: sexist and racist implications', in Maria Mies and Vandana Shiva (eds), *Ecofeminism*. Halifax: Fernwood. pp. 174–97.

Miller, Peter (1994) 'Accounting and objectivity: the invention of calculating selves and calculable spaces', in A. Megill (ed.), *Rethinking Objectivity*. Durham, NC: Duke University Press. pp. 239–64.

Miller, Stuart (1990) *Understanding Europeans*. Santa Fe, NM: Muir.

Mills, C. Wright (1956) *The Power Elite*. Oxford: Oxford University Press.

Minc, Alain (1993) *Le Nouveau Moyen Âge*. Paris: Gallimard.

Mintzberg, Henry (1983) *Power in and around Organizations*. Englewood Cliffs, NJ: Prentice-Hall.

Mintzer, Irving and Leonard, J. (eds) (1994) *Negotiating Climate Change: the Inside Story of the Rio Convention*. Cambridge: Cambridge University Press.

Moglen, Eben (1998) 'Antitrust and American democracy', *The Nation*, 267 (18): 11–15.

Morriss, Peter (1987) *Power: a Philosophical Analysis*. Manchester: Manchester University Press.

Morss, Elliot (1991) 'The new global players: how they compete and collaborate', *World Development*, 19 (1): 55–64.

Newland, Kathleen (1999) 'Workers of the world, now what?', *Foreign Policy*, 114 (Spring): 52–65.

Nordberg-Hodges, Helena (1996) 'The pressure to modernize and globalize', in Jerry Mander and Edward Goldsmith (eds), *The Case against the Global Economy*. San Francisco, CA: Sierra. pp. 33–46.

Nordby, Trond (1994) *Korporatisme på norsk 1920–1990*. Oslo: Universitetsforlaget.

Nye, Joseph S. Jr (1993) *Understanding International Conflicts: an Introduction to Theory and History*. New York: HarperCollins.

Offe, Claus (1977) 'Einleitung', in Peter Bachrach and Morton S. Baratz (eds), *Macht und Armut*. Frankfurt am Main: Suhrkamp. pp. 7–34.

Olsen, Johan P. (1983) *Organized Democracy: Political Institutions in a Welfare State – the Case of Norway*. Oslo: Universitetsforlaget.

Opedal, Ståle and Rommetvedt, Hilmar (1995a) *Miljøvernorganisasjonenes påvirkningsstrategier – korporatisme, lobbyisme, aksjonisme*. Stavanger: Rogalandsforskning, arbeidsnotat 95/052.

Opedal, Ståle and Rommetvedt, Hilmar (1995b) *Nærings- og miljøorganisasjonenes politiske påvirkning*. Stavanger: Rogalandsforskning, arbeidsnotat 95/111.

Opedal, Ståle and Farsund, Arild Aurvåg (1997a) 'Miljøhensyn og lokal sysselsetting: Avgiften på engangsemballasje', in Jan Erling Klausen and Hilmar Rommetvedt (eds), *Miljøpolitikk: Organisasjonene, Stortinget og forvaltningen*. Oslo: Tano Aschehoug. pp. 58–73.

Opedal, Ståle and Farsund, Arild Aurvåg (1997b) 'Klassisk naturvern: Bevaring av barskog', in Jan Erling Klausen and Hilmar Rommetvedt (eds), *Miljøpolitikk: Organisasjonene, Stortinget og forvaltningen*. Oslo: Tano Aschehoug. pp. 94–112.

Osborne, David and Gaebler, Ted (1992) *Reinventing Government: How the Entrepreneurial Spirit is Transforming the Public Sector, from Schoolhouse to Statehouse, City Hall to the Pentagon*. Reading, MA: Addison-Wesley.

Parsons, Talcott (1963) 'On the concept of political power', *Proceedings of the American Philosophical Society*, 107: 232–62.

Parsons, Talcott (1986) 'On the concept of political power' (1963), in Steven Lukes (ed.), *Power*. New York: New York University Press. pp. 94–143.

Pateman, Carole (1970) *Participation and Democratic Theory*. Cambridge: Cambridge University Press.

Pells, Richard (1997) 'The local and global loyalties of Europeans and Americans', *The Chronicle of Higher Education*, 2 May.

Peters, Bernhard (1993) *Die Integration moderner Gesellschaften*. Frankfurt am Main: Suhrkamp.

Pettman, Jindy J. (1996) *Worlding Women: a Feminist International Politics*. London: Routledge.

Phillips, Kevin (1990) *The Politics of Rich and Poor: Wealth and the American Electorate in the Reagan Aftermath*. New York: Random House.

Pitkin, Hanna F. (1967) *The Concept of Representation*. Berkeley, CA: University of California Press.

Pitkin, Hanna F. (1972) *Wittgenstein and Justice*. Berkeley, CA: University of California Press.

Polanyi, Karl (1944) *The Great Transformation: the Political and Economic Origins of Our Time*. New York: Rinehart.

Polsby, Nelson W. (1960) 'How to study community power: the pluralist alternative', *Journal of Politics*, 22: 474–84.

Potter, David (1996) 'Non-governmental organizations and environmental policies', in A. Blowers and P. Glasbergen (eds), *Environmental Policy in an International Context. Volume III: Prospects for Environmental Change*. London: Arnold. pp. 25–50.

Princen, Thomas (1994) 'The ivory trade ban: NGOs and international conservation', in Thomas Princen and M. Finger (eds), *Environmental NGOs in World Politics: Linking the Local to the Global*. London: Routledge. pp. 121–59.

Pulkkinen, Tuija (1996) *The Postmodern and the Political Agency*. Helsinki: Hakapaino.

Putnam, Robert D. (1988) 'Diplomacy and domestic policy: the logic of two-level games', *International Organization*, 42: 427–60.

Ransom, John S. (1997) *Foucault's Discipline: The Politics of Subjectivity*. London: Duke University Press.

Rawls, John (1971) *A Theory of Justice*. Oxford: Oxford University Press.

Rawls, John (1993) *Political Liberalism*. New York: Columbia University Press.

Ray, James L. (1987) *Global Politics*, 3rd edn. Boston: Houghton Mifflin.

Rhodes, Richard (1995) *Dark Sun: the Making of the Hydrogen Bomb*. New York: Simon & Schuster.

Rhodes, Roderick (1997) 'Foreword', in Walter Kickert, Erik-Hans Klijn and Joop Koppenjan (eds), *Managing Complex Networks: Strategies for the Public Sector*. London: Sage. pp. xi–xv.

Rhodes, Roderick A.W. (1996) 'The new governance: governing without government', *Political Studies* 19: 652–67.

Rhodes, Roderick and Marsh, David (1992) 'New directions in the study of policy networks', *European Journal of Political Research*, 21: 181–205.

Richardson, James L. (1997) 'Contending liberalism: past and present', *European Journal of International Relations*, 3 (1): 5–33.

Riker, William H. (1964) 'Some ambiguities in the notion of power', *American Political Science Review*, 58: 341–9.

Ritzer, George (1998) *The McDonaldization Thesis: Explorations and Extensions*. London: Sage.

Robertson, Roland (1992) *Globalization: Social Theory and Global Culture*. London: Sage.

Roche, Maurice (1992) *Rethinking Citizenship: Welfare, Ideology and Change in a Modern Society*. Cambridge: Polity.

Rokkan, Stein (1966) 'Norway: numerical democracy and corporate pluralism', in Robert A. Dahl (ed.), *Political Oppositions in Western Democracies*. New Haven, CT: Yale University Press. pp. 70–115.

Rommetvedt, Hilmar (1997a) 'Utviklingsfaser i det norske organisasjon/statforholdet', in Guy-Erik Isaksson (ed.), *Inblickar i nordisk parlamentarism*. Åbo: Åbo Akademi, Statsvetenskapliga institutionen, Series A, 470: 129–56.

Rommetvedt, Hilmar (1997b) 'Næringslivets politiske påvirkning', in Morten Malmø (ed.), *Politisk årbok 1997*. Oslo: Andante. pp. 98–114.

Rommetvedt, Hilmar (1998) 'Norwegian parliamentary committees: performance, structural change and external relations', in Lawrence D. Longley and Roger H. Davidson (eds), *The New Roles of Parliamentary Committees*. London: Cass. pp. 60–84.

Rommetvedt, Hilmar and Opedal, Ståle (1995) 'Næringskorporatisme og miljølobbyisme? Norske miljø- og næringsorganisasjoners politiske påvirkning', *Nordisk Administrativt Tidsskrift*, 76: 277–302.

Rommetvedt, Hilmar, Farsund, Arild Aurvåg and Melberg, Kjersti (forthcoming) 'Corporatism and lobbyism in Norwegian environmental policy-making', in Stuart Nagel (ed.), *Handbook of Global Technology Policy*. New York: Marcel Dekker.

Rose, Nikolas and Miller, Peter (1992) 'Political power beyond the state: the problematics of government', *British Journal of Sociology*, 43 (2): 173–207.

Rosenau, James N. (1992) 'Governance order and change in world politics', in James N. Rosenau and Ernst-Otto Czempiel (eds), *Governance without Government: Order and Change in World Politics*. Cambridge: Cambridge University Press. pp. 1–29.

Rosenau, James N. (1997) *Along the Domestic–Foreign Frontier: Exploring Governance in a Turbulent World*. Cambridge: Cambridge University Press.

Rowlands, Ian H. (1995) *The Politics of Global Atmospheric Change*. Manchester: Manchester University Press.

Rowlands, Ian H. and Greene, Malory (eds) (1992) *Global Environmental Change and International Relations*. London: Macmillan.

Ruggie, John Gerard (1993) 'Territoriality and beyond', *International Organization*, 47: 139–74.

Sarcinelli, Ulrich (1987) *Symbolische Politik*. Opladen: Westdeutscher.

Sassen, Saskia (1999) 'Global financial centers', *Foreign Affairs*, 78 (1): 78–87.

Schaap, Linze and van Twist, Marcus (1997) 'The dynamics of closedness in networks', in Walter Kickert, Erik-Hans Klijn and Joop Koppenjan (eds), *Managing Complex Networks: Strategies for the Public Sector*. London: Sage. pp. 62–78.

Scharpf, Fritz W. (1978) 'Interorganizational policy studies: issues, concepts and perspectives', in Kenneth Hanf and Fritz W. Scharpf (eds), *Interorganizational Policy Making: Limits to Coordination and Central Control*. London: Sage.

Scharpf, Fritz, Reissert, Bernd and Schnabel, Fritz (1976) *Politikverflechtung: Theorie und Empirie des kooperativen Föderalismus in der Bundesrepublik*. Kronberg: Scriptor.

Schmitt, Carl (1989) *Verfassungslehre* (1928). Leipzig. Reprinted Berlin: Duncker & Humblot.

Schmitter, Philippe C. (1979) 'Still the century of corporatism?', in Philippe C. Schmitter and Gerhard Lehmbruch, *Trends towards Corporatist Intermediation*. London: Sage. pp. 7–52.

Schmitter, Philippe C. (1982) 'Reflections on where the theory of neo-corporatism has gone and where the praxis of neo-corporatism may be going', in Gerhard Lehmbruch and Philippe C. Schmitter (eds), *Patterns of Corporatist Policy-Making*. London: Sage. pp. 259–79.

Scott, William R. (1987) 'The adolescence of institutional theory', *Administrative Science Quarterly*, 32 (4): 493–511.

Self, Peter (1985) *Political Theories of Modern Government*. London: Allen & Unwin.

Sewell, Graham and Wilkinson, Barry (1992) '"Someone to watch over me": surveillance, discipline and the just-in-time labour process', *Sociology*, 26 (2): 271–89.

Shiva, Vandana and Holla-Bhar, Radha (1996) 'Piracy by the patent: the case of the neem tree', in Jerry Mander and Edward Goldsmith (eds), *The Case against the Global Economy*. San Francisco: Sierra. pp. 146–59.

Singer, Max and Wildavsky, Aaron (1993) *The Real World Order: Zones of Peace/Zones of Turmoil*. Chatham, NJ: Chatham.

Smend, Rudolf (1956) 'Integrationslehre', in *Handwörterbuch der Sozialwissenschaften*, vol. 5. Göttingen. pp. 299–302. Also in Rudolf Smend, *Staatsrechtliche Abhandlungen*, 2nd edn. Berlin: Duncker & Humblot, 1968. pp. 475–81.

Smend, Rudolf (1968) 'Verfassung und Verfassungsrecht' (1928), in *Staatsrechtliche Abhandlungen*, 2nd edn. Berlin: Duncker & Humblot. pp. 119–276.

Sorauf, Frank J. (1972) *Party Politics in America*, 2nd edn. Boston: Little, Brown.

Spruyt, Hendrik (1994) *The Sovereign State and its Competitors: an Analysis of Systems Change*. Princeton, NJ: Princeton University Press.

Spybey, Tony (1996) *Globalization and World Society*. Cambridge: Polity.

Stiglitz, Joseph (1998) 'The East Asian miracle and the crisis'. Talk presented at University of Malaya, Kuala Lumpur, 16 March.

Stokman, F.N. (1994) 'Besluitvormingsmodellen binnen beleidsnetwerken', in L. Huberts and J. Kleinnijenhuis (eds), *Methoden van invloedsanalyse*. Meppel: Boom. pp. 165–87.

Strange, Susan (1996) *The Retreat of the State: the Diffusion of Power in the World Economy*. Cambridge: Cambridge University Press.

Talbott, Strobe (1997) 'East meets West: regional integration in an era of global interdependence'. Speech at the Meeting of the World Affairs Council of Northern California, San Francisco, 18 September.

Taylor, Charles (1975) *Hegel*. Cambridge: Cambridge University Press.

Taylor, Charles (1989) *Sources of the Self: the Making of the Modern Identity*. Cambridge: Cambridge University Press.

Thompson-Feraru, A. (1974) 'Transnational political interests and the global environment', *International Organization*, 28: 31–60.

Truman, David B. (1951) *The Governmental Process: Political Interests and Public Opinion*. New York: Knopf.

Van der Schot, Jos and van de Veen, Hans (1997) 'De nieuwe macht van NGO's', in K. Waagmeester (ed.), *Houdbare Economie. Kroniek van Duurzaam Nederland*. Amsterdam: NCDO/Kok Agora. pp. 197–209.

Van Elteren, Mel (1996) 'Conceptualizing the impact of US popular culture globally', *Journal of Popular Culture*, 30 (1): 47–89.

Van Krieken, Robert (1996) 'Proto-governmentalization and the historical formation of organizational subjectivity', *Economy and Society*, 25 (2): 195–221.

Van Noort, Wim, Huberts, Leo and Rademakers, Leo (1987) *Protest en Pressie: Een systematische analyse van collectieve actie.* Assen: Van Gorcum.

Van Schendelen, M.P.C.M. (1981) 'Politieke invloed', in M.P.C.M. van Schendelen (ed.), *Kernthema's van de politicologie.* Meppel: Boom. pp. 11–138.

Van Tatenhove, Jan (1993) 'Milieubeleid onder dak? Beleidsvoeringsprocessen in het Nederlandse milieubeleid in de periode 1970–1990; nader uitgewerkt voor de Gelderse Vallei'. PhD thesis, WAU, Wageningen.

Van Tatenhove, Jan and Leroy, Pieter (1995) 'Beleidsnetwerken: een kritische analyse', *Beleidswetenschap*, 9 (2): 128–45.

Van Tatenhove, Jan, Arts, Bas and Leroy, Pieter (2000) *Political Modernization and the Environment: The Renewal of Environmental Policy Arrangements.* Dordrecht: Kluwer.

Van Waarden, Frans (1992) 'Dimensions and types of policy networks', *European Journal of Political Research*, 21: 29–52.

Verschuren, Piet and Doorewaard, Hans (1995) *Het ontwerpen van een onderzoek.* Utrecht: Lemma.

Visser, Jelle and Hemerrijck, Anton (1998) *'Een Nederlands Mirakel', beleidsleren in de verzorgingsstaat ('A Dutch Miracle': Policy Learning in the Welfare State).* Amsterdam: Amsterdam University Press.

Voegelin, Eric (1952) *The New Science of Politics.* Chicago: University of Chicago Press.

VROM (1991) *Report of the Dutch Delegation to INC3.* The Hague.

VROM (1994) *Report of the Dutch Delegation to INC10.* The Hague.

Wallace, William and Zielonka, Jan (1998) 'Misunderstanding Europe', *Foreign Affairs*, 77 (6): 65–79.

Walsh, Kieron, Hinings, Christopher R., Greenwood, Royston and Ransom, Stuart (1981) 'Power and advantage in organizations', *Organization Studies*, 2 (2): 131–52.

Walt, Stephen M. (1998–9) 'The ties that fray: why Europe and America are drifting apart', *The National Interest*, 54 (Winter): 3–11.

Waltz, Kenneth N. (1979) *Theory of International Politics.* Reading, MA: Addison-Wesley.

Wartenberg, Thomas E. (1990) *The Forms of Power: from Domination to Transformation.* Philadelphia: Temple University Press.

Waste, Robert J. (1986a) 'Community power and pluralist theory,' in Robert J. Waste (ed.), *Community Power: Directions for Future Research.* Beverly Hills, CA: Sage.

Waste, Robert J. (ed.) (1986b) *Community Power: Directions for Future Research.* Beverly Hills, CA: Sage.

Waters, Malcolm (1995) *Globalization.* London: Routledge.

Weber, Max (1948) *The Theory of Social and Economic Organization*, trans. Talcott Parsons and A. M. Henderson. New York: Free Press.

Weber, Max (1978) *Economy and Society* (1922), ed. Guenther Roth and Claus Wittich. Berkeley, Los Angeles, London: University of California Press.

Wendt, Alexander E. (1992) 'Anarchy is what states make of it: the social construction of power politics', *International Organization*, 46: 391–425.

Westerheijden, D. (1987) 'The substance of a shadow: a critique of power measurement methods', *Acta Politica* (1): 39–59.

White, Randall (1995) *Global Spin: Probing the Globalization Debate: Where in the World Are We Going?* Toronto: Dundurn.

Whitman, Marina v. N. (1999) 'Global competition and the changing role of the American corporation', *The Washington Quarterly*, 22 (2): 59–82.

Wilks, Stephen and Wright, Maurice (eds) (1987) *Comparative Government–Industry Relations: Western Europe, the United States and Japan.* Oxford: Clarendon.

Willets, Peter (ed.) (1982) *Pressure Groups in the Global System.* London: Pinter.

Williamson, Peter J. (1989) *Corporatism in Perspective: an Introductory Guide to Corporatist Theory*. London: Sage.

Wittgenstein, Ludwig (1968) *Philosophical Investigations*, trans. G. E. M. Anscombe. Oxford: Blackwell.

Wittgenstein, Ludwig (1969) *The Blue and Brown Books*. Oxford: Oxford University Press.

Woerdman, Edwin (1997) 'Internationale onderhandelingen over klimaatbeleid: emissiereductie, Joint Implementation, en verhandelbare emissierechten', *Milieu*, no. 5: 218–27.

Wrong, Dennis H. (1988) *Power: Its Forms, Bases and Uses*. Chicago: University of Chicago Press.

Yearley, Stephen (1996) *Sociology, Environmentalism, Globalization*. London: Sage.

Zuckerman, Mortimer B. (1998) 'A second American century', *Foreign Affairs*, 77 (3): 18–31.

Index